Dr. William Allchorn

Moving beyond Islamist Extremism: Assessing Counter Narrative Responses to the Global Far Right

ANALYZING POLITICAL VIOLENCE

Edited by Bethan Johnson and John Richardson

1 *Nasser Kurdy, David Tucker*
  A Reply to Hate: Forgiving My Attacker
  ISBN 978-3-8382-1558-7

2 *Michael Colborne*
  From the Fires of War:
  Ukraine's Azov Movement and the Global Far Right
  ISBN 978-3-8382-1508-2

3 *Dr. William Allchorn*
  Moving beyond Islamist Extremism:
  Assessing Counter Narrative Responses to the Global Far Right
  ISBN 978-3-8382-1490-0

Dr. William Allchorn

MOVING BEYOND ISLAMIST EXTREMISM

Assessing Counter Narrative Responses to the Global Far Right

Bibliografische Information der Deutschen Nationalbibliothek
Die Deutsche Nationalbibliothek verzeichnet diese Publikation in der Deutschen Nationalbibliografie; detaillierte bibliografische Daten sind im Internet über http://dnb.d-nb.de abrufbar.

Bibliographic information published by the Deutsche Nationalbibliothek
Die Deutsche Nationalbibliothek lists this publication in the Deutsche Nationalbibliografie; detailed bibliographic data are available in the Internet at http://dnb.d-nb.de.

Cover image: 142212921 © motortion | Dreamstime.com

ISBN-13: 978-3-8382-1490-0
© *ibidem*-Verlag, Stuttgart 2021
Alle Rechte vorbehalten

Das Werk einschließlich aller seiner Teile ist urheberrechtlich geschützt. Jede Verwertung außerhalb der engen Grenzen des Urheberrechtsgesetzes ist ohne Zustimmung des Verlages unzulässig und strafbar. Dies gilt insbesondere für Vervielfältigungen, Übersetzungen, Mikroverfilmungen und elektronische Speicherformen sowie die Einspeicherung und Verarbeitung in elektronischen Systemen.

All rights reserved. No part of this publication may be reproduced, stored in or introduced into a retrieval system, or transmitted, in any form, or by any means (electronic, mechanical, photocopying, recording or otherwise) without the prior written permission of the publisher. Any person who does any unauthorized act in relation to this publication may be liable to criminal prosecution and civil claims for damages.

Printed in the EU

Table of Contents

Table of Contents 5
List of Figures 11
List of Tables 15
Introduction—Stochastic Far-Right Terrorism & The New 'Fifth Wave' of Violent Extremism 17
Chapter 1: The Journey of (Contested) Concepts Narratives, Counter Narratives and its Application to Far-Right Extremism 31
    Introduction 31
    Addressing the Lacuna: Violent Far-Right Narratives under the Fifth Wave of Stochastic Terrorism 33
        1.   Cultural Threat Conspiracy-Theory Narrative 33
        2.   Ethnic Threat Conspiracy Theory Narrative 34
        3.   Accelerationist Narrative 36
        4.   Anti-Establishment Narrative 37
        5.   Misogynist Narrative 38
        6.   Environmental Narrative 39
        7.   Victimhood Narrative 40
    The Journey of a (Contested) Concept—Counter Narratives, Islamist Extremism and its Application to Far-Right Extremism 42
    Evaluating Far-Right Counter-Narratives: Testing Effectiveness and Impact 45
        1.   Define the Context and State the Problem being addressed 46
        2.   Develop a 'Theory of Change' (ToC) and write a detailed ToC Statement 49
    Theory of Change Statement 51

1. Identify the Goals & Objectives of the Campaign and quantify/link them to each intervention 52
2. Determine the Key Indicators and measure success based on the state goals and objectives 53
3. Determine the Tools & Collection Methods used to obtain the desired data 57
4. Determine Whether Staff Have the Appropriate Capacity 58
5. Assess the Results on the basis of data collected 59

Conclusion 61

Chapter 2: Far-Right Extremist Narratives and Counter-Narratives in Western Europe — The Cases of the UK and Germany 63

Introduction 63

Violent Far-right Extremist Groups and Narratives in the UK & Germany: Ascendant Anti-Muslim Populism, Declining Ethno-Nationalism, Ascendant Chauvinism, Neo-Nazism, & Anti-Globalism 67

    I. Violent Far-Right Extremist Groups in the UK 67
        a) Combat 18 (C18) *67*
        b) National Action *69*
        c) Sonnenkrieg Division (SKD) *71*
        d) System Resistance Network (SRN) *72*
        e) Order of Nine Angles (O9A) *74*
        f) Misanthropic Division (MD) *75*
    II. Violent Far-Right Extremist Groups in Germany 77
        a) Blood & Honour (B&H) *77*
        b) Combat 18 (Germany) *79*
        c) The Third Path *81*
        d) Revolution Chemnitz *83*
        e) Group Freital *85*

Summary 87

Violent Far-Right Counter Narratives & Counter Narrative Campaigns in the UK and Germany: Tapping into Anti-Muslim Populist, Ethno-Nationalist, Neo-Nazi, Masculinist and Anti-Globalist Positions 88

Recommendations and Conclusions 104

Chapter 3: Far-Right Extremist Narratives and Counter-Narratives in North America — The Cases of the US and Canada 107

Introduction 107

Violent Far-Right Extremist Narratives in North America: Common Narratives of Ascendant Chauvinism & Accelerationism, added to Persistent White Supremacism and Anti-Government Extremism 111

    I.   Violent Far-Right Extremist Groups in the US 111
        a) The Base *111*
        b) Atomwaffen Division *114*
        c) Proud Boys *116*
        d) Rise Above Movement (R.A.M.) *119*
        e) Patriot Prayer *121*
        f) Oath Keepers *124*
        g) III%ers (Three Percenters) *126*
    II.   Violent Far-Right Extremist Groups in Canada 128
        a) Atalante-Quebec *128*
        b) Aryan Guard *130*
        c) Church of the Creator *132*
        d) Heritage Front *133*
        e) Blood and Honour (Club 28) *135*

Summary 137

Violent Far-Right Counter-Narratives in North America: Tapping into White Supremacist, Neo-Nazi/Fascist, Anti-Immigration, Antisemitic, Anti-Muslim, Chauvinist and Anti-Government Narratives 140

Conclusions and Recommendations 159

Chapter 4: Far-Right Extremist Narratives and Counter Narratives in Australasia — The Cases of Australia and New Zealand 163

Violent Far-Right Extremist Groups and Narratives in Australasia: Ascendant Anti-Muslim Populism, Ethno-Nationalism, White Supremacism and Chauvinism 165

    I. Violent Far-Right Extremist Groups in Australia 166
        a) United Patriots Front (UPF) 166
        b) Lads Society 167
        c) Combat 18 (Australia) 170
        d) True Blue Crew (TBC) 172
        e) The Dingoes 174

    II. Violent Far-Right Extremist Groups in New Zealand 176
        a) New Zealand National Front 176
        b) Right Wing Resistance 178
        c) Unit 88 180
        d) Wargus Christi 182

Summary 184

Violent Far-Right Counter Narratives & Counter Narrative Campaigns in Australasia: Tapping into Anti-Muslim, Populist, Ethno-Nationalist, White Supremacist and Ultra-Nationalist Narratives 186

Conclusions and Recommendations 198

Chapter 5: Testing the Words vs. Deeds Nexus — A Facebook Pilot Study of UK Far-Right Counter Narratives in the Online Space 201

Introduction 201

Dialing Back Hatred: Research Context, Objectives, Hypotheses and Methodology for Testing Far-Right Counter Narrative Effectiveness 203

Phase 1: Focus Group Testing of Far-Right Counter Narrative
Content 206

    I.   Introduction 206
    II.   Focus Group-Tested Far-Right Counter
        Narrative Content 207
    III. Trusted Organisations & Messengers 211
    IV. Mocked-Up Facebook Page 214

Findings 215

    I.   Issues Important to Target Audience 215
    II.   Behaviour of Target Audience on Social Media 217
    III. Responses to Focus Group Tested Far-Right
        Counter Narrative Content: What Worked
        Well, Not So Well and Fairly Well 218
        1. Far-Right Counter Narrative Content that Worked Well... 219
        2. Far-Right Counter Narratives that worked Fairly Well 223
        3. Far-Right Counter Narratives that Worked Not So Well... 225
    IV. Focus Group-Tested Responses to 'Everybody
        Makes Britain Great' Page 238
    Conclusions from Focus Group Testing 239

Phase 2: Online Survey & Facebook Ads Testing of
Far-Right Counter Narrative Content 240

    I.   Introduction 240
    II.   Online-Tested Far-Right Counter Narrative
        Content 241

Findings 251

Facebook Ads Testing: Measuring Levels of Engagement
with Far-Right Counter Narrative Content 251

Pre- and Post-Test Survey: Measuring the Impact of
Far-Right Counter Narratives 267

    I.   Survey Design, Rollout & Responses 267
    II.   Survey Findings 272

Conclusion 279

Conclusion — Revisiting Counter Narratives (Lessons, Recommendations and Ways Forward for Combating Far-Right Extremism) 283

    Key Findings — Global Far-Right Narratives and Counter Narratives in the Fifth Wave 285

    Lessons and Policy Recommendations — The Current State of Counter Narrative Responses to the Global Far-Right 288

    Concluding Remarks — Immunised Democracy & The Role of Counter Narratives within a Broader Counter-Terrorism Framework 290

Bibliography 295

    Books and Journal Articles 295

    Non-Anglophone Books and Articles 299

    Reports 300

List of Figures

Figure 1: Total Publications Per Year on the Subject of 'Counter Narratives', 1990–2019 20

Figure 2: Total Publications Per Year on the Subject of 'Far Right Counter Narratives', 1990-2019 20

Figure 3: Terrorist Attacks by Type, 1970-2018 23

Figure 4: Frequency of Far-Right Terror Attacks, 1970–2018 24

Figure 5: Example Indicators for a Far-Right Counter-Narrative Campaign 56

Figure 6: Number of racially or religiously aggravated offences recorded by the police by month in the UK, April 2013 to March 2018 65

Figure 7: Right-Wing Hate Crime Rate in Germany, 2002-2016 66

Figure 8: T-Shirt before and after washing 92

Figure 9: Screenshot from English Disco Lover's Promotional Video 94

Figure 10: Screenshot of 'Britain Furst' Parody Tweet 95

Figure 11: Rudolf-Hess-Memorial March and Exit-Germany campaign banner "Donate The Hate" 97

Figure 12: Donate the Hate campaign 98

Figure 13: Exit UK 'Stories' Page 99

Figure 14: London Grid for Learning's 'Counter-Extremism' resource video 100

Figure 15: Reach and Engagements with Moonshot CVE's Redirect Method 102

Figure 16: Response of Far-right Extremist to One-to-One Outreach 103

Figure 17: Message Content of One-to-One Outreach 104

Figure 18: US Right-Wing Terror Incidents & Attacks vs. Other Western Nations, 2002–2019 109

Figure 19: Canada's Global Terrorism Index Score, 2010–2018 109

Figure 20: Screen Grab from 2011 Hours Against Hate Campaign 'Launch' Video 147

Figure 21: Age Range of Twitter Users from the Extreme Dialogue Dashboard 146

Figure 22: Overview of EXIT USA (2015) Counter Narrative Videos 147

Figure 23: Example of Direct Message from Exit USA Campaign 149

Figure 24: Before and After Engagement Statistics for EXIT USA Campaign 149

Figure 25: Example Infographic from the 'Know Extremism' Instagram Account 152

Figure 26: Screen Grab from OSCE video reviewing the Voices Against Extremism Project 153

Figure 27: Screen Grab from 'Peer-to-Peer: Facebook Global Digital Challenge' Video, "Who do you want to be?" 155

Figure 28: Picture of 'Landscape of Hate' Project in Action 156

Figure 29: Statistics and Facts used on "We are Free Radicals: Finding Our Way Again" website 158

Figure 30: Front Cover of the November 2019 Edition of 'Ctrl+Alt+Del-Hate' 159

Figure 31: Linkages between Australia Far-Right and Christchurch Attacker 184

Figure 32: All Together Now (2019) "FAQs" Page. 190

Figure 33: Top 10 "White Power? Discussion Page" Discussion Starters (Discussion Types-IB = Ideologically-based & GI= Group Identification-based) 193

Figure 34: New Zealand Prime Minister, Jacinda Ardern, talking to the families of victims after the Christchurch attack... 196

Figure 35: Anti-Muslim Populism Counter Narrative Content .. 207

Figure 36: Ethno-Nationalist Counter Narrative Content............ 208

Figure 37: Masculinist Counter Narrative Content....................... 209

Figure 38: Populist, Anti-Establishment & Victimhood Counter Narrative Content... 210

Figure 39: Topical Counter Narrative Content............................... 211

Figure 40: Tested UK Brand Messengers.. 212

Figure 41: Tested UK Political Messengers 213

Figure 42: Tested UK Online Influencer & Media Messengers ... 213

Figure 43: Tested Mock-up of 'Everybody Makes Britain Great' Seed Page... 214

Figure 44: Screenshot of Coca-Cola 'Where Everyone Plays' Video 220

Figure 45: Screenshot of Open Your Eyes to Hate 'Captain David Wiseman' Video.. 221

Figure 46: Screenshot from BBC One 'Cornershop Heroes' Video 222

Figure 47: Screenshot of Original Content: 'Ghurka' Meme............ 223

Figure 48: Screenshot of Original Content: 'Chelsea Football Match' Meme 224

Figure 49: Screenshot of Original Content: 'EDL March' Meme.. 225

Figure 50: Screenshot of Original Content: Memes on the topics of LGBT equality, Gender equality and the importance of voting in the UK....................................... 227

Figure 51: Screenshot of Armed Forces Muslim Association 'Our Heroes: Ali Haidar' Video 228

Figure 52: Screenshots of Original Content: 'Covid-19 Boris Johnson & Corner shop' Memes 230

Figure 53: Screenshots of Original Content: 'Far-Right Protestor' & 'Tommy Robinson' Memes 233

Figure 54: Screenshots of Original Content: 'Channel Migrants' Memes 235

Figure 55: Screenshots of Original Content: 'UK Cabinet' & 'Sheerin-Capaldi' Memes 237

Figure 56: ITV 'We are Changed by What We See' Britain's Got Talent Advert (featuring Diversity) 238

Figure 57: Mockup of 'Everybody Makes Britain Great' Seed Page 239

Figure 58: Flow Diagram of Online Far-Right Counter Narrative Rollout 249

Figure 59: Race Warrior-Shared Passions 1 (Video Optimisation) 254

Table 14: Pre-Test Survey Questionnaire Name, Audience and Total Responses 268

Figure 61: Attitudinal Question Items for Pre-Test and Post-Test Surveys 270

Figure 62: Everybody Makes Britain Great Survey — Most Shared, Representative and Favourite Image 275

Figure 63: Overall Attitudinal Responses in Pre-Test Survey 276

Figure 63: Overall Attitudinal Responses in Post-Test Survey ... 277

Figure 64: Global Far-Right Counter Narratives within a Broader CT Strategy 292

List of Tables

Table 1: Push & Pull Factors into Violent Far-Right Extremism 47

Table 2: Examples of Far-Right Counter Narrative Scenarios 48

Table 3: Online Tested Far-Right Counter Narrative Content 241

Table 4: Summative Cost, Reach and Engagement Metrics from Facebook Ads Testing 252

Table 5: Views of Shared Passion Videos (Segmented by View Rate) 255

Table 6: Summative Table of Cost, Reach and Engagement Metrics for Football Facebook Ads 256

Table 7: Breakdown of Cost, Reach and Engagement Metrics for Football Facebook Ads 258

Table 8: Highest-Ranking Meme & Video Content Across All Themes 260

Table 9: Levels of Reach and Engagement among Working Class Warriors 263

Table 10: Levels of Reach and Engagement among Race Warriors 264

Table 11: Levels of Reach and Engagement among Conspiracy Joe 265

Table 12: Levels of Reach and Engagement among Conspiracy Jane 266

Table 13: Adverts used to Promote Pre-Test & Post-Test Surveys on Facebook 267

Table 15: Post-Test Survey Questionnaire Name, Audience and Total Responses 269

Table 16: Attitudinal Shift Scores (% Change in Average for Each Response Category) 273

Table 17: Standard Deviations for Attitudinal Scores
(Pre-Test Survey) 278

Table 18: Standard Deviations for Attitudinal Scores
(Post-Test Survey) 279

Introduction — Stochastic Far-Right Terrorism & The New 'Fifth Wave' of Violent Extremism

At 1.40pm on 15 March 2019, Christchurch shooter, Brenton Heston Tarrant, approached the Al-Noor Mosque near the city's Hagley Park. Greeted by a septuagenarian usher at Friday prayers, Tarrant opened fire on worshippers for six minutes. He only stopped to reload and to gather more ammunition and weapons from his car outside before continuing his bloody rampage. Returning to his vehicle at 1.46pm, the terrorist then drove for seven minutes (6.5km) across town to the Linwood Islamic Centre, where he began firing through the Centre's windows at worshippers gathering inside.[1] Challenged by a congregant, Tarrant then fled the scene of his second massacre at 1.56pm before being arrested at 1.59pm.

Whilst the use of a manifesto, video livestreaming over the internet and the transnational nature of the attacker's networks set a trend of far-right terrorism in 2019 & 2020,[2] a vital detail remains unique to Christchurch: It is the site of one of the deadliest far-right terror attacks within that wave. In total, 51 people were killed and another 50 seriously wounded, with the attacker foiled from targeting a third location and setting fire to the Muslim places of worship.[3] A week after the one-year anniversary of his shooting spree,

---

[1] Bostock, B., Corcoran, K, & Logan, B., 'This timeline of the Christchurch Mosque terror attacks shows how New Zealand's deadliest shooting unfolded', *Insider*, 19 March 2019, online at: https://www.insider.com/christchurch-shooting-timeline-49-killed-new-zealand-mosques-2019-3.

[2] See the following: Macklin, G., 'The Christchurch Attacks: Livestream Terror in the Viral Video Age', *CTC Sentinel*, 12 (6), July 2019, online at: https://ctc.usma.edu/christchurch-attacks-livestream-terror-viral-video-age/ & Macklin, G., 'The El Paso Terrorist Attack: The Chain Reaction of Global Right-Wing Terror', *CTC Sentinel*, 12(11), December 2019, online at: https://ctc.usma.edu/el-paso-terrorist-attack-chain-reaction-global-right-wing-terror/.

[3] Fattal, I., 'New Zealand Went More Than 20 Years Between Mass Shootings', *The Atlantic*, 15 March 2019, online at: https://www.theatlantic.com/politics/archive/2019/03/new-zealands-history-mass-shootings-christchurch/585052/.

however, Tarrant unexpectedly pleaded guilty to 51 charges of murder, 40 charges of attempted murder, and one charge of terrorism (unexpectedly because by pleading this way he forwent a jury trial and thereby a potential platform for his far-right extremist views.[4]) Several months later, he was later given a life sentence without parole for committing the atrocities of March 15 — the first time in New Zealand history that a defendant has been handed such a sentence.[5] It is unlikely that the attacker will ever leave prison.

One aspect that was less unique to the attacker, however, was the use of narratives and grand narratives to valorise and mythologise his deadly rampage that had already been in existence eight years prior. Both the conspiracy theory that became the title of Tarrant's manifesto ("The Great Replacement") and the use of anti-Muslim ideology had already become a common place eight years prior (on 22 July 2011) when Anders Behring Breivik shot up a Labour-Party summer camp on the island of Utoya, just outside of Norway — believing in a fable story about Europe becoming a "Eurabia", aided and abetted by left-wing politicians — and a book of a similar name was released by far-right thinker, Renaud Camus. Going further back to perhaps the most infamous far-right terror attacks in modern history, the perpetrator of the 1995 Oklahoma City Bombings Timothy McVeigh (with his accomplice, Terry Lynn Nichols) was similarly inspired by a work of far-right fiction — with a highway patrol officer finding an excerpt from the far-right anti-government polemic, *The Turner Diaries*, in McVeigh's car as he fled the scene of his mass atrocity.

What was then new about the events of March 2019 was the extent to which it started a cumulative[6] (or what others have called

---

4   *BBC News*, 'Christchurch shootings: Brenton Tarrant pleads guilty to 51 murders', 26 March 2020, online at: https://www.bbc.co.uk/news/world-asia-52044013.

5   *BBC News*, 'Christchurch mosque attack: Brenton Tarrant sentenced to life without parole', 27 August 2020, online at: https://www.bbc.co.uk/news/world-asia-53919624.

6   Macklin, G., Op Cit.

a 'hive' or 'stochastic')[7] moment that would reverberate around the globe in summer and autumn of 2019 and early 2020 also, providing an ignition switch for various other attacks. From El Paso, to Halle and Hanau, several far-right terror attacks began to be inspired and connected together by scholars, commentators and online far--right communities in what some have tentatively queried as a new wave of global far-right terrorism, reverberating beyond European shores and into North America and Australasia.[8] This maps onto reporting of a 320% rise in far-right terror incidents globally in the past five years[9] as well as national level reporting that suggest that cases to government-run counter-radicalisation programmes have also increased markedly in recent years.[10]

---

[7] Daily Kos, 'Stochastic Terrorism: Triggering the shooters', 11 January 2011, online at: https://www.dailykos.com/stories/2011/1/10/934890/-Stochastic-Terrorism:-Triggering-the-shooters; Hamm, M.S. & Spaaij, R. The Age of Lone Wolf Terrorism. New York: Columbia University Press, 2017, pp. 84–89, & Woo, G., 'Quantitative terrorism risk assessment', Journal of Risk Finance. 4 (1): 7–14, 2002, doi:10.1108/eb022949.

[8] Augur, V.A., 'Right-Wing Terror: A Fifth Global Wave?' Perspectives on Terrorism, 14(3): 87-97, June 2020, online at: https://www.universiteitleiden.nl/binaries/content/assets/customsites/perspectives-on-terrorism/2020/issue-3/auger.pdf & Weinberg, L. & Eubank, W., 'An End to the Fourth Wave of Terrorism?', Studies in Conflict and Terrorism, 33(7): 594-602, 2015, DOI: 10.1080/1057610X.2010.483757.

[9] Institute for Economics & Peace, ,Global Terrorism Index 2019: Measuring the Impact of Terrorism', Sydney, November 2019, online at: http://visionofhumanity.org/app/uploads/2019/11/GTI-2019web.pdf.

[10] Dodd, V. & Grierson, J., 'Fastest-growing UK terrorist threat is from far-right, say police', The Guardian, 19 September 2019, online at: https://www.theguardian.com/uk-news/2019/sep/19/fastest-growing-uk-terrorist-threat-is-from-far-right-say-police & Dearden, L., 'UK saw highest number of far-right terror attacks and plots in Europe in 2019, Europol says', The Independent, 23 June 2020, online at: https://www.independent.co.uk/news/uk/home-news/terror-attacks-far-right-islamist-europe-uk-stanwell-2019-a9581921.html.

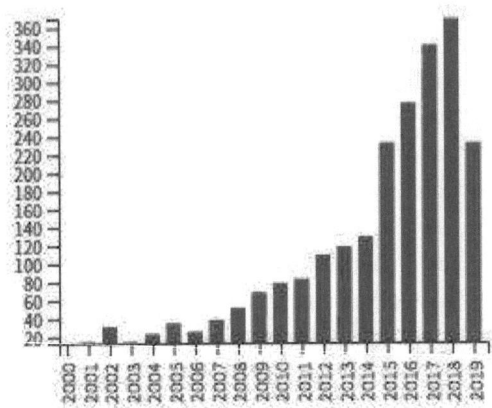

Figure 1: Total Publications Per Year on the Subject of 'Counter Narratives', 1990–2019.[11]

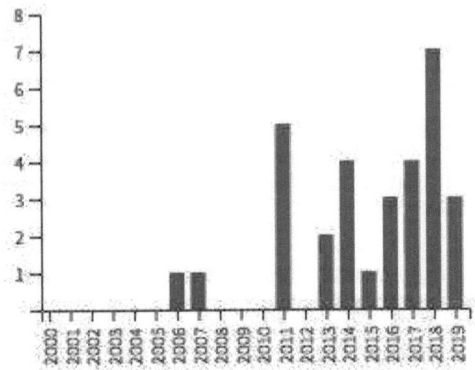

Figure 2: Total Publications Per Year on the Subject of 'Far Right Counter Narratives', 1990-2019.

---

[11] This (and Figure 2) below were sourced in late 2019 from the Web of Science journal article database, searching for 'Counter Narratives' and 'Far Right Counter Narratives'.

When compared with other forms of terrorism, however, little research has been devoted to the study of far-right violence in general and the role of narratives in particular to elicit—but also to combat (as shown in Figure 1 and 2 above)—far-right violence.[12] Moreover, and over the past decade and a half, counter narratives—defined as "a message that ... [demystify] deconstruct or delegitimise extremist narratives"[13]—have become a key part of western counter terrorism toolkits. However, little is known about how we should structure them as a technique and the extent to which they work in stopping individuals from escalating from radicalism to extremist violence. Apart from some notable key exceptions, there are few academic studies aimed at putting counter narratives on a firmer, more empirically rigorous footing. A key aim of this book is to elucidate better how we might go about this—with the use of original data from a UK-based online pilot.

Looking more broadly, however, it is true that certain key factors have frustrated these efforts to tackle far-right radicalisation and violence. Firstly, and most important, the range of ideologies and conspiracy theories that make up the far-right render it a difficult extremist threat to combat. Whether it is more anti-Islam forms of cultural nationalism at the more radical end or neo-Nazi forms of racial nationalism,[14] the diverse nature of far-right ideology frustrates efforts to isolate the ideological inspiration that we are countering.[15] Indeed, at the time of writing, scholars and counter-terrorism officers in the UK were reporting the 'pick and mix' nature of

---

[12] Schuurman, B., 'Topics in terrorism research: reviewing trends and gaps, 2007-2016.' Critical Studies on Terrorism. 12(1), 2019, pp. 463-480.

[13] Tuck, H. & Silverman, H., 'The Counter Narrative Handbook', London: ISD, 2016, p.65, online at: https://www.isdglobal.org/wp-content/uploads/2016/06/Counter-narrative-Handbook_1.pdf.

[14] For more on definitions and conceptualisations of the global far-right, see: Bjørgo, T., & Ravndal, J.A., 'Extreme-Right Violence and Terrorism: Concepts, Patterns, and Responses', ICCT Paper, 23 September 2019, online at: https://icct.nl/publication/extreme-right-violence-and-terrorism-concepts-patterns-and-responses/.

[15] Here 'far-right extremism' is used to describe a broad plethora of cognate paramilitary groups, groupuscules and lone-actor terrorists that could be considered as harbouring violent nativist, authoritarian and (sometimes) non-violent

narratives and conspiracy theories used by terror referrals.[16] Secondly, and added on to this, the definitional issue has filtered down into how national governments define terrorism and what ideologies are included and excluded from government proscription and sanction, with some governments only starting to proscribe far-right extremist groups under terror sanctions relatively recently.[17] The third and most uncomfortable truth is the inherent racialisation in how we talk about communities susceptible to terrorism and the lack of active reflection and introspection where far-right terrorism has become a problem, reaching back into policy debates of what we should and should not define as terrorism.[18] The fourth is the change in threat picture facing Western policymakers that has shifted in the past five years from Islamist extremism as being the predominant threat to far-right extremism. To some extent there is a politics of catch-up here that is lagging behind the threat picture. The fifth (and

---

populist policy ideas (Mudde, C., *Populist Far right in Europe*, Cambridge: Cambridge Uniersity Press, 2007). Far-Right Extremism includes individuals and groups who actively "espouse violence" and "seek the overthrow of liberal democracy" entirely (Eatwell 2003, Ten Theories of the Extreme Right, 14) rather than those who offer "a critique of the constitutional order without any anti-democratic behaviour or intention" (Carter, *The Extreme Right in Western Europe: Success or Failure?*, Manchester: Manchester University Press, 2005, p. 22). Those with such a propensity towards violence and/or anti-system values are historically referred to as the extreme right rather than the far-right, and such individuals and groups range from non-violent anti-Islam groups to a range of formally constituted neo-fascist and neo-Nazi political parties that inspire terrorist action, as well as lone-actor terrorists.

16   Allen, C., 'Extreme far right: 'pick'n'mix' ideologies and direct messaging online make for deadly new combination', *The Conversation*, 19 March 2019, online at: https://theconversation.com/extreme-far-right-picknmix-ideologies-and-direct-messaging-online-make-for-deadly-new-combination-112331 & Baldét, W., 'Preventing violent extremism: we need to talk about Kieron', *Open Democracy*, 25 February 2020, online at: https://www.opendemocracy.net/en/countering-radical-right/prevent-and-terrorism-act-we-need-talk-about-kieron/.

17   Examples of this include: the National Action in the UK, the Russian Imperial Movement in the US and Combat 18/Blood and Honour in Canada.

18   For more on this, see: Groothuis, S., 'Researching race, racialisation, and racism in critical terrorism studies: clarifying conceptual ambiguities', *Critical Studies on Terrorism*, 2020, https://doi.org/10.1080/17539153.2020.1810990.

perhaps most important) factor is a belief that it is predominantly social and not ideological factors drive forms of far-right terrorism.[19] We see this in media depictions of far-right terrorists as mentally unwell, loners without addressing the problematic ideas that lead them down the road of violent action and the uncomfortable mainstreamness of those ideations in the first place.[20]

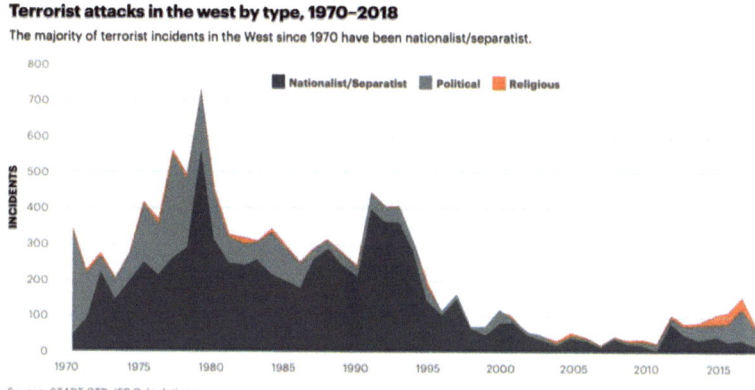

Figure 3:   Terrorist Attacks by Type, 1970-2018[21]

---

[19] For more on this, see: Holbrook, D & and Horgan, J., 'Terrorism and Ideology: Cracking the Nut', Perspectives on Terrorism, 13(6): 2-15, online at: https://www.universiteitleiden.nl/binaries/content/assets/customsites/perspectives-on-terrorism/2019/issue-6/01-holbrook-and-horgan.pdf.

[20] For more empirical evidence of this argument, see: Mudde, C., 'The Populist Far right: A Pathological Normalcy', Western European Politics, 33(6): 1167-1186, online at: https://doi.org/10.1080/01402382.2010.508901.

[21] Institute for Economics & Peace, 'Global Terrorism Index 2019: Measuring the Impact of Terrorism', p. 47, online at: https://reliefweb.int/sites/reliefweb.int/files/resources/GTI-2019web.pdf.

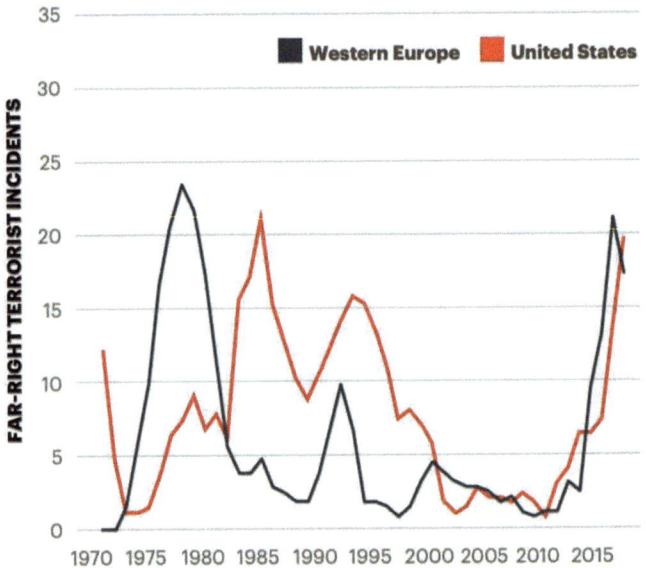

Figure 4: Frequency of Far-Right Terror Attacks, 1970–2018[22]

In any case, and as shown in figure 3 and 4, we now live in an age of far-right violence. As recent terrorist attacks and spikes in hate crimes in the US, Europe and Australia have shown, ideas and messages propagated by far-right actors do lead to organised, violent political action on a scale that is equal (or if not greater) than Islamist extremism. The pertinent question therefore becomes: how do we respond to this? This book aims to identify and evaluate the power of far-right narratives (as a phenomenon in themselves) that are echoing around online extremist ecosystems, terror cells and

---

[22] Ibid, p. 50.

street-based groups at the time of writing and making sense of efforts to counter this in our current epoch. It includes some of the preliminary results of an online pilot to test far-right counter narratives, with much of the material coming from online research, country and region-specific case studies as well as original quantitative study of the effectiveness of far-right counter narratives in one of the locations discussed. It is designed to give a panoptic overview of the global far-right that has been largely lacking in the mainly Eurocentric studies of this phenomenon, knitting together the online and offline networks in North America and Australia that have contributed to this burgeoning fifth wave of extremist violence.[23]

Wave Theory and Terrorism: Contextualising the Current Fifth Wave of Far-Right Extremist Violence

Wave theory has come to be widely accepted in political as a useful historical model in order to describe generational changes in terrorism and extremism over the modern period. According to Rappoport (2004), the principal proponent of wave theory in terrorism research, we can identify four waves of terrorism in the modern era. These include: an 1) Anarchist Wave (1878–1919) spurred by democratic and egalitarian ideals of the French Revolution and characterised by solo-actor assassinations, 2. Anti-Colonial Wave (1920s-1960s) that embraced the post-World War I ideal of national self-determination and tended to use bombings and guerrilla tactics, 3. New Left Wave (mid 1960s-1990s) that was inspired by Marxist-Leninist ideology and a reaction to the Vietnam War, and 4. Religious Wave (1979-present) that was initiated by revolutions and invasions in Middle Eastern countries (notably Iran and Afghanistan).[24] The generational nature of wave theory is a major strength,

---

[23] For more on this critique, see: Gattinara, P.C., 'The study of the far right and its three E's: why scholarship must go beyond Eurocentrism, Electoralism and Externalism', French Politics, https://doi.org/10.1057/s41253-020-00124-8.

[24] Rappoport, D., 'The Fourth Wave: September 11 in the History of Terrorism', Current History, December 2001, pp. 419-424.

although the religious wave does seem to defy the single generation life span allotted to each wave. Wave theory also allows us to identify key characteristics of each wave (e.g., ideology/theology, strategy/tactics, and the use of communications) as well as the persistence of certain trends across time (e.g., the rise and fall of international terroristic movements).

Wave Theory—like other academic theories—has its limits, however. In particular, scholars have criticised it for being analytically blind to groups (such as the IRA and PLO) that have outlived several waves (Kaplan 2016).[25] Moreover, others have suggested that it underplays the trans-historical nature of some terrorist tactics and ideological causes. For example, Parker & Sitter (2015) suggest that we should instead see terrorism evolving through strains and contagion—with four distinct strains in total (Socialist, Nationalist, Religious, and Exclusionist) that can be traced back to the 1850s.[26] Other criticisms of wave theory are based on its analytical utility when explaining the more recent European home-grown jihadism that we see and the predicted decline of the fourth wave. For example, can current home-grown jihadism be powered by the political impulse of events that happened as far back as 1979 (i.e., the Islamic Revolution in Iran and the Soviet invasion of Afghanistan)?[27] Moreover, does not the rise of the Islamic State, the resultant flood of refugees into Western Europe, and the numbing series of high casualty terrorist attacks from 2013 to present suggest that the end of the fourth wave in 2019 is too early to call?

In any case, some suggest that we can add to Rappoport's initial fourth waves with a fifth wave of terrorism—animated by white

---

[25] Kaplin, J., 'Waves of Political Terrorism', In: Oxford Research Encyclopedia of Politics, November 2016, DOI: 10.1093/acrefore/9780190228637.013.24

[26] Parker, T. & Sitter, N., 'The Four Horsemen of Terrorism: It's Not Waves, It's Strains, Terrorism and Political Violence', Terrorism and Political Violence, 28(2): 197-216, 2016, https://doi.org/10.1080/09546553.2015.1112277.

[27] Proshyn, D., 'Breaking the Waves: How the Phenomenon of European Jihadism Militates Against the Wave Theory of Terrorism', International Studies: Interdisciplinary Political and Cultural Journal, 17 (1): 91-107, 2015, online at: http://cejsh.icm.edu.pl/cejsh/element/bwmeta1.element.hdl_11089_17468/c/ipcj-2015-0007.pdf. P.105.

identity and white supremacist concerns. Leonard Weinberg and William Eubank (2012), for example, argue whether we are living in a new age of far-right terrorism whereby the targets are minorities, the modus operandi is gun violence and the mass communicator is the internet.[28] Moreover, and in keeping with the strain theory above, others have predicted a far-right element to the fifth wave premise. D. K. Gupta, for example, suggests that if a fifth wave arrives, it "should exhibit a collective consciousness "either based on ethno-nationalism, religious identity, or economic class."[29] Moreover, Jeffrey Kaplan suggests that the fifth wave should be thought to be composed of "ethnic utopians" trying to remake their societies, following the example of Cambodia's Khmer Rouge.[30] Finally, Jeffrey Simon asserts that the fifth wave will be a "Technological Wave", characterised by "lone operators" using the internet and cyber tools in a similar way to which we have seen in recent far-right terror attacks in North America and Europe.[31]

Equally, and on the other hand, some scholars (Kaplan 2016) — writing before the incidents of 2019 and 2020 — have pointed out that it is largely too early to suggest that a new far-right wave is occurring.[32] In fact, they suggest that we can see the far-right wave fitting into the fourth wave quite easily — with religiosity and a sense of political religion being deep at the heart of the far-right, be it in every stage of the Ku Klux Klan, the Turkish Grey Wolves, the Christian Identity movement, or any of the many varieties of post-War National Socialism. Moreover, much of the modus operandi and mass communicators used by far-right terrorists trade off of the

---

[28] Weinberg, L., & Eubank, W. Op Cit.

[29] Gupta, D.K., 'Waves of international terrorism: An explanation of the process by which ideas flood the world,' in Jean E. Rosenfeld, ed. *Terrorism, Identity and Legitimacy: The Four Waves theory and political violence*. (New York: Routledge, 2011), p. 40.

[30] Kaplan, J., 'Terrorism's Fifth Wave: A Theory, a Conundrum and a Dilemma,' *Perspectives on Terrorism*, 2:2 (January 2008), pp. 12-24.

[31] Simon, J.D., 'Technological and lone operator terrorism: Prospects for a Fifth Wave of Global Terrorism,' in Rosenfeld ed., op. cit., pp. 44-65

[32] Kaplan, J. Op Cit.

same techniques used by ISIS terrorists in the present that might suggest too much of a blurring between a fourth and fifth wave.

What is however clear is that the current fifteen-year epoch of terrorism globally has seen both a qualitative and quantitative shift in the nature of far-right terrorism. As Augur (2020) argues, the expansion of far-right political violence in Europe and North America over the past 10-15 years, the cohesive transnational character of such violence, the similarity of trigger events (e.g., the rising levels of migration and right-wing populist movements), as well as a "common predominant energy" (or cause) around the "awakening the white race to the danger of migration" and changing demographic trends, all provide evidence for Augur's (2020) argument that "right-wing terror does meet the criteria for a wave", which does not appear to be abating anytime yet. [33]

Outline of Book

As we can see from the above overview of the current fifth wave of stochastic far-right terrorism, far-right extremist narratives have provided both the motive and ideological of terrorist action. Various screeds of the Oslo, Christchurch, El Paso, Halle and Hanau shooters demonstrate the awesome power of civilizational narratives and their ability to inspire like-minded actors to carry out 'copy-cat' acts of violence. The good news is that counter narratives posed in contradiction to such narratives can also act as a means of countering terrorism violence. As some scholars have argued, this is not just about micro-interventions but thinking about macro-narratives and the shaping of culture such that individuals, society groups and countries as a whole are able to combat the throes of far-right extremist violence at its earliest stages.[34] It will also take insertion of such counter narratives into online echo chambers at the hard end and a global cultural shift at the soft end to mitigate

---

[33] Augur (Ibid, PP. 89-90).

[34] Glazzard, A. 'Losing the Plot: Narrative, Counter-Narrative and Violent Extremism'. ICCT Research Paper, May 2017, online at: https://icct.nl/wp-content/uploads/2017/05/ICCT-Glazzard-Losing-the-Plot-May-2017.pdf.

far-right extremist messages and movements — weaving such counter narratives into our culture and way of life — if we are truly going to scotch those engaging in this new wave of terrorism at its early stages.

Chapter one will act as a grounding for the rest of the book — reviewing the existing theoretical and empirical academic literature on extremist counter narratives, alternative narratives and strategic communications campaigns. It will track the history of the concept and addresses the hot debates that often surround the use of counter narratives techniques. In the second half of the chapter, we will outline the narrative structure and overarching types of far-right extremist narratives at the present time as well as the array of far-right ideologies 'out there.' It will also outline a new methodology for assessing the strength and effectiveness of far-right narratives and counter narratives — using insights gleaned from the communication studies literature on media effects.

Moving on from chapter one, we will start our journey across six geographical contexts that have become the home of the violent far-right in the past ten to fifteen years, with a comparison of the UK and Germany. Open-source statistical data and online violent extremist literature will be harvested and compared in order to identify the particular far-right extremist narratives in each case. In particular, this chapter will hone in on issues surrounding German reintegration and British national identity, and how these factors enter into the narratives of far-right extremists as well as counter narrative efforts.

Finally, and to complete our journey of the global far-right, we will look beyond Europe among the contexts that are currently animating the most sustained concern among scholars and policymakers when it comes to the violent far-right. Starting with North America first, chapter 3 will compare the far-right extremist scenes in the US and Canada at the present time — with a particular focus on online terroristic subcultures and offline terrorist action. In particular, the chapter will explore civil war nostalgia and perceptions of white marginalization within the narratives of far-right groups in both geographical contexts. Chapter 4 will examine compare the far-right extremist scenes in the Australia and New Zealand—with the latter under renewed attention at the present time.

The book will end with the results of a tie-up between CARR and Facebook aimed at empirically testing five far-right counter narratives amongst individuals in the UK considered being at the tipping point of in the process of radicalizing towards far-right extremist activism. It will lay out the experimental methodology and recruitment method used, the theoretical framework employed, the findings of the study and an assessment of the attitudinal change among participants. This will lead nicely into the final chapter that will outline lessons, recommendations and ways forward for counter narratives when combating the global far-right. Future avenues of research will be mapped out. In particular, a strong emphasis will be put on a shift away from an obsession in terrorism studies of solely looking at Islamist extremism and towards a research agenda that incorporates all extremisms; both violent and non-violent. Notably, there has been little in the way of empirical studies looking at far-right terrorism and possible responses to it—a problem that this book aims to partially remedy.

Chapter 1: The Journey of (Contested) Concepts — Narratives, Counter Narratives and its Application to Far-Right Extremism

Introduction

Narratives[35] have been an important form of political persuasion throughout human history. Aristotle's Poetics (c. 335 BCE), the first surviving text of literary studies, is probably one of the original texts about the study of narratives, or narratology. It was Aristotle who first distinguished two of the fundamental elements of narrative — ordering events into a sequence (what he called "mythos"), and using characters to experience the events (what he called "ethos"). Added to "ethos" (or the character of the messenger), Aristotle also later added that messages need a compelling emotional element (what he called "pathos") and a rational sense of coherence (what he called "logos") in order to persuade an audience.[36] In this book, we define narratives as "any cohesive and coherent account of events ... about characters engaged in acts that result in questions or conflicts for which answers or resolutions are provided".[37] At its core, any good narrative will have an orientation statement (i.e., who, what, where, how & when), action statement (i.c., evaluation of orientation) and resolution statement (i.e., prescribed course of action).[38] It will also have an inner coherence (i.e., have a traceable

---

[35] Here, we see ‚narratives' as one side of the same coin as ideology, with narratives acting as real-world manifestations (or 'vehicles') of ideology.

[36] Braet, A., 'Ethos, Pathos and Logos in Aristotle's Rhetoric: A Re-Examination', *Argumentation*, 6:307-320, 1992.

[37] Braddock, K., *Weaponized Words: The Strategic Role of Persuasion in Violent Radicalization and Counter-Radicalization*, Cambridge: Cambridge University Press, 2020, pp. 59-60.

[38] This is a simplified version of a similar schema, laid out in: Labov, W., & Waletzky, J., 'Narrative analysis: Oral versions of personal experience', *Journal*

and believable logic) and external fidelity (i.e., a resonance with what is going on external to the immediate scenario at play) that make it believable and intelligible.[39]

Far-right terrorist and extremist actors are no different from more mainstream political activists. They use narratives to recruit new members, broadcast their activities and mobilise their individuals into violent action. Most existing models of terrorist narratology suggest that there are many different versions of narratives developed and expounded upon by terrorist organisations but do not take account of the far-right. According to Ashour (2010), for example, there are five key terrorist meta-narratives, which include a: 1. Political Narrative (emphasising the grievances suffered and culprit for said grievances); 2. Historical Narrative (episodes that further evidence the grievance-culprit dichotomy); 3. Socio-psychological Narrative (affective (usually transcendental) appeals revolving around heroism of violent acts linked to core grievance narrative); 4. Instrumental Narrative (e.g., addresses the effectiveness of a particular mode of violent activism for achieving socio-political goals); and 5. Theological Narrative—emphasises the religiously legitimate aspects of activism linked again to the core grievance narrative, including ethical and moral issues (e.g., decadent west) within this narrative. Whilst of course numbers 1-4 apply to the far-right, the last is largely confined to extreme Islamist violence.

Picking up on this gap and exploring this issue further, this chapter outlines the key narratives animating far-right extremists' movements at this current time and then moves on to suggest how counter narratives might be used to reduce appeals to joining the violent far-right. Part of this will be placating a robust framework for the construction and testing of far-right counter narratives that will continue to frame discussion in the rest of the book.

---

of Narrative & Life History, 7(1-4), 1997, 3-38, online at: http://dx.doi.org/10.1075/jnlh.7.02nar

[39] Ashour, A., 'Online De-Radicalization? Countering Violent Extremist Narratives Message, Messenger and Media Strategy', *Perspectives on Terrorism*, 4(6): 15-19, December 2010.

Addressing the Lacuna: Violent Far-Right Narratives under the Fifth Wave of Stochastic Terrorism

When it comes to the far-right, there are a wide range of crisis narratives that far-right actors in the fifth wave of terrorism are currently using to persuade individuals into violent activism. These might be ethno-nationalist messages that suggest there are irreversible demographic trends are leading to the endangerment of Western culture or racially nationalistic notions that a holy war between different ethnic groups is somehow inevitable, with the latter being accelerated through acts of terrorism, political violence and the destruction of the prevailing liberal democratic system.[40] Building on Expert Workshop and Country Reports from CARR and Hedayah's Radical Right Counter Narratives (RRCN) Project (2019-2020),[41] the most prevalent narratives within far-right extremist circles at the present moment (in 2020) are:

1. **Cultural Threat Conspiracy-Theory Narrative**

   Example: "Cultural identities are under threat, elites are complicit in this, and this will end in either a clash of civilisations and/or a "great replacement" of indigenous European culture."[42]

---

[40] Here we can see how conspiracy theories act as a radicalisation multiplier to far-right extremist narratives. See for more information: Emberland, T., 'Why conspiracy theories can act as radicalization multipliers of far-right ideals', *CREX Right Now!* Blog, 24 February 2020, online at: https://www.sv.uio.no/c-rex/english/news-and-events/right-now/2020/conspiracy-theories-radicalization-multipliers.html.

[41] The RRCN country reports are one of many resources as part of Hedayah's Radical Right Counter-Narrative Collection. They give an up-to-date look at far-right extremist trends, groups, narratives, and counter-narrative interventions in nine countries and regions (UK, US, Canada, Germany, Ukraine, the Balkans, New Zealand, Australia and Scandinavia), surveying issues related to far right extremism globally. To access these reports, register for Hedayah's Counter-Narrative Library at: https://www.cn-library.com.

[42] This (and narratives #2, #4, #5, & #7) have been adapted from CARR-Hedayah Far right Counter Narratives Project, 'Expert Workshop Report', London/Abu Dhabi: CARR/Hedayah, pp. 3-6.

One of the most common far-right narratives at the present moment is related to a cultural threat conspiracy theory, a threat perceived as being especially to the 'Christian West' from Islam and 'Islamisation'. Cultural-threat conspiracy theories connected to demographic-based conspiracy theories are circulated by Identitarian groups such Generation Identity, and centre around ideas of a 'Great Replacement' or 'Eurabia' whereby elites (often dubbed 'cultural Marxists') are complicit in the replacement of Christian culture by an 'Islamic Other'. Cultural-threat conspiracy theories, participants noted, are connected with anxieties around the 'push factor' (noted above) of sudden change or loss of culture and/or national identity.

Expert have noted that this sort of narrative connected to micro-level narratives related to the 'threat' of: the subjugation of women, the imposition of sharia law, the building of mosques, the presence of halal food and concerns around child sexual exploitation (often referred to by the far-right in the UK context as 'Muslim Grooming Gangs'). On the more violent end of the spectrum, these concerns were linked to the idea of a modern-day "crusade" against the East, using memory of previous military battles to justify the use of violence.[43]

2. Ethnic Threat Conspiracy Theory Narrative

> "Ethnic identities are under threat, elites are complicit in "white genocide", and this will end in holy racial war."[44]

Another common far-right conspiracy-theory narrative identified in both in the RRCN Project centred around an ethnic threat, a more 'blood and soil' form of racism that tends to map onto ethno-nationalist parts of far-right extremist ideology. This ethnic-threat conspiracy-theory narrative can also be further connected to both

---

[43] Key examples here including the likes of Anders Breivik (2011) and Brenton Tarrant (2019) who dubbed themselves as crusaders and Christian martyrs hoping to bring about a violent 'Christian resistance' against the Muslim 'Other'.

[44] Again, as above, this is a 'mocked up' example (i.e. it is abstracted from similar, real-world far-right extremist narratives).

antisemitic and white-supremacist conspiracy theories circulated by openly neo-fascist and neo-Nazi groups, such as the Azov Battalion in the Ukraine and Combat 14/8 in Europe more generally, as well as (democratically elected) illiberal authoritarian regimes in Eastern and Central Europe that use anti-Soros conspiracy theories.[45] Specific issues connected with ethnic-threat narratives include the use of nationalist histories and 'golden-age' nostalgia, attachment to a homeland and anxieties over 'degeneracy' connected with non-EU migration's 'erosion' of separation between different ethnic groups (i.e., ideas of ethnopluralism). In relation to this form of xenophobia, it can be noted that welfare-state nationalism (or welfare chauvinism) was a "winning formula" of far-right political parties, with a classic example being the French Front National's fusing of anti-immigration and economic nationalist sentiments.[46]

On the more violent end of the spectrum, such narratives can escalate into the idea of the need for a 'racial holy war' (or RaHoWa), in which essentialised and mutually incompatible racial and ethnic groups come into conflict with each other. Variations between mainstream notions of antisemitism (e.g., global elites dictating the 'rules of the game') and xenophobia (e.g., 'migrants taking our X') can be compared to the more extreme narratives of fringe, extremist far-right subcultures (e.g., the idea of Zionist Occupied Governments in the West being controlled by the 'Jews'). In the light of the far-right terror attack in Hanau, Germany, some analysts have suggested that such conspiratorial narratives serve as "radicalisation multiplier" for those involved in violent extremist

---

[45] An example of this is Hungarian Prime Minister, Viktor Orban's claim that global financier, George Soros, has a secret plot to flood Hungary with migrants and thereby destroy their nation. For other examples see: www.bbc.co.uk/news/stories-49584157.

[46] For academic examples of a "winning formula" for far-right extremist parties, see: Rydgren, J., 'Is extreme right-wing populism contagious? Explaining the emergence of a new party family', European Journal of Political Research, 44(3): 413-437, online at: https://doi.org/10.1111/j.1475-6765.2005.00233.x.

milieus, locking violent extremists into a form of thinking that explains their marginality compared to mainstream society.[47] It is advised that practitioners involved in deconstructing such conspiratorial narratives do so with great caution, carefully researching the content, structure and logics of such conspiracies before attempting to counter them.[48] In other words, by attempting to deconstruct these narratives, the narratives of marginality may actually be reinforced, rather than countered.

3. Accelerationist Narrative

> "The Western capitalist system is degenerate and corrupt. We must therefore engage in violent socio-political and economic conflict in order to bring about the revolution and race war that will hasten in a new 'pure' & 'white' system or world order."[49]

One emergent narrative that can be found in the locations outlined in the following chapters is the idea of a revolutionary-right overthrow of democratic systems through a race war or even more apocalyptic scenarios. Attributable to the 'Siege Culture' works of James Mason and adopted by a number of fringe neo-Nazi terror cells, accelerationism has its origins in an anti-democratic neo-reactionary doctrine from the 1990s found in Nick Land's *Dark Enlightenment*, which has since been reinterpreted and adopted by far-right extremist terrorists to justify hastening the overthrow of democratic order. In particular, several groups have subscribed to this doctrine recently, including Atomwaffen Division and the Base in the US, Sonnenkrieg Division in the UK, Antipodean Resistance in Australia, and Feuerkrieg Division in the Baltics. All of these groups are explicitly nihilistic and violent in their scope and have conceived several plots and attacks in the US and Europe in the past two years

---

[47] Emberland, T., Op Cit.

[48] For an indicative example, see: Baele, S., 'Conspiratorial Narratives in Violent Political Actors', Journal of Language and Social Psychology, 38 (5-6), 2019, 706–734, 2019.

[49] This narrative was found to be particularly prevalent among emergent violent far-right extremist groups in the Far-Right Counter-Narrative project's Country Reports for the US, Australia, and New Zealand.

alone.[50] In the UK, for example, Sonnenkrieg Division activists suggest that: "When the day comes, we will not ask whether you swung to the right or whether you swung to the left; we will simply swing you by the neck."[51] Similarly, Antipodean Resistance have talked about the need to "Legalise the execution of Jews."[52] Added to this, links to neo-Nazi satanic and occult groups in their respective locales act to further radicalise individuals involved in these movements, connecting them to an international network of covens and noxious radical groups.

4. Anti-Establishment Narrative

> "Governments, the EU, NATO, the UN & multinational companies have too much power over us, their role is to ostensibly to keep 'the people' down, we therefore need to rise up against them."[53]

One key narrative animating far-right extremism at the time of writing, and connected with narratives 1 & 2 above, is a sense of anti-establishment sentiments by far-right groups aimed against certain policies and elites for letting down so-called 'ordinary people'. Connected with racialized perceptions of economic depriva-

---

[50] Thompson, A.C. & Hanrahan, J., 'Inside Atomwaffen As It Celebrates a Member for Allegedly Killing a Gay Jewish College Student', *ProPublica*, 23 February 2018, online at: https://www.propublica.org/article/atomwaffen-division-inside-white-hate-group; Hawkins, D., & Knowles, H., 'Alleged members of white supremacy group 'the Base' charged with plotting to kill antifa couple', *Washington Post*, 18 January 2020, online at: https://www.washingtonpost.com/national-security/2020/01/18/the-base-white-supremacist-arrests/; & *BBC News*, 'Teenage neo-Nazis jailed over terror offences', 18 June 2019, online at: https://www.bbc.co.uk/news/uk-48672929.

[51] Subcommandante, '[Brief] New Sonnenkrieg Division Propaganda Shared on Fascist Forge', 16 January 2019, online at: https://medium.com/americanodyssey/new-sonnenkrieg-division-propaganda-appears-on-fascist-forge-forum-bb488cefbe53.

[52] Nathan, J., 'Antipodean Resistance: The Rise and Goals of Australia's New Nazis', *ABC News*, 20 April 2018, online at: https://www.abc.net.au/religion/antipodean-resistance-the-rise-and-goals-of-australias-new-nazis/10094794.

[53] Again, as above, this is a 'mocked up' example (i.e. it is abstracted from similar, real-world far-right extremist narratives).

tion and a sense of 'losing out to globalisation', this far-right narrative taps into a wider range grievance to do with multiculturalism, political correctness, political corruption, and the government not providing for 'ordinary' (white) citizens.

Both the expert workshop and country reports for the CARR-Hedayah RRCN project picked up specific instances of this narrative being mobilised. In particular, this anti-establishment narrative was found to exist: 1) in a more diluted version as antisemitic tropes and conspiracy theories (i.e., a nefarious global banking elite); 2) through the idea of a 'deep state' or 'hidden strong powers' who (supposedly) advocate entrenched interests against the 'will of the people'; and 3) through (perceived) covert collaborations deemed t0 advantage Muslim or migrant communities over the native, white community. On the more violent end of the spectrum, such narratives were said to escalate to the idea of the need for attacks against government institutions and officials (supposedly and symbolically) connected with resistance to policy programmes or positions deemed 'against', or a 'threat' to, the 'people'.

5. Misogynist Narrative

> "Societies are under threat because men cannot live 'according to their nature', feminists are traitors, we must return to a heteronormative past."[54]

Another narrative that has gained popularity among far-right extremist groups stems from an endangered form of masculinity. Experts connect this with a sense of nostalgia and traditionalism that hark back to times where culturally expected norms around the family, gender, and sexuality were of a fixed and heteronormative variety. More extreme manifestations of male supremacism were noted by participants, emanating from the alt-right involuntary celibate movement (i.e., 'incel') as well as online gaming subcultures (e.g., Gamergate) as part of a larger online ecosystem of alt-right activism.

---

[54] Again, as above, this is a 'mocked up' example (i.e. it is abstracted from similar, real-world far-right extremist narratives).

While patriarchal ideology runs through all sections of the far-right, it was also noted that divisions exist between different sections. For example, while some sections of the extreme far-right are more firmly patriarchal and traditionalist, others give the appearance of being more progressive. This latter trend can be seen in the leadership of gay (e.g., Pim Fortuyn) and female members (e.g., National Rally's Marine Le Pen and Brothers of Italy's Georgia Meloni), and/or advocating for LGBT and women's rights issues. This use of progressive language is often done, however, in order to counterpoise Western civilization against an essentialised and 'regressive' Muslim 'Other', leading back to the nativist core of far-right ideology.[55] Examples of where more extreme male-supremacist ideas have played a role in recent acts of far-right violence include the Toronto Van Attacker Alek Minassian[56] and Florida Yoga Club Shooter Scott Beierle, who were ultimately enacting violent fantasies on a gendered 'other'.[57]

6. Environmental Narrative

> *Example:* "The earth is running out of resources. Overcrowding by the overbreeding of non-whites is a tangible threat. Not everyone will be able to hold out. It is therefore vital to ensure that 'our' (i.e. white) people survive."[58]

One other emergent narrative being used by far-right extremists is the idea of demographic endangerment related to theories of overpopulation by non-whites and the depletion of an ethnically 'pure' homeland as a result. Coming to prominence in far-right solo-actor manifestoes of the Christchurch and El Paso shooters, so-called

---

[55] See Chapter 1 of Mudde, C., *Populist Radical Right Parties in Europe*, Cambridge: Cambridge University Press, 2007, PP. 11-31.

[56] Zaveri, M., Jacobs, J. and Mervosh, S., 'Gunman in Yoga Studio Shooting Recorded Misogynistic Videos and Faced Battery Charges.' *New York Times*, 3 November 2018, Hyperlink: https://www.nytimes.com/2018/11/03/us/yoga-studio-shooting-florida.html.

[57] *BBC*, 'Alek Minassian Toronto van attack suspect praised 'incel' killer', 25 April 2018, online at: https://www.bbc.co.uk/news/world-us-canada-43883052.

[58] This narrative was found to be particularly prevalent among Identitarian far-right extremist groups in New Zealand.

'eco-fascists' portray ecological decay and crisis as a threat to the racial integrity of the white race with the only possible resolution being an end to mass immigration and uncontrolled urbanization under a form of authoritarian leadership.[59] In New Zealand, for example, Action Zealandia and the (now defunct) Dominion Movement talk about how more established left-wing and right-wing actors have failed to be "environmentally conscious in their governance", and therefore betrayed 'the people' in favour of multiculturalism and capitalism.[60] Here, we can see how far-right extremists try to use emerging, socio-cultural wedge issues, such as the environment and law and order, to exploit a niche within public discourse into which they insert their own exclusionary narratives and anti-democratic processes.[61]

7. Victimhood Narrative

> Example: "Governments favour ethnic and religious minorities over the majority white population. Anti-Politically-Correct (PC) comments lead to persecution. Ordinary people are being silenced."[62]

One final narrative, largely connected with the above anti-establishment sentiments, evinces a sense of victimhood, marginalisation or silencing in political affairs. This victimhood narrative is a recent *cause célèbre* among far-right actors concerning 'free speech' and the idea of certain unorthodox viewpoints being stifled by 'political correctness'. Compared to more mainstream, populist grievances,

---

[59] Bernhard, F., 'Eco-fascism: justifications of terrorist violence in the Christchurch mosque shooting and the El Paso shooting', *Open Democracy*, 13 August 2019, online at: https://www.opendemocracy.net/en/countering-far right/eco-fascism-justifications-terrorist-violence-christchurch-mosque-shooting-and-el-paso-shooting/.

[60] Power, G., 'Nationalism and the Environment', *Action Zealandia* Website, 26 August 2019, online at: https://action-zealandia.com/articles/nationalism-and-the-environment.

[61] See the following for examples: Callahan, D., 'How New Wedge Issues are Dividing the Right', *Demos*, 7 November 2013, online at: https://www.demos.org/blog/how-new-wedge-issues-are-dividing-right.

[62] Again, as above, this is a 'mocked up' example (i.e. it is abstracted from similar, real-world far-right extremist narratives).

however, this victimhood narrative has a more ethnic and religious hue to it—blaming deprivations on elites (allegedly) listening to one racial or religious community over another. As one workshop participant pointed out, reinforcement of this narrative is seen in local 'folklore' around priority housing, criminality, and lenient prison sentences for minority communities, while 'white' citizens are viewed by the elites (including the media) as an underclass of 'bad people'. A particular UK-based example given of this victimhood narrative was the summer 2018 'Free Tommy' protests at the trial of former EDL leader, Tommy Robinson (aka Stephen Yaxley Lennon), for contempt of court charges.[63] Other examples are the 2011 and 2016 court trials against Geert Wilders[64] and the 2017 campus tours carried out by alt-right influencer Milo Yiannopoulos, whereby both these far-right actors were able to frame opposition to their viewpoints in terms of denials of free speech.[65]

---

[63] Staff Reporter, 'Far-right activists stage violent protest calling for Tommy Robinson to be freed.' *The Independent,* 9 June 2018, online at: https://www.independent.co.uk/news/uk/crime/tommy-robinson-protest-london-far-right-police-arrest-geert-wilders-a8391596.html.

[64] See *BBC News,* 'Dutch anti-Islam MP Geert Wilders goes on trial.', 4 October 2010, online at: https://www.bbc.co.uk/news/world-europe-11464025 & Boztas, S., 'Trial of anti-Islamic politician Geert Wilders begins in Netherlands over his 'fewer Moroccans' comment', *The Telegraph,* 31 October 2016, online at: https://www.telegraph.co.uk/news/2016/10/31/trial-of-anti-islamic-politician-geert-wilders-begins-in-netherl/.

[65] Svrluga, S., 'UC-Berkeley says 'Free Speech Week' is cancelled. Milo Yiannopoulos says he's coming anyway.' *Washington Post,* 23 September 2017, online at: https://www.washingtonpost.com/news/grade-point/wp/2017/09/23/uc-berkeley-says-free-speech-week-is-canceled-milo-yiannopoulos-says-hes-still-coming-to-campus/?utm_term=.2086d6df7ad7.

The Journey of a (Contested) Concept—Counter Narratives, Islamist Extremism and its Application to Far-Right Extremism

Over the past decade, counter narratives—defined as messages that can "[demystify], deconstruct or delegitimise extremist narratives"[66]—have become a key part of western efforts to combat terrorism. Placed at the softer end of counter-terrorism (CT) tactics, the use of communications in order to disrupt organisations committed to violent extremist causes has come to occupy the 'upstream' space of preventative measures available to governments, non-governmental organisations (NGOs), and civil-society actors wishing to counter political violence at the ideational level. Such a communications-focused approach has become especially important as terrorist organisations have become more adept at using social media in order to radicalise and recruit. The internet and social media have been used to circumvent traditional forms of media and face-to-face encounters in order to spread messages using targeted propaganda techniques. As far-right terrorism picks up momentum, a 'war of words and ideas,' in addition to counter-terrorism actions on the ground, is much-needed in order to combat the threat of far-right extremist violence In particular, and as seen through the examples of attacks in Christchurch, El Paso, Halle, and Hanau,[67] the use of manifestos, online meme culture and conspiracy theories has knit together disparate, transnational groups of far-

---

[66] Tuck, H. and Silverman, T., 'The Counter Narrative Handbook', London: ISD, 2016, 65, online at: https://www.isdglobal.org/wp-content/uploads/2016/06/Counter-narrative-Handbook_1.pdf.

[67] Helsel, P., 'Suspect in Christchurch mosque shootings charged with terrorism', *NBC News*, 21 May 2019, online at: https://www.nbcnews.com/news/world/suspect-christchurch-mosque-shootings-charged-terrorism-n1008161; Romo, V. 'El Paso Walmart Shooting Suspect Pleads Not Guilty,' *NPR*, 10 October 2019, online at: https://www.npr.org/2019/10/10/769013051/el-paso-walmart-shooting-suspect-pleads-not-guilty; *BBC*, 'German Halle gunman admits far-right synagogue attack', 11 October 2019, online at: https://www.bbc.co.uk/news/world-europe-50011898; Hucal, S., 'Racially motivated terror attack in Hanau puts Germany's right wing extremism into focus', *ABC*

right actors in favour of accelerationist, political violence.[68] The seemingly sporadic and solo actor nature of the attacks has posed a key challenge to Countering Violent Extremism (CVE) practitioners.

Despite this renewed challenge and imperative, little guidance is available to practitioners, civil society, and NGOs on how to design successful counter narrative campaigns specific to the far-right. Indeed, the majority of articles, handbooks, guidance notes, and briefing documents on the topic tend to privilege either an ideologically agnostic approach, or one specific to Islamist extremism.[69] Some studies have bucked this trend but don't generally focus on the far-right per se. In order to address this lacuna, it is best to return back to the fundamentals of narratology and see how the above emergent narratives might be best countered.

If attempting to construct counter narratives in order to disrupt, delegitimise and/or devalue the appeal of the above narratives, for example, it is useful to identify what we can call 'entry points' within the structure of extremist narratives in order to unpick their veracity, authenticity and believability. As suggested in the introduction to this chapter, such far-right counter narratives can be done by breaking down such narratives into their orientation statement (i.e., who, what, where, how & when), action statement

---

News, 27 February 2020, online at: https://abcnews.go.com/US/racially-motivated-terror-attack-hanau-puts-germanys-wing/story?id=69128298.

[68] For a good overview of the 2019 wave of far-right extremist attacks, see: Macklin, G., 'The El Paso Terrorist Attack: The Chain Reaction of Global Right-Wing Terror', *CTC Sentinel*, December 2019, online at: https://ctc.usma.edu/app/uploads/2019/12/CTC-SENTINEL-112019.pdf.

[69] See: Briggs, R. & Feve, S., 'Review of Programs to Counter Narratives of Violent Extremism', London: ISD, 2013; Tuck, H. & Silverman, H., 'The Counter Narrative Handbook', London: ISD, 2016; Reynolds, L & Tuck H., 'The Counter Narrative Monitoring and Evaluation Handbook', London: ISD, 2016: Silverman, Stewart, Amanullah and Birdwell, 'The Impact of Counter Narratives'. London: ISD, 2016; & Hedayah/ICCT, 'Developing Effective Counter-Narrative Frameworks for Countering Violent Extremism'. Hedayah/ICCT: Abu Dabi/Hague, September 2014.

(i.e., evaluation of orientation) and resolution restatement (i.e., prescribed course of action).[70] Whilst it might be unprofitable to contest the factual veracity of the orientation statement, both the action and solution statements of the narrative might be more profitably contested. The rationale behind such a technique is that far-right extremists tend to do most harm in how they interpret and offer solutions to what is happening 'out there', and how they frame reality. Opinions are also a softer target than facts, and this maps onto how extremists use grievances to add their own ideological 'twist' on real world events. Therefore, disputing the action and resolution statement are more profitable as it means practitioners are disputing the ideological interpretation of the truth (or factual reality) presented, rather than the reality itself. Below are some key counter-narratives that could deployed by practitioners to respond to the violent far-right extremist messages identified above, and could include:

1. **Factual or Historical Counter Narrative** — "Seeing society through a racialized lens breaks down bonds of togetherness which ultimately leads to a worse outcome for everyone. By seeing what unites us, we can move forward, stronger together."
2. **Ideological Counter Narrative** — "Social separation is what fosters misunderstandings and hatred between different people groups. Mixing fosters understanding and shows that shared social, economic and political resources work. Notions of superiority fail to recognise the good in other cultures and religions and the bad in our own."
3. **Economic Counter Narrative** — "Being subject to impersonal economic forces is trying for all citizens, we are all negatively affected by economic disadvantage equally, the solution is working together to make sure that globalisation and the economic system works for all."

---

[70] This is a simplified version of a similar schema, laid out in: Labov, W., & Waletzky, J., 'Narrative analysis: Oral versions of personal experience', *Journal of Narrative & Life History*, 7(1-4), 1997, 3-38, online at: http://dx.doi.org/10.1075/jnlh.7.02nar.

4. **Alternative or Positive Narrative**—"X is a feminist activist but engages in the same everyday activity as you and I. They are engaged in social action and do not take preferences or sides. Their activism helps increase the pool of rights we all enjoy."
5. **Political Counter Narrative**—"There are problems and deficits within all democracies. Governments and elected officials provide a directly accountable individual for each citizen. By standing for office or voting in elections, you will be able to change the system from the insider."

Evaluating Far-Right Counter-Narratives: Testing Effectiveness and Impact

Despite their widespread popularity, the effectiveness of counter-messaging interventions has become a hot topic of debate in recent years, with better efforts adopted more recently to robustly assess and evaluate whether such programmes lead to sustained attitudinal and behavioural change.[71] Nowhere else has this debate been more evident in the field of counter-narratives used as a soft counter-terrorism approach in order to prevent and counter violent extremism. In particular, the issue of empirical effect of whether words change deeds and small-scale evidence base for what makes

---

[71] See: Dawson, L., Edwards, C.,& Jeffray, C., 'Learning and Adapting: The Use of Monitoring and Evaluation in Countering Violent Extremism', London: RUSI, 2014; Helmus, T.C. et al, 'RAND Programme Evaluation Toolkit for Countering Violent Extremism', Santa Monica, Ca: RAND Corporation, Holmer, G. & Bauman, P., 'Measuring Up: Evaluating the Impact of P/CVE Programmes', Washington, DC: United States Institute of Peace; Lewis, J., Knott, K., & Marsden, S., 'Countering Violent Extremism II: A Guide to Good Practice', Lancaster, UK: Centre for Evidence on Security Threats, Mattei, C. & Zeiger, S., 'Evaluate Your CVE: Projecting Your Impact', Hedayah: Abu Dhabi, 2018; & RAN Network, 'Guideline Evaluation of PCVE Programmes and Interventions', Brussels: RAN, July 2018.

a successful counter-narrative intervention has come under the microscope.[72] In order to expand such an evidence base, robust metrics and statistics to test the effectiveness of counter-narrative campaigns in diverting individuals away from far-right milieus should therefore be at the forefront of practitioners and NGOs approaches to designing, conducting, and evaluating such interventions.

In this vein, campaign metrics are key to testing the success of any prospective far-right counter-narrative campaign. As highlighted below, there is an emerging consensus on the metrics — when assessing the effectiveness of any counter-messaging campaign, which now revolve around awareness, engagement, & impact indicators. For practitioners, it can be argued that it is key to the success of any campaign to be conscious of these metrics, how they contribute to the main objective of an intervention and the extent to which they help quantify the goals of a campaign from the start. Such a proactive approach has the additional advantage of reducing the risk of data lost due to ignorance — and therefore valuable statistical information that can help inform and evaluate counter-narrative efforts. In this part of the chapter, we will move through each of the steps needed to thoroughly evaluate the impact and effectiveness of a far-right counter-narrative campaign — useful to both academics and practitioners in this field of study.

Define the Context and State the Problem being addressed

Understanding the context of the country or local community is important to designing a far-right counter-narrative campaign, which ultimately influences monitoring, measurement and evaluation. In identifying the local context, it is important to consider how the campaign counters the 'push', 'pull' & 'enabling' factors related to the type of far-right extremism being targeted (see table 1 below), as well as how it may be perceived or received by the far-right ex-

---

[72] For an in-depth rehearsal of some of these arguments, see: Ferguson, K., 'Countering violent extremism through media and communication strategies', University of East Anglia: Partnership for Conflict, Crime & Security Research, pp. 10-16.

tremist community or target audience that is the focus of a campaign (see table 2 for examples of localised scenarios and audiences).

The ultimate goal of evaluation (also based on 'Theory of Change' developed in step two) should be to measure how far a campaign has gone in addressing the problem identified (e.g., radicalisation of youth (aged 11-18) at the site of far-right extremist demonstrations or young adults (aged 18-35) on far-right extremist social media boards or channels) and that it is grounded in the context in which it is situated. Whether that be online or offline, the evidence suggests that it needs to be localised to the area, grievances and drivers of far-right extremist activism that is being targeted (e.g., young far-right extremist foreign fighters (ages of 18-35) who have been or are returning from the Ukraine).

Table 1: Push & Pull Factors into Violent Far-Right Extremism

Push Factors/Structural Motivators	Pull Factors/Individual Incentives
Social/Psychological Sense of Religious, Ethnic or Cultural Marginalisation, Loss & Endangerment (related to Religious, Ethnic or Cultural Changes) Broader Processes of Social Fragmentation, Isolation & Disintegration Childhood Trauma (e.g., Bullying, Abuse & Emotional Disintegration) Poor Mental Health (e.g., Autism, Depression & Personality Disorders) Economic Sudden Global Economic Change or Upheaval – either through Recession or Substantial Shift in means of Production Unemployment, Low Levels of Educational Attainment & Career Success	Psychological 'Buzz' or Thrill Seeking within Direct Action Activism Attractiveness of Violent and/or Performative Masculinity Social Offer of Brotherhood, Belonging & Comradery Offer of Social Empowerment and/or Social Engagement Political/Ideological Attractiveness of Control or Sense-Making over 'Outside Forces' Attractiveness of Alternative Outlet for Political Engagement and Activism

Political Loss of Political Trust in Mainstream Actors around Handling of Migration, as well as associated Cultural and Security Politics Sense of Political Silencing & Exclusion from Mainstream Political Institutions	
Enabling Factors	
Contact with 'Person of Influence' or activists within Far-right Extremist Milieus, either online or offline 'Calls to action' by extremist groups after particular flashpoints (e.g., child sexual exploitation, inter-racial rioting or Islamist terror attack) Availability of Extremist Texts (such as William Pierce's *Turner Diaries* or Renaud Camus' *Great Replacement*) Online Forums and Communities (such as Iron March, 8Kun, and neo-Nazi Telegram Channels)	

Table 2: Examples of Far-Right Counter Narrative Scenarios

Scenario	Target Audience	Counter-Narrative Campaign Example
You have been tasked to put together a far-right counter-narrative campaign in the wake of a neo-Nazi terror attack.	Young people using alternative social media or gaming platforms between the ages of 18-35.	Peer-to-Peer online counter-narrative interventions designed to delegitimise forms of violence.
You have been tasked with diverting people away from online clandestine neo-Nazi networks.	Young people (aged 18-35) involved in online clandestine neo-Nazi networks but exist normally in the 'outside world'.	Platform-endorsed messaging targeting such users and aimed at delegitimising racially nationalist and dehumanising language.
You are situated in an area with a high frequency of sizeable anti-Islam protests.	Young adults (aged 11-18) who live in a peripheral or post-industrial town who might get sucked into these protests.	Social media and offline schools-based educational programmes designed at highlighting risks of engaging in such protests.
You are situated in an area with a high frequency of commemorative marches that glorify Nazism.	Older people (aged 40-65) who live in a relatively affluent but homogenously white Western	Innovative offline advertising campaign at site of protest highlighting donations to anti-racist

	city who have low levels of political education.	charities for each mile marched.
You are situated in an area with a recent increase of refugees and asylum seekers.	Older people (aged 40-65) who live in such areas.	Innovative offline billboard advertising campaign highlighting stories and similarities with refugees and asylum seekers.
You are situated at a university with a high frequency of Identitarian activism and 'stickering' campaigns.	University students (ages of 18-25) who are situated in such an area.	Creative counter-'stickering'[73] campaign involving humorous depictions of hipster Nazi's.
You are situated in a country with a large number of returning far-right extremist fighters.	Young far-right extremist foreign fighters (ages of 18-35) who have been or are returning from the Ukraine.	Peer-to-Peer offline counter-narrative interventions designed to delegitimise forms of violence.
You are situated in an East German town with an annual White Power Music festival.	Young far-right extremist heavy metal fans (ages of 18-35) who visit White Power Music festivals.	A clandestine distribution of counter-narrative T-shirts that reveal a counter-narrative message once washed.

Develop a 'Theory of Change' (ToC) and write a detailed ToC Statement

Another key element of campaign design with regards to goals and objectives should be to ensure a RRCN campaign has a logical Theory of Change (ToC). This means that the inputs, activities, outputs and outcomes should all connect to the goal or objective of a campaign through a specific correlational logic.

---

[73] Here, 'Stickering' is defined as the act of putting up small poster-like stickers conveying far-right propaganda. It has become especially popular with Identitarian groups (such as Generation Identity Europe, Identity Australia, and Action Zealandia) and Neo-Nazi cells (such as National Action) as stickers can be easily downloaded and printed from templates online.

A ToC explains therefore how the activities and results of the campaign are connected to each other.[74] It offers a testable hypothesis for determining the impact of a counter-narrative campaign on its target audience (e.g., significantly decreasing the number of neo-Nazi's wishing to join the violent far-right extremist battalion to under 100.). The ToC incorporates three types of projected results that should be articulated based on this correlational logic:

a) **Outputs** are measurable products (usually quantitative) of a campaign's activities. Often outputs are recorded measures in terms of units completed. For example, number of participants with an increased understanding of risks of far-right extremist activism after a campaign.
b) **Outcomes** are the intended results of campaign activities (usually qualitative). Often outcomes are expressed in terms of change in behaviour or attitudes. For example, the enhanced understanding of the contradictions in far-right extremist ideology might be a campaign outcome amongst the recipients.
c) **Impact** refers to the ultimate goal or objective of the campaign, affiliated with both the recipients and larger target population of far-right leaning individuals.

Often impact (e.g., diversion away from far-right ideology) is the most difficult component to measure. However, outputs and outcomes should support the measurement of impact through the ToC derived from the outset. This means that although impact (e.g., diversion away from far-right ideology) might not be visible or measurable immediately, it is still possible to reasonably consider its projection (e.g., numbers leaving far-right extremist groups), through the ToC.

---

[74] For an example of a more sophisticated Theory of Change map, see: Mattei, C. & Zeiger, S., 'Evaluate Your CVE: Projecting Your Impact', Hedayah: Abu Dhabi, 2018, p. 17.

Theory of Change Statement

As part of developing a ToC for a RRCN intervention, an intervention designer should take into consideration the underlying assumptions outlined in step 1 and articulate them in a concise statement that maps the logical flow of the inputs, activities, outcomes and projected impact. In its simplest form, a ToC Statement can be expressed through an "IF", "THEN" and "BECAUSE" statement. The ToC statement can help to articulate the broader ToC of the RRCN campaign in a succinct and useful way, particularly in reporting to donors and partners. Several examples of simplified ToC Statements are below:

Campaign A: Diversion of neo-Nazis away from a Violent Far right Extremist Battalion
IF neo-Nazis sympathetic to battalion Group G receive warnings and diluted negative information about the negative activities of Group G
AND
IF neo-Nazis suspect it as part of an infiltration effort
THEN they will reject entreaties to join the violent far right extremist battalion
BECAUSE Group G has been delegitimised in their eyes (both from an ideological but also a strategic standpoint)

Campaign B: Diverting older people away from Violent Far-right Extremist Protest
IF older people (aged 40–65) are situated in an area with a recent increase of refugees and asylum seekers receive messages highlighting positive stories and similarities with refugees and asylum seekers
AND are saturated with those messages over a sustained period

Identify the Goals & Objectives of the Campaign and quantify/link them to each intervention

The goal or objective of a far-right counter narrative campaign should be focused on changing attitudes and behaviours of participants, because of the campaign. Within the overarching category of goal and objectives, it may be decided to insert sub-goals and sub-objectives in order to complete these larger macro-objectives. When setting evaluating a programme, it is important to keep in mind the resources available for the programme. The goals should be realistic as per the available resources and activities, and should not try to achieve too much or too little. For an example of goal setting (based on what has been said so far), see the below case study example:

> **EXIT Deutschland 'Nazis against Nazis' Campaign (2014)**
> Description: From 2001 until today, there is a commemorative march for Hitlers' deputy, Rudolf Heß, held in the Upper Franconian German city of Wunsiedel, where he was buried. The city has become a pilgrimage destination for neo-Nazis. Exit Germany designed a campaign against these marches with a simple idea: Adopt a charity run model of miles run but apply it to the neo-Nazis' march. With every meter achieved by the far-right extremist participants, they unlocked 10 Euros of (previously raised) funds for the EXIT Deutschland and its activities. So, the demonstrators faced the dilemma of demonstrating and donating or not demonstrating and admitting defeat. On 15 November 2014, the campaign started.
>
> **Step 1: Assess Push and Pull Factors**
> Push Factors:
> Sense of Religious, Ethnic or Cultural Loss & Endangerment
> Broader Processes of Social Fragmentation, Isolation & Disintegration
> Loss of Political Trust in Mainstream Actors around Handling of Migration, as well as associated Cultural and Security Politics
> Sense of Political Silencing & Exclusion from Mainstream Political Institutions
> Pull Factors:
> 'Buzz' or Thrill-seeking within Direct Action Activism
> Violent and/or Performative Masculinity
> Need for Brotherhood, Belonging & Comradery
> Need for Social Empowerment or Engagement
> Control or Sense-Making over 'Outside Forces'
> Alternative Outlet for Political Engagement and Activism
> Enabling Network:

Contact with 'Person of Influence' or activists within Far-right Extremist Milieus, either online or offline.

Step 2: Identify Target Audience
Sympathizers & Justifiers
The immediate target audience were, of course, the 250 neo-Nazi's who took to the streets in Wunsiedel that November, but also the press and local residents of the town.

Step 3: Identify Violent Extremist Narrative Being Countered
Like Exit Germany's Trojan Horse T-Shirt campaign, the violent extremist narratives being countered were around: 1) the implicit control that far-right-wing extremist actors had over their activities, 2) the personal narratives of demonstrators that they were 'free' to go about these activities without interference, and 3) the belief that to the solemn and serious nature of the marches could not be subverted — in this case by decorating the streets with jovial signs and slogans.

Step 4: Set Clear Goals and Objectives for Interventions

Goal 1:
Raising Awareness (and funds) for the work of Exit Germany in far-right de-radicalisation and disengagement within non-aligned audiences and the extremist scene at large.
Goal 2:
Diverting those advancing in their commitment to white supremacist belief systems through questioning the control and freedom that they had to march.
Goal 3:
Undermining Appeal through parodying solemn parades Neo-Nazis and poking fun at key ideological slogans and epithets.

Determine the Key Indicators and measure success based on the state goals and objectives

The key indicators should always refer to goals and objectives and should actually be able to measure the change of the status quo in the progression towards a far-right counter narrative campaign's goals and objectives. When developing key indicators and measures, it is important to take into consideration the methods utilised for evaluation (again, the logic model should be considered holistically as a later step might affect the previous one). Key Indicators may be either qualitative or quantitative:

- **Quantitative Measures** are numerical and have the advantage that they are easier to compare over time. For quantitative measures, it is also often possible to use visualization (graphics or charts) and statistical methods to analyse and compare the dataset.
- **Qualitative Measures** are descriptions of change over time (i.e., behaviours, attitudes or institutions) that are not captured in a numerical format. Qualitative measures may not be able to be analysed using statistical data (although qualitative descriptions can sometimes be coded), and may be assessed subjectively or based on a particular context.

In Country X, there is a problem with a large number of far-right extremists joining a violent extremist battalion, Group G, from abroad and engaging in raids against domestic military units and populations. Group G aims to support the overthrow of a democratically elected government in Country X and (at least theoretically) institute a fascist, authoritarian political system where white people will 'reign supreme'. Group G recruits young people on the internet on alternative social media platforms and bulletin boards that are popular among neo-Nazi's (e.g., Telegram, VK, 4Chan, 8Kun, and Neinchan). They also expand their recruiting efforts through infiltrating other far-right extremist groups in other countries within the region.

Counter-Narrative Program

Counter-narrative developers decide to develop a campaign to raise awareness of negative consequences of joining Group G in Country X.[75] This will be done through three channels:

---

[75] Zeiger, S., Op Cit.,p. 30.

1. Posting on Chan-type image boards connected to Group G, including the re-mixing of their propaganda in a satirical and humorous fashion;

2. Social media information campaigns designed to delegitimise the proxy war in the eyes of white nationalists (both in Country X and elsewhere);

3. Warnings posted to far-right extremist VK and Telegram groups warning of infiltration by 'Group G' in the wider regional context.

Goal:

Significantly decreasing the number of neo-Nazi's wishing to join the violent far-right extremist battalion to under 100.

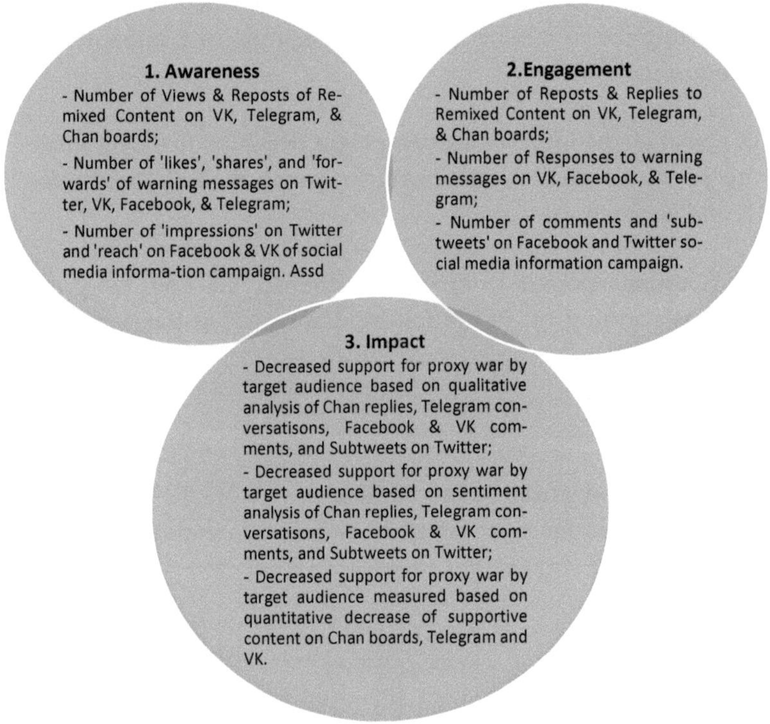

1. Awareness
- Number of Views & Reposts of Remixed Content on VK, Telegram, & Chan boards;
- Number of 'likes', 'shares', and 'forwards' of warning messages on Twitter, VK, Facebook, & Telegram;
- Number of 'impressions' on Twitter and 'reach' on Facebook & VK of social media informa-tion campaign. Assd

2. Engagement
- Number of Reposts & Replies to Remixed Content on VK, Telegram, & Chan boards;
- Number of Responses to warning messages on VK, Facebook, & Telegram;
- Number of comments and 'subtweets' on Facebook and Twitter social media information campaign.

3. Impact
- Decreased support for proxy war by target audience based on qualitative analysis of Chan replies, Telegram conversatisons, Facebook & VK comments, and Subtweets on Twitter;
- Decreased support for proxy war by target audience based on sentiment analysis of Chan replies, Telegram conversatisons, Facebook & VK comments, and Subtweets on Twitter;
- Decreased support for proxy war by target audience measured based on quantitative decrease of supportive content on Chan boards, Telegram and VK.

Figure 5: Example Indicators for a Far-Right Counter-Narrative Campaign

Determine the Tools & Collection Methods used to obtain the desired data

There are multiple formative and summative evaluation techniques and tools that can be used to elicit both quantitative and qualitative data tied to a far-right counter-narrative campaign. This can be through opinion polls with target audiences, personal testimonies from intervention providers, interviews with those have reached out as a result of an intervention, focus groups to pilot key messages before the main campaign, media monitoring during the campaign, and experimental randomised control research to again pilot key messages. When it comes to far-right extremism, the first hand, research (as described above) might be difficult to negotiate, especially when there is a suspicious or hard-to-reach audiences. Here, trust and openness are important when doing such first-hand data collection. Moreover, in order to obtain a clear measure of a campaign, it is important use data to measure the overall impact of sustained attitudinal and behavioural change (e.g., less support for far-right extremist ideas and activism) as a result of the intervention as this will give practitioners and academics a better steer of what does and does not work with a target audience.

Sometimes it might not however be practicable to directly test this with a target audience. In this case, it might be good to find proxy test subjects (e.g., government officials, practitioners, or social workers) who have contact with a target audience and who will be able to answer questionnaires and surveys containing specific and tailored questions to how the target audience is now thinking and behaving (online and offline) as a result of the counter-narrative campaign.

Some tools and collections methods helpful for measuring the effects of far-right counter-narrative campaigns include the following (with # 2 better for piloting and & #1 & # 3 better for testing summative outcomes of a RRCN campaign):

- **Awareness** (e.g., no. of impressions, views, frequency and reach beyond initial audience) — metrics here are about how, when and where users are exposed to a campaign, and which parts of the campaign reached them, added to this it is useful

to know the broad demographic characteristics of those exposed to the campaign.
- **Engagement** (e.g., likes, shares, retweets, comments, direct messages and email) — metrics here provide an indication of the quality and frequency of interactions between audiences and a campaign. For some campaigns (especially with those at risk of violent extremism), higher levels of engagement might be a more appropriate gauge of success. Added to this, it might also be important to measure how long and in what way users react to the content.
- **Impact** — understanding the definite impact of online counter narrative campaigns is tricky but involves using both awareness and engagement statistics to measure whether the goals set for the campaign have been met. Follow-up questionnaires, data mining techniques (e.g., sentiment and key word analysis), and expert reviews can be used to aid this process. Both Louis Reynolds and Henry Tuck (2016) suggest campaigns should be differentiated between Upstream (i.e., general public) and Downstream (i.e., those interested in — or engaged in the dissemination of — extremist propaganda) users.[76]

Determine Whether Staff Have the Appropriate Capacity

When evaluating a far-right counter-narrative campaign, there is always the need for pragmatism. When defining the goals and objectives of the campaign, practitioners need to define the key indicators and measures, the methods and tools that will be used to evaluate, but it also necessary to give affordances for the capacity and limitations of the team behind the intervention when evaluating a counter-narrative project.

Counter-narrative campaign organisers should at least take into consideration the training, resources and capacity available for MM&E when setting goals and objectives of the campaign. However, sometimes goals and objectives are set by donors, and may not be able to be

---

[76] Reynolds, L & Tuck H., "The Counter Narrative Monitoring and Evaluation Handbook", London: ISD, 2016.

adjusted. If there are limitations to MM&E capacity and resources, the counter-narrative campaign organiser may need to recognize that concrete results for evaluation may be limited, or reach out to a third-party-organisation (such as a research centre or academic body) to carry out an independent evaluation on their behalf.

Being realistic here about the competencies of the team you're evaluating (both in terms of content-specific expertise to do with understanding the grievances, drivers and activism of far-right but also moderation and ability to collect data plus the time they have set aside for MM&E) is therefore vitally important in order to capture good quality data on a particular far-right counter-narrative intervention.

Assess the Results on the basis of data collected

Evaluations should refer back to the ToC and goals and objectives (set back in steps 2 & 3), and should inform current and future campaigns. If measurement and monitoring activities are properly set up at the start of the campaign, early results can also be included in feedback loops throughout the campaign to optimise the effectiveness of campaign interventions. The below is a recap of Outputs, Outcomes and Impacts used to evaluate RRCN campaign examples and to elaborate on information set out in step 2:

- **Outputs** are measurable products (usually quantitative) of a campaign's activities. Often outputs are recorded measures in terms of units completed. For example, number of participants with an increased understanding of the risks of far-right extremist activism after the campaign. Some examples of outputs include:
    o Number of recipients with an increased understanding of far-right extremism.
    o Presence/absence of new report or publication resulting from the campaign.
    o Presence/absence of a new policy approach or government communications strategy resulting from the campaign.

- **Outcomes** are the intended results of campaign activities (usually qualitative). Often outcomes are expressed in terms of change in behaviour or attitudes. For example, the enhanced understanding of far-right ideology might be a campaign outcome amongst the target audience. Some examples of outcomes include:
    o Increased knowledge of far-right extremist ideology.
    o Decreased number of those active in far-right extremist milieus.
    o Changes in behaviour of adherents as a result of increased knowledge of far-right extremist ideology.
    o Changes in behaviour of wider community to promote pro-migrant, inclusive identities and community cohesion.

- **Impact** refers to the ultimate vision of the campaign, affiliated with both the recipients and target population. Often impact is the most difficult component to measure. However, outputs and outcomes should support the definition of projected impact through the ToC derived from the outset. Some examples of impact include:
    o At-risk individuals prevented from joining violent far-right extremist organizations.
    o Increasing the number and effectiveness of far-right counter-messages that influence the behaviour of a target audience.
    o Increasing in number of fully de-radicalized/disengaged and/or rehabilitated far-right extremist activists.

Both the preliminary and final results of the MM&E should inform the decision-making and design of current and future RRCN projects. Therefore, based on certain preliminary results the counter-narrative campaign team might realise that there could be the need to re-set/change goal and objectives or stop a programme. This should be identified in any official documents for the RRCN campaign under evaluation.

Conclusion

As this chapter has noted, a lack of rigour pervades when it comes to testing and evaluating counter-narratives in general but also violent far-right narratives in particular. This chapter has attempted to address this problem through setting out an analytical framework that can be used by practitioners and scholars to analyse far-right counter-narrative interventions. Perhaps more pertinent at this moment of fifth-wave terrorism has been the identification of archetypal far-right narratives and conspiracy theories used to inspire far-right terrorism and violence. As we shall see in other chapters below, these common narratives have inspired violent extremist far-right groups in such differing contexts as Australasia, Europe and North America, with the internet providing the key communication vector in this broader global far-right movement. Starting with the UK and Germany, we will look at how transnational and mediatised the narratives of the global far-right have become, and most importantly how we can use counter-narrative techniques to undermine their attempts at mobilisation in various localised contexts.

Chapter 2: Far-Right Extremist Narratives and Counter-Narratives in Western Europe — The Cases of the UK and Germany

Introduction

The spectre of rising far-right violence in the UK and Germany has become an increasing concern to policy makers, academic researchers and practitioners. To some extent, this is not unexpected; in both countries, far-right parties and protest movements have been largely unsuccessful in making their exclusionist politics known at the ballot box or on the streets of both countries. Whether it be the neo-Nazi NPD in Germany or the neo-fascist BNP in the UK, both parties have failed to chalk up successful national victories in their respective contexts. Moreover, even as anti-Islam street protest has become a stable feature of extra-parliamentary far-right activism over the last ten years, they have signally failed in adding the more extreme iterations of their policies to the mainstream issue agendas of their respective countries. Added to this, both countries have also managed to censure and limit the mobilisations of far-right parties and social movement organisation through hostile electoral systems and legal measures designed at curbing racist hate speech. This has somewhat closed down the political opportunity structure for legitimate offline action

Accordingly, however, this has seen the spectre of non-aligned and organised forms of far-right political violence rear its ugly head over the past five to ten years — with increases in identity-based violence[77] (IBV) against minorities happening after the so-

---

[77] Here, 'Identity-Based Violence' is defined as forms of "violence [that are] directed against an individual or group because of their identity (as perceived by the perpetrator)" (Ferguson, 2016, *Countering violent extremism through media and communication strategies*, 4). This can range from isolated forms of hate crime to

called 'Refugee Crisis' and Islamist terror attacks from 2013 to 2017. Added to this, several far-right terror attacks were perpetrated on UK and German soil in 2016, 2017, 2019 and 2020 — that claimed the lives of 32 people.[78] Zooming out, and hovering in the background at this time of transition, far-right extremists in both countries have also been involved in championing anti-elitist and Eurosceptic causes in the past few years — using traditionalist, populist and nationalist concerns to mainstream their messages.[79] Like with recent terror attacks, there has also been an increase in right-wing motivated hate crimes since the so-called 2015 'Refugee Crisis' in Germany and the 2016 EU referendum in UK[80] (see Figure 6 & 7 below). Whilst far-right terror attacks in both countries have not been as frequent as in the US (19 in the UK and 10 in Germany versus 37 in the final 2016-2020 period recorded by the Global Terrorism Database),[81] there does however appear to be a concerning upstream picture of far-right extremist violence that has become the 'fastest-growing' source of work for counter terror officials tasked with preventing, contesting and disrupting terrorist violence in the UK.[82]

---

more concerted forms of extermination and genocide. In this case, we are concerned with the former as an extension of more deadly forms of political violence (i.e., far-right terrorism).

[78] This analysis was conducted comparing counts of violent far-right extremist attacks (i.e., Neo-Nazi, White Supremacist, Anti-Muslim Extremist and Anti-Semitic attacks) available at START's Global Terrorism Database here: https://www.start.umd.edu/gtd/.

[79] See Meyjes, T., 'Some of the BNP's 2005 elections pledges are now mainstream policy', *The Metro*, 27 April 2017, online at: https://metro.co.uk/2017/04/27/some-of-bnps-2005-election-pledges-are-now-mainstream-policy-6599296/?ito=cbshare.

[80] Devine, Daniel, 'The UK Referendum on Membership of the European Union as a Trigger Event for Hate Crimes', 5 February 2018, online at: https://ssrn.com/abstract=3118190 or http://dx.doi.org/10.2139/ssrn.3118190.

[81] This analysis was conducted comparing counts of violent far- right extremist attacks (i.e., Neo-Nazi, White Supremacist, Anti-Muslim Extremist and Anti-Semitic attacks) available at START's Global Terrorism Database here: https://www.start.umd.edu/gtd/.

[82] Dodd, V. & Grierson, J., 'Fastest-growing UK terrorist threat is from far right, say police ', *The Guardian*, 19 September 2019, online at: https://www.theguardian.com/

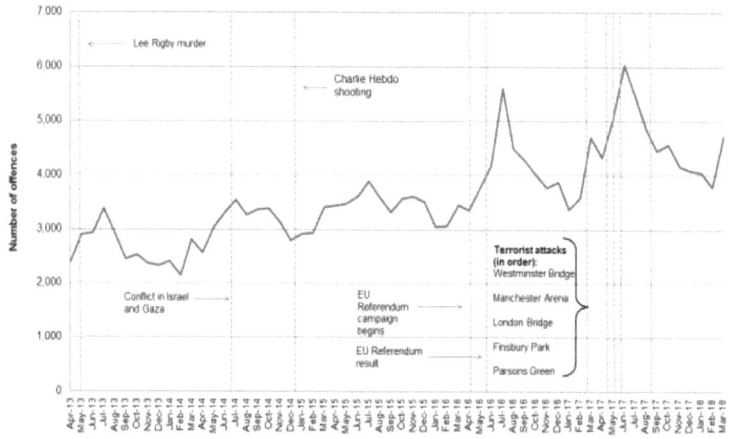

Figure 6:   Number of racially or religiously aggravated offences recorded by the police by month in the UK, April 2013 to March 2018[83]

uk-news/2019/sep/19/fastest-growing-uk-terrorist-threat-is-from-far-right-say-police.

[83] UK Home Office, ‚Hate Crime: England and Wales, 2018/2019', London: HM Goverment, 2019, P.8, online at: https://assets.publishing.service.gov.uk/government/uploads/system/uploads/attachment_data/file/839172/hate-crime-1819-hosb2419.pdf.

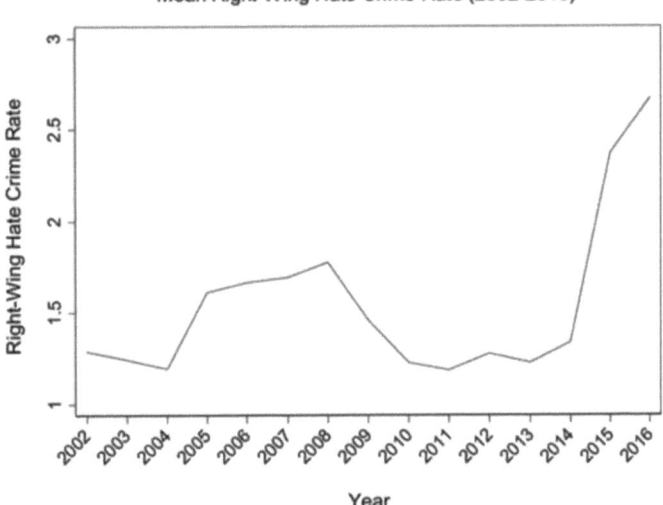

Figure 7: Right-Wing Hate Crime Rate in Germany, 2002-2016[84]

This chapter then focuses on the UK and Germany at a time of heightened far-right extremist concern. The first part chapter surveys the activities of several, key far-right extremist groups in both contexts and the anti-Muslim populist, ethno-nationalist, neo-Nazi, masculinist and anti-globalist narratives that they propagate at the present moment. Using these case study examples, the second part will then suggest guidance for – and examples of – counter narratives that can be posed in relation to these dominant frames. This will flow into the next section that will focus on existing counter narrative campaigns in the UK and German contexts. Finally, the chapter will conclude with further recommendations for practitioners when conducting campaigns to counteract violent far-right extremist messages.

---

[84] Piatkowska, S.J., Andreas Hövermann, Tse-Chuan Yang, Immigration Influx as a Trigger for Right-Wing Crime: A Temporal Analysis of Hate Crimes in Germany in the Light of the 'Refugee Crisis', The British Journal of Criminology, Volume 60, Issue 3, May 2020, Pages 620–641, https://doi.org/10.1093/bjc/azz073. Cited: P. 629.

Violent Far-right Extremist Groups and Narratives in the UK & Germany: Ascendant Anti-Muslim Populism, Declining Ethno-Nationalism, Ascendant Chauvinism, Neo-Nazism, & Anti-Globalism

Despite being electorally moribund, a plethora of far-right extremist protest movements & groupuscules[85] still animate the far-right extremist landscape in both countries. Within each of these categories, each mobilise around a wide range of different ideologies, grievances and modes of action. Moreover, the liminality between non-violence and violence within the narratives presented by these groups is important to observe (see figure 3 below).[86] Below therefore is a list of violent far-right organisations that are active at the present time in both contexts. This includes examples of key narratives that they are presenting at the present moment in both contexts and a short summary of each group.

I. Violent Far-Right Extremist Groups in the UK

a) Combat 18 (C18)
Leader: William Browning
Membership: 30-40
Ideology: Neo-Nazism, Ethno-Nationalism, Anti-Semitism

Description:
Founded in the UK in the early 1990's to provide street protection for the neo-fascist BNP, Combat 18 has transformed through many

---

[85] Here, 'Groupuscules' are defined as tiny, often neo-Nazi, bands of far-right extremists that establish a milieu with reference points that stretch out internationally as well as into the past as well (Jackson 2014, *National Action and National Socialism for the 21st Century*, 101).

[86] For a pertinent example, see: Allen, C., 'National Action: links between the far right, extremism and terrorism', Commission for Countering Extremism Research Paper Series, 2019, online at: https://assets.publishing.service.gov.uk/government/uploads/system/uploads/attachment_data/file/827232/Chris_Allen_-_National_Action_Post_Publication_Revisions.pdf.

iterations and — more recently — periods of dormancy. Nowadays the group largely consists of social gatherings rather than any serious, organised political activity. In 2018, the group put on several music concerts in the UK through ideologically aligned 'Oi music' bands, such as 'No Remorse' and 'Last Orders'. In the UK, it therefore exists largely to support a tightly network group of Neo-Nazi activists and as a sub-cultural milieu — largely concentrated in the South East of England. Other international chapters of Combat 18 have however been more active — with one German-based activist being implicated in the assassination of CDU politician, Walter Lübcke, in June 2019.[87] Moreover, in the same month, the Canadian Government added Combat 18 to its list of illegal terrorist organisations — making it the first time a far-right group to enter onto the list. The UK Chapter of Combat 18 has a long history of violence — with one of its former members, David Copeland, behind several deadly attacks in April 1999.[88]

Narrative Examples:

Neo-Nazism: "We must secure the existence of our people and a future for white children."

- 14 words from David Lane's Turner Diaries — a key text for Combat 18 activists.[89]

Ethno-Nationalism: "Whatever it takes, oderint dum metuant, White Revolution is the only solution."

---

[87] Aderet, O., 'German Authorities Suspect neo-Nazi Terror Group Was Behind Politician's Assassination', *Haaretz*, 28 June 2019, online at: https://www.haaretz.com/world-news/europe/.premium-german-authorities-suspect-neo-nazi-terror-group-behind-politician-s-assassination-1.7420449.

[88] Bilani, S., 'The Far-Right Views Behind the London Bombings of 1999', *Vice News*, 25 April 2019, online at: https://www.vice.com/en_uk/article/597bdb/the-far-right-views-behind-the-london-bombings-of-1999.

[89] Meleagrou-Hitchens, A. and Standing, E., 'Blood and Honour: Britain's Far-Right Militants', (London: Henry Jackson Society, 2010), online at: http://henryjacksonsociety.org/wp-content/uploads/2013/01/BLOOD-AND-HNOUR.pdf.

- Combat 18 motto.⁹⁰

Anti-Semitism: "Zyklon-B: over six million satisfied customers. Manufactured by Combat 18."

- Poster produced by South African National Socialist group and inspired by Combat 18.⁹¹

b) National Action
Leaders: Benjamin Raymond and Alex Davies
Membership: Unknown
Ideology: Neo-Nazism, Anti-Semitism, Anti-Establishment

Description:
Now proscribed as a terrorist organisation, National Action emerged as a website in the summer of 2013 and proceeded to start small-scale stunts, street demonstrations, and online campaigns later that year. Deliberately distinguishing itself from more mass based protest organisations, NA increasingly took on a terroristic and aesthetically distinctive approach—framing its activities as provocative and extreme as well as dressing in black clothing reminiscent of interwar fascist movements. Two years after its formation, a more terroristic and extreme form of activism became apparent– with one of its members attempting to murder a Sikh doctor in 2015, its proscription by the UK Government in December 2016 and the prosecution of Jack Renshaw for the attempted murder of a UK Member of Parliament in 2019.⁹² Apart from other UK

---

⁹⁰ Street, Z., 'Sun Front Page Nazi Shame', *Byline Times*, 25 June 2016, online at: https://www.byline.com/column/20/article/1123.

⁹¹ Goodricke-Clarke, N., *Black Sun: Aryan Cults, Esoteric Nazism, and the Politics of Identity*, (New York: NYU Press, 2003), 45, online at: https://bit.ly/2H2egEi.

⁹² *BBC News*, 'Lee Rigby revenge attacker Zack Davies given life sentence', 11 September 2015, online at: https://www.bbc.co.uk/news/uk-wales-north-east-wales-34218184; UK Home Office, 'National Action becomes first extreme right-

far-right organisations, then, National Action furrowed a distinctively pernicious and actively violent seam – giving rise to some of the offshoots noted below.

Narrative Examples:

Neo-Nazism: #Hitlerwasright
- Garron Helm's antisemitic tweet directed at former Jewish MP Luciana Berger.[93]

Antisemitism: "Weakness on the Jewish question is simply unforgivable, ignorance is inexcusable."

- Interview with National Action activists.[94]

Anti-Establishment: "Death to traitors, freedom for Britain"

- Slogan on National Action Website and Slogan of Thomas Mair.[95]

---

wing group to be banned in UK', Press Release, 16 December 2016, online at: https://www.gov.uk/government/news/national-action-becomes-first-extreme-right-wing-group-to-be-banned-in-uk; & *BBC News*, 'Jack Renshaw: MP death plot neo-Nazi jailed for life', 17 May 2019, online at: https://www.bbc.co.uk/news/uk-england-lancashire-48306380.

[93] Perraudin, F., 'Man jailed for antisemitic tweet to Labour MP', *The Guardian*, 20 October 2014, online at: https://www.theguardian.com/uk-news/2014/oct/20/man-jailed-antisemitic-tweet-labour-mp.

[94] Allen, C., 'National Action: links between the far right, extremism and terrorism', (London: Commission for Countering Extremism, August 2019), online at: https://assets.publishing.service.gov.uk/government/uploads/system/uploads/attachment_data/file/834342/Chris_Allen_-_National_Action_Post_Publication_Revisions.pdf.

[95] Allen, C., 'Proscribing National Action: Considering the Impact of Banning the British Far-Right Group', *The Political Quarterly*, 88(4), January 2017, 654, online at: https://onlinelibrary.wiley.com/doi/full/10.1111/1467-923X.12368.

c) Sonnenkrieg Division (SKD)
Leaders: Andrew Dymock and Oskar Koczorowski
Membership: Unknown
Ideology: Neo-Nazism, Satanism, Violent Misogyny.

Description:
Started in 2018, Sonnenkrieg Division (or SKD) is the third iteration of proscribed UK Neo-Nazi terror group, National Action. Fostering links with similarly violent Neo-Nazi groups in the US as part of a broader transnational Siege sub-culture,[96] SKD has used online 'gaming' forums (such as Discord) to communicate secretly and anonymously between its members. Using largely the same ideology as NA, SKD has demonstrated a trend towards Satanism, paedophilia and rape — sectioning itself off at the very extremes of the UK far-right. Last December (2018), SKD co-leader, Oskar Koczorowski, pleaded guilty in court to two counts of encouraging terrorism,[97] while sexual offence allegations against another member of SKD are currently outstanding. Like SRN, SKD has largely acted as a discussion forum — though reports emerged of torture directed against one of its female members in December 2018. The BBC investigation also unearthed artwork calling for the assassination of Prince Harry, Duke of Sussex, and police officers.[98]

Narrative Examples:
Neo-Nazism: "When the day comes, we will not ask whether you swung to the right or whether you swung to the left; we will simply swing you by the neck."

---

[96] Counter Extremism Project, 'Siege's Ties to Extremists', 2019, online at: https://www.counterextremism.com/siege-ties-to-extremists.
[97] *BBC News*, 'Teenage neo-Nazis jailed over terror offences', 18 June 2019, online at: https://www.bbc.co.uk/news/uk-48672929.
[98] Ibid.

72   MOVING BEYOND ISLAMIST EXTREMISM

- SKD poster shared on Fascist Forge website.[99]

Satanism: "When there's nowhere to hide and there's nowhere to run. All you can do is look to the Sun."

- SKD poster shared on Sonnenkrieg Division's Gab.ai account.[100]

Violent Misogyny: "Race Mixing Whores. Get the f***ing rope."

- SKD poster shared on Gab.ai user Commando's account.[101]

d) System Resistance Network (SRN)
Leaders: Alex Davies & Austin Ross
Membership: 10
Ideology: Neo-Nazism, Anti-Establishment Extremism, Homophobia

Description:
Now largely defunct, System Resistance Network (or SRN) became active in 2017 after the proscription of National Action (NA) as a terrorist organisation by the UK Home Office. Mainly NA activists — using similar forms of Nazi ideology and violent extremism — until August 2018 when the group disbanded, therefore populated it.[102] Previously named Vanguard Britannia, small pockets of SRN activists were involved in putting up anti-leftist, homophobic and

---

[99] Subcomandante X, '[Brief] New Sonnenkrieg Division Propaganda Shared on Fascist Forge', *The Medium*, 16 January 2019, online at: https://medium.com/americanodyssey/new-sonnenkrieg-division-propaganda-appears-on-fascist-forge-forum-bb488cefbe53.

[100] Ibid.

[101] Ibid.

[102] In the periods after proscription, a former National Action activists also existed as part of Telegram group named the 'Triple K Mafia' (or Ku Klux Klan mafia) – a nod to US white supremacism.

anti-refugee posters in Dundee, Swansea, Cardiff and Bristol during its short existence.[103] After their 2018 fallout, SRN members then went on to create the UK chapter of the violent US Neo-Nazi group, Atomwaffen Division — calling itself 'Sonnenkrieg Division' or 'Sun War Division', a version of Atomwaffen Division but with 'less guns'.[104] The group was therefore largely a 'front' organisation for NA activists from the previously proscribed far-right terror group and lived a relatively short existence.

Narrative Examples:

Neo-Nazism: "The National Socialist never capitulates. He will never negotiate away his freedom. He will never compromise his ideals. We are revolutionary National Socialists united by struggle: the struggle against the System."

- An excerpt from SRN's website. [105]

Extreme Anti-Establishmentarianism: "Our imperative is the destruction of the System. A system that imports non-Whites en masse to rape our children and colonise our country whilst criminalising any pushback from the public."

- An excerpt from SRN's website.[106]

Homophobia: "AIDS isn't a disease, it's a cure to fa**otry. Hail AIDS."

- Excerpt from SRN postering campaign in Dundee, Scotland.[107]

---

[103] BBC News, 'System Resistance Network: Neo-Nazi group 'should be illegal'', 3 December 2018, online at: https://www.bbc.co.uk/news/uk-wales-46292599.

[104] Macklin, G., 'The Evolution of Extreme-Right Terrorism and Efforts to Counter It in the United Kingdom', CTC Sentinel 12(1), January 2019, 17, online at: https://ctc.usma.edu/app/uploads/2019/01/CTC-SENTINEL-012019.pdf.

[105] Briggs, B., 'Banned terrorist group is behind latest neo-Nazi outfit in Scotland', The Ferret, 4 January 2018, online at: https://theferret.scot/system-resistance-network/.

[106] Ibid.

[107] Morkis, S., 'Anti-Nazi rally planned for Dundee in response to fascist poster campaign', The Courier, 9 December 2017, online at: https://www.

e) Order of Nine Angles (O9A)
Leaders: David Myatt, Richard Moult, Michael Mouthwork.
Membership: Unknown.
Ideology: Neo-Nazism, Satanism, Aryanism

Description:
The O9A was formed in the 1960s by the coming together of three Shropshire-based Dark Pagan covens — Camlad, the Temple of the Sun and the Noctulians. A Nazi-Satanist group, O9A deifies Hitler and the Third Reich, which are regarded as having attempted to create a "Satanic empire" in order to achieve the destiny of the western world. One of its earliest adherents was David Myatt who has written most of the group's literature. In the 1990s, the group's leadership was taken over by a former Combat 18 activist and National Social Movement activist, Richard Moult. Disruption and subversion are two tactics widely encouraged by the O9A. Destablising society through terror and acts of sabotage formed a central theme of Myatt's writings while he was associated with C18 (see above). Like Woden Folk, O9A has been linked to other violent Neo-Nazi groups in the UK, including National Action and its later iteration of Sonnenkrieg Division. It also has inspired other international covens of Nazi-Satanism, including New Zealand-based 'The Black Order', the Australian-based 'Temple of Them' and Californian-based 'White Star Association'. UK anti-fascist collective, *Hope Not Hate*, suggest that the violent extremist threat posed by O9A is currently being under-estimated or ignored — with literature and rituals commissioned by the group said to encourages racism, violence, sexual abuse and murder as ritual sacrifice; both targeted at its own members and those outside the group.[108]

---

thecourier.co.uk/fp/news/local/dundee/560659/anti-nazi-rally-planned-for-dundee-in-response-to-fascist-poster-campaign/.

[108] Lowles, N., 'Order of the Nine Angles', *Hope Not Hate* Website, 16 February 2019, online at: https://www.hopenothate.org.uk/2019/02/16/state-of-hate-2019-order-of-nine-angles/.

Narrative Examples:
Neo-Nazism: "Adolf Hitler was sent by our gods. To guide us to greatness."

- Words contained in Mass of Heresy in O9A's *Black Book of Satan*.[109]

Satanism: "as originally used and meant, the term satan refers to some human being or beings who 'diabolically' plot or who scheme against ... the Jews."

- Words of David Myatt in a 2013 interview.[110]

Aryanism: "We believe in the inequality of the races. And in the right of the Aryans to live. According to the laws of the folk."

- Words contained in Mass of Heresy in O9A's *Black Book of Satan*.[111]

f) Misanthropic Division (MD)
Leaders: Francesco Saverio Fontana, Jimmy Hey, and Robin Gray.
Membership: Unknown
Ideology: Neo-Nazism, Ethno-Nationalism, Violent Chauvinism.

Description:
Largely a recruiting body for sending UK Neo-Nazis to be involved in the Ukrainian civil war, Misanthropic Division (or MD) provides

---

[109] Ibid.

[110] *Order of the Nine Angles*, 'The Geryne of Satan', 2014, online at: https://archive.org/stream/MSS2014/ONA%20-%20The%20Geryne%20of%20Satan_djvu.txt.

[111] Kaplan, J., *Encyclopaedia of White Power: A Sourcebook on the Radical Racist Right*, (Oxford: Rowman & Littlefield, 2000), 237, online at: https://bit.ly/39eDziK.

a mirror image to Jihadist-aligned individuals being sent to fight in Syria—showing the UK far-right's violent intent beyond the borders of the UK. With strong connections to Poland, Japan and South America, Misanthropic Division's operations were disrupted in 2017 due to reports of the group's activities being shared with Ukraine's embassy in the UK. Previously active in Greater Manchester, West London, and the Republic of Ireland, mass arrests in June 2017 led to the group's operations grinding to a halt until more stable lines of recruitment can be re-opened with the pro-Nazi Ukraine-based militia, called 'Azov Battalion'.[112] Latest reports show that the group's international chapters are still active on 'surface web' platforms, such as Facebook, but with no real offline activity.[113]

Narrative Examples:

Neo-Nazism: "Misanthropic Division is a NS Brotherhood exclusive to european and eurodescendent men. We live accordingly the principles of Nature and we denounce the modern political and corrupt system with his multicultural society."

- Number one of fourteen guiding principles published by Misanthropic Division International.[114]

Ethno-Nationalism: "No more refugees. Stop Immigration. Stop the Invasion."

---

[112] Richardson, O., 'Neo-Nazis From Misanthropic Division Given Jail Sentence in Moscow', *Stalker Zone,* 22 June 2017, online at: http://www.stalkerzone.org/neo-nazis-misanthropic-division-given-jail-sentence-moscow/.

[113] Dearden, L., 'Neo-Nazi groups allowed to stay on Facebook because they 'do not violate community standards"', *The Independent,* 24 March 2019, online at: https://www.independent.co.uk/news/uk/home-news/facebook-new-zealand-neo-nazis-white-supremacists-a8837886.html.

[114] *FOIA Research,* '14 Points of the Misanthropic Division International', 1 June 2019, online at: https://www.foiaresearch.net/organization/misanthropic-division.

- Poster at Edinburgh March 2016 demonstration.[115]

Violent Chauvinism: "While you are sitting around on Vkontakte. Or hanging out with your friends. Every day I'm training, To f**k up my opponent in a fight. We are the sober and angry youth!"

- Popular Song among Azov Battalion fighters.[116]

II. Violent Far-Right Extremist Groups in Germany[117]

a) Blood & Honour (B&H)

Leader: Unknown
Membership: Unknown
Ideology: Neo-Nazism, 'Revisionism', Ethno-Nationalism

Description:
B&H was founded in 1987 in the UK in order to promote neo-Nazism through "White Power" music by bands like "Skrewdriver" and "No Remorse". Due to the infamy of the former band, B&H quickly became an international organization. National divisions and regional sections extended across much of the whole world, above all in Europe, North America and Oceania. By the late 1980s and early 1990s, B&H had become notorious Scandinavia (especially Sweden and Denmark) and Germany. A German division

---

[115] *Tell MAMA*, 'Scottish Defence League Protest Falls Flat but Brings Together Hardened Neo-Nazis', 22 March 2016, online at: https://tellmamauk.org/scottish-defence-league-protest-falls-flat-brings-together-hardened-neo-nazis/.

[116] Kuzmenko, O., 'The Straight-Edge Neo-Nazi Group that Attacked a Ukrainian Roma Camp', *Bellingcat*, 26 June 2018, Hyperlink: https://www.bellingcat.com/news/uk-and-europe/2018/06/26/straight-edge-neo-nazi-group-attacked-ukrainian-roma-camp/.

[117] Group profiles and narratives here have been extracted from the Hedayah Radical Right Counter Narrative Project Germany Country Report, see the original here:https://www.hedayahcenter.org/resources/reports_and_publications/germany_radical_right_cve_narratives/.

was founded in 1994 but was banned in September 2000 by the Federal Minister of the Interior, alongside its youth organisation "White Youth" (founded in 1997). The German division and its member became, especially Jan Werner and Thomas Starke, became well known for their long-lasting support of the NSU, with money, infrastructure, and contacts to survive in the underground. Furthermore, B&H collected money at concerts "for the three" which was brought to the NSU core trio by B&H members. Key features of this movement still include promotion of white power music through concerts, music production and transnational distribution.[118] After the ban several groups continued cooperate under names like "Brotherhood 28" or "Division 28". These underground organisations drew upon the infrastructure and labels of foreign divisions with close ties to German activists—especially in Belgium (Wallonia and Flanders), France and Hungary.[119] In addition to white power music, B&H is well known for close association with its paramilitary wing, Combat 18.

Narrative Examples:
Neo-Nazism: "Blood and Honour" [Blut und Ehre]

- Motto inscribed on the travelling knifes of the Hitler Youth from 1933 until 1938.[120]

---

[118] See Sebastian Gräfe, '"Blood & Honour": „Trotz Verbot nicht tot?". Bedeutung in Gegenwart und Vergangenheit' In: Uwe Backes & Steffen Kailitz (eds.), Sachsen – eine Hochburg des Rechtsextremismus? (Göttingen: V&R 2020), 299-314.

[119] See NRW rechtsaußen, 'NRW: „Blood & Honour"-Konzert in Belgien mit „German Support"', Lotta Magazin, 14 July 2011, online at: http://lotta-magazin.de/nrwrex/2011/07/nrw-blood-honour-konzert-belgien-mit-german-support; Antifaschistisches Infoblatt, 'Nazi-Gedenken ohne Ende – Tag(e) der Ehre in Budapest', Antifaschistisches Infoblatt, 26 May 2019, online at: https://www.antifainfoblatt.de/artikel/nazi-gedenken-ohne-ende-%E2%80%93-tage-der-ehre-budapest; Antifaschistisches Infoblatt, 'Die Ermittlungen gegen „Blood & Honour" Nachfolger', Antifaschistisches Infoblatt, 21. September 2016, online at: https://www.antifainfoblatt.de/artikel/die-ermittlungen-gegen-%E2%80%9Eblood-honour%E2%80%9C-nachfolger.

[120] See Heinz Schreckenberg, Erziehung, 'Lebenswelt und Kriegseinsatz der deutschen Jugend unter Adolf Hitler', p. 213; Picture online at: https://www.the-

Historical Revisionism: "We are the streets and we are the law, the 4th Reich is what we are fighting for."

- B&H band 'Race War' from Germany with their Title 'Hail Blood And Honour' from their 2001 album 'The White Race will Prevail'.[121]

Ethno-Nationalism: "The purpose of the Blood & Honour movement must be to attract and activate young Whites through White Power music and other White Pride cultural activities."

- Max Hammer (Erik Blücher), Blood & Honour Field Manual[122]

b) Combat 18 (Germany)
Leaders: Torsten Heise, Robin Schmiemann, Marco Gottschalk, Stanley Röske, Marco Eckert, & Lars Bergeest
Membership: c. 20-60 (2019)[123]
Ideology: Neo-Nazism, Ethno-Nationalism, Vanguardism

Description:
C18 was founded in the UK in 1992 and, like its umbrella B&H (see above), quickly expanded to other countries, resulting in up to 25 official divisions worldwide today. One of the most active and influential is in Germany, consisting of three known and verifiable

---

saleroom.com/en-gb/auction-catalogues/walldorf/catalogue-id-auktio10012/lot-a19643bf-8ac0-4194-b72a-a5c50098a150.

[121] Race War, 'Hail Blood And Honour', The White Race Will Prevail, Micetrap Records 2001.

[122] See Max Hammer (Erik Blücher), Blood & Honour Field Manual, 2000.

[123] See Exif-Recherche, '«Combat 18» Reunion ', Exif-Recherche, 16 July 2018, online at: https://exif-recherche.org/?p=4399.

(regional) sections, all lead by the confidant of the movement's founder, Will Browning, Thorsten Heise and his right-hand man Robin Schmiemann. The oldest section gathers around Marco Gottschalk, singer of the C18 band "Oidoxie", and his "Oidoxie Streetfighting Crew". They are located in and around the city of Dortmund, one of the few local strongholds of the extreme right in West Germany. The second section gathers around Stanley Röske (including the suspected murderer of CDU politician Walter Lübcke, who was closely linked to the Nordhessen Crew, a precursor of this section), and is located around the city of Kassel. The third section builds on the remains of Combat-18 Pinneberg, a paramilitary group existing from 2001 until 2003. Leaders of this section are purported to be Marco Eckert and Lars Bergeest. C18 was involved in the reemerging concert business, band promotion (especially of C18 bands like Oidoxie, TreueOrden and Erschießungskommando) as well as networking and combat training.[124] In January 2020 "Combat 18 Germany" was banned by German Federal Minister of the Interior but—much like B&H once again- have continued under another label. Called the "Brothers of Honour", the group now wears branded clothes of other divisions to conceal their identities; for example, as Combat 18 Sweden.[125] Beyond the combat training and resulting verdicts the homes of several members were searched in the light of the ban of C18 Germany. The headquarter of Thorsten Heise was searched several times and he was found guilty of hate speech, the production and distribution of race baiting CDs and the illegal possession of firearms.

Narrative Examples:

Neo-Nazism: "We must secure the existence of our people and a future for white children."

---

[124] See Maximilian Kreter, 'Die deutsche Rechtsrockszene. Integraler Bestandteil der rechtsextremen Bewegung oder isolierte, subkulturelle Szene', Jahrbuch Extremismus & Demokratie 31, 2019, 159-173, here: 169-172.

[125] See Sebastian Weiermann, ' Wirkungsloses Verbot', Neues Deutschland, 23 January 2020, online at: https://www.neues-deutschland.de/artikel/1131902. combat-wirkungsloses-verbot.html.

- David E. Lane, member of 'The Order'.[126]

Ethno-Nationalism: "Fighting for better nations, we want our cities clean. This is the terror machine, this is Combat 18."

- The band 'Oidoxie' from Dortmund with the title 'Terrormachine' from the 2006 album 'Terrormachine'.[127]

Violent Masculinity: "Silent Brotherhood — whatever it takes — C18."

- Combat 18 motto, Tattoo on the lower leg of Robin Schmiemann,[128]

c) The Third Path
Leader: Klaus Armstroff
Membership: 530 (2018)[129]
Ideology: Neo-Nazism; 'Revisionism'; Anti-Globalism

Description:
The Third Path is minor Neo-Nazi party founded in 2013 as a camouflage organisation for the banned "Free Network South" (*Freies Netz Süd*). Given this precursor organisation, their local strongholds were based in North Eastern Bavaria/Franconia, South West Saxony and Western Rhineland-Palatine. Members take part in elections even if, according to the statements of their chairman, Klaus Armstroff, they are not interested in traditional party politics. Instead, they focus on movement and street politics (such rallies in

---

[126] See George Michael, 'David Lane and the Fourteen Words', Totalitarian Movements and Political Religions. 10 (1), 2009, 43-61.

[127] See Oidoxie, 'Terrormachine', Terrormachine, WB-Versand 2006.

[128] See Antifa Recherche Dortmund, 'Aushängeschild für C18. Robin Schmiemann: Vom Handlanger zur Symbolfigur', Lotta-Magazin, 29 June 2019, online at: http://www.lotta-magazin.de/ausgabe/online/aush-ngeschild-f-r-c18-0.

[129] See Bundesministerium des Innern, für Bau und Heimat (eds.), 'Verfassungsschutzbericht 2018', p. 80.

their strongholds and visits to foreign countries like Hungary). The group also offers martial arts and transnational networking with other fascist and extremist organizations, in which they make clear reference to the NSDAP and the Nazism at these events. Furthermore, their only programmatic document ever published was a ten-point manifesto, which bears compositional and terminological similarities to the 25-point manifesto of the NSDAP.[130] Besides the large criminal records and extremist activities of their members – e.g., Martin Wiese: planned bomb attack on Jewish Cultural Center in Munich, member of a terrorist organisation; Maik Eminger: close supporter of the National Socialist Underground (brother André sentenced to 2.5 years in prison for direct support of the NSU), former co-leader of the free comradeship "White Brotherhood Erzgebirge" [Weiße Bruderschaft Erzgebirge]; Matthias Fischer: former leader of the "Free Network South", served at least two years in prison for several crimes – The Third Path unfolds its activities in marches resembling the SA-tradition, i.e., on 1 May 2019 in Plauen.[131]

Narrative Examples:
Neo Nazism: "Creation of German Socialism […] German children for the country."

- 10-point manifesto of The Third Path[132]

---

[130] See Marc Brandstetter, M., 'Parteigründungen als Reaktionen auf staatliche Verbote', Jahrbuch Extremismus & Demokratie 28, 2016, 188-206; Maximilian Kreter, 'Die deutsche Rechtsrockszene. Integraler Bestandteil der rechtsextremen Bewegung oder isolierte, subkulturelle Szene', Jahrbuch Extremismus & Demokratie 31, 2019, 159-173, here: 166-167.

[131] See Marc Brandstetter, M., 'Parteigründungen als Reaktionen auf staatliche Verbote', Jahrbuch Extremismus & Demokratie 28, 2016, 188-206; Jonas Miller, 'Die bayerische Neonaziszene verliert einen führenden Kopf', Zeit Stöungsmelder, 12 July 2014, online at: https://blog.zeit.de/stoerungsmelder/2014/07/12/die-bayerische-neonaziszene-verliert-einen-fuehrenden-kopf_16687; Tim Mönch, 'Weniger Neonazis in Plauen als erwartet', Belltower News, 2 May 2019, nline at: https://www.belltower.news/aufmarsch-am-1-mai-weniger-neonazis-in-plauen-als-erwartet-84665/.

[132] See Der Dritte Weg, ' 10 Punkte Programm der Partei DER DRITTE WEG', online at: https://der-dritte-weg.info/zehn-punkte-programm/.

Historical Revisionism: "Germany is larger than the FRG."

- 10-point manifesto of The Third Path]¹³³

Anti-Globalism: "No German Blood for foreign interests."

- 10-point manifesto of The Third Path.¹³⁴

d) Revolution Chemnitz
Leader: Christian K.
Membership: 8¹³⁵
Ideology: Neo-Nazism, Great Replacement
conspiracy theory, Vanguardism

Description:
Revolution Chemnitz (RC) started as out as a Telegram chat group of this name on 10th September 2018, in the aftermath of the extreme right Chemnitz riots that late August.¹³⁶ They aimed to "change Germany's history" and threatened to make the NSU appear as an "kindergarten preschool group" in comparison to what they planned. Members have their roots in the local and regional extreme right skinhead, hooligan, and Neo-Nazi scene, especially in the surroundings of Sturm 34, a banned organization from Mittweida, whose members were found guilty of a long list of

---

[133] Ibid.

[134] Ibid.

[135] See ARD, 'Haftstrafen für „Revolution Chemnitz"', tagesschau.de, 24 March 2020, online at: https://www.tagesschau.de/inland/urteil-revolution-chemnitz-101.html.

[136] See Matthias Bartsch, Maik Baumgärtner, Jörg Diehl, Jan Friedmann, Lothar Gorris, Nils Klawitter, Martin Knobbe, Beate Lakotta, Katharina Meyer zu Eppendorf, René Pfister, Christopher Piltz, Sven Röbel, Fidelius Schmid, Charlotte Schönberger, Andreas Ulrich, David Walden, Wolf Wiedmann-Schmidt, Steffen Winter, 'The Riots in Chemnitz and Their Aftermath', Spiegel Online, 31 August 2018, online at: https://www.spiegel.de/international/germany/the-riots-in-chemnitz-and-their-aftermath-the-return-of-the-ugly-german-a-1225897.html.

crimes ranging from hate speech to assaults. Only four days after its foundation the RC started a "test run" as a vigilante group. They checked IDs in Chemnitz and attacked both Germans and foreigners ahead of a series of planned attacks on 3rd October, German Unity Day, a public holiday with ceremonies all over the country. On 1st October the police arrested six out of the eight members before they could carry out an assault.[137] All six were found guilty of having membership in a terrorist organization (129a§ German Penalty Code), while the leader, Christian K. was also found guilty of founding a terrorist organisation.[138]

Narrative Examples:

Neo-Nazism: "Struggle against state and capital. Free, social national."

- Self description of RC on Facebook[139]

Great Replacement conspiracy theory : "Time does not stand still, ‚Volkstod' is near. Time for Revolution, forward with us. Revolution Chemnitz."

- Screenshot of picture posted on Facebook[140]

Violent Masculinity: "Assault on the media dictatorship and its slaves [...] and the NSU was intended to be made looking like a kindergarten preschool group in comparison to Revolution Chemnitz."

---

[137] See Julia Jüttner, 'Rechtsextremes Klassentreffen in Handschellen', Spiegel Online, 30 September 2019, online at: https://www.spiegel.de/panorama/justiz/revolution-chemnitz-prozessauftakt-rechtsextremes-klassentreffen-a-1289362.html.

[138] See ARD, 'Haftstrafen für „Revolution Chemnitz"', tagesschau.de, 24 March 2020, online at: https://www.tagesschau.de/inland/urteil-revolution-chemnitz-101.html.

[139] See Revolution Chemnitz Facebook "Logo", online at: https://web.achive.org/web/20181001164726/https://www.facebook.com/Revolution-Chemnitz-ANW-447800521999813/.

[140] Revolution Chemnitz, Facebook site, online at: https://image.stern.de/8385312/16x9-20481152/6d877c772c3b54a1fbd346fcce4dba44/dq/chemnitz-screenshot-x4.jpg

- Facebook post and an excerpt of a Telegram chat of Revolution Chemnitz[141]

e) Group Freital
Leader: Timo S. & Patrick F.
Membership: 8[142]
Ideology: Neo-Nazism, Ethno-Nationalism, Anti-Immigration Sentiment

Description:
The Group Freital started on Facebook as a vigilante group in March 2015. Taking place in the wake of the so-called refugee crisis, the group first announced itself as the "Civil Defence Corps FTL/360" (Bürgerwehr FTL/360) in the Saxon city of Freital (next to Dresden). The head of the group was the same Timo S. was a member of the alleged terrorist group, the White Wolves Terror Crew (Weisse Wölfe Terrorcrew, WWT). It was also established that Timo S. supported the White Power band "Weisse Wölfe", (comparable to "Oidoxie" and the "Oidoxie Streetfighting Crew"). His co-leader was Patrick F., who had close ties to Dynamo Dresden's radical right football firm, "Fist of the East" (Faust des Ostens). Group Freital's then gathered five more men and one woman. The group made its first major public appearance during the racist riots of Heidenau in August 2015. Between July and November 2015, they

---

[141] See https://web.archive.org/web/20181001164726/https://www.facebook.com/Revolution-Chemnitz-ANW-447800521999813/;
Telegram chat cited in: Andrea Hentschel, 'In Sachsen stehen acht Männer der Gruppe „Revolution Chemnitz" vor Gericht', General Anzeiger Bonn, 1 October 2018, online at: https://www.general-anzeiger-bonn.de/news/politik/deutschland/in-sachsen-stehen-acht-maenner-der-gruppe-revolution-chemnitz-vor-gericht_aid-46205445.

[142] See Sebastian Gräfe, Sven Segelke, 'Rechte Hassgewalt in Sachen, 2011 bis 2016' In: Uwe Backes, Sebastian Gräfe, Anna-Maria Haase, Maximilian Kreter, Michail Logvinov, Sven Segelke (eds.), Rechte Hassgewalt in Sachsen. Entwicklungstrends und Radikalisierung (Göttingen: V&R 2019), 53-136, here: pp. 106-111.

launched several arson attacks against refugee hostels as well as against cars and offices belonging to politicians of the party The Left (Die Linke); one attack was also carried out alongside with the Free Comradeship Dresden). All 8 members were convicted of membership in a terrorist organisation (129a§ German Penalty Code), bomb attacks and attempted murder.[143] Responses in Freital were striking in that some from civil society tried to downplay the deeds and the role by declaring it a "boyish prank" or the like, rather than violent, terrorist attacks.[144]

Narrative Examples:
Neo-Nazism: "We're Nazis until the bitter end."

- Facebook comment by Philipp W. on 23 September 2015[145]

Anti-Immigration Sentiment: "Please keep on fleeing! No housing available!"

- Sticker found at Philipp W.s home[146]

Ethno-Nationalism: "Germany awakes! Loving your country is not a crime."

- Facebook comment by Mike S. on 28 August 2015[147]

---

[143] Ibid.

[144] See Robert Bongen, Thomas Datt, Philipp Hennig, Johannes Jolmes ,‚‚‚Lausbuben": Wie man in Freital Terroristen verharmlost', Panorama, 14 December 2017, online at: https://daserste.ndr.de/panorama/archiv/2017/Lausbuben-Wie-man-in-Freital-Terroristen-verharmlost,freital112.html.

[145] See Der Generalbundesanwalt beim Bundesgerichtshof, Anklageschrift, Az 2 BJs 38/16-5, 2 StE 19/16-5, p. 43.

[146] Ibid.

[147] See: Der Generalbundesanwalt beim Bundesgerichtshof, Anklageschrift, Az 2 BJs 38/16-5, 2 StE 19/16-5, p. 47.

Summary

As we can see from the above survey of UK and German-based violent far-right extremist actors at this time, most groups appear to revolve around a constellation of anti-Muslim populist, ethno-nationalist, masculinist & anti-globalist positions—with a large dose of victimhood, accelerationism and imminence in the way that the narratives are delivered. Such narratives—particularly amongst the street protest scene—are symptomatic of a broader shift by Western far-right groups away from the toxicity of anti-semitism and towards more mainstream forms of anti-Muslim prejudice (though neo-Nazism is very much present and active).[148] We can also see how the immediate and simplified nature of these narratives have the potential to be perceived as a 'call of action' for those on the fringes of these movements—heightening the possibility of narrative escalation that might ultimately lead to terrorist violence.[149]

Drawing on a recent RAN meeting note for inspiration,[150] these narratives can be simplified to the following broad positions—characterised by an:

1. **Anti-Muslim Populism Narrative**– i.e., national & cultural identities are under threat because of Islam, elites are complicit, this ends in clash of civilisations.
2. **Ethno-Nationalist Narrative**—i.e., ethnic identities are under threat, elites are complicit in 'white genocide', this ends in race war and/or a 'great replacement'.

---

[148] For more, see Zúquete, José Pedro, 'The European Extreme Right and Islam: New Directions?', *Journal of Political Ideologies*, 13 (3), 2008, 321-345.

[149] Indeed, in Sarah Cobb's (2013) book on *Narrative Dynamics in Conflict Resolution*, she finds that conflict escalation is inversely related to narrative complexity – the simpler and harder line the narrative, the more likely it will lead to conflict (p.88).

[150] RAN, 'Ex Post Paper: Current and Future Narratives and Strategies of Far-Right and Islamist Extremism', May 2019, online at: https://ec.europa.eu/home-affairs/sites/homeaffairs/files/what-we-do/networks/radicalisation_awareness_network/ran-papers/docs/ran_pol_cn_most_often_used_narratives_stockholm_05042019_en.pdf.

3. **Neo-Nazism and Nazi 'Revisionism' Narrative** – i.e., advocating extreme right ideological stances rooted in fascism and National Socialism, while simultaneously defending or minimising the crimes of historical National Socialism, above all the Holocaust.
4. **Masculinist Narrative** – i.e., societies are under threat because men cannot live 'according to their nature', feminists & LGBT community are considered traitors.
5. **Anti-Globalist Narrative** – i.e., the EU, NATO, the UN & multinational companies have too much power over us, their role is ostensibly to keep 'the people' down, we must withdraw with immediate effect.
6. **Victimhood Narrative** – i.e., Governments favour ethnic and religious minorities over the majority white population, anti-PC comments lead to persecution, our views are being silenced and suppressed at the expense of freedom of speech.

Violent Far-Right Counter Narratives & Counter Narrative Campaigns in the UK and Germany: Tapping into Anti-Muslim Populist, Ethno-Nationalist, Neo-Nazi, Masculinist and Anti-Globalist Positions

Constructing counter narratives in order to disrupt, delegitimise and devalue the appeal of these narratives, it is useful to identify 'entry points' within the structure of extremist narratives in order to unpick the veracity, authenticity and believability of such narratives. As modelled in the examples suggested in the above summary, this can be done by breaking down such narratives into their orientation (i.e., who, what, where, how & when), action (i.e., evaluation of orientation) and resolution (i.e., prescribed course of action) structure.[151] Whilst it might be unprofitable to contest the fac-

---

[151] This is a simplified version of a similar schema, laid out in: Labov, W., & Waletzky, J., 'Narrative analysis: Oral versions of personal experience'm *Journal*

tual veracity of the orientation statement, both the action and solution sections of the narrative might be more profitably contested. Below are some key counter-narratives that could deployed by practitioners to respond to the UK and German violent far-right extremist messages could identified above:

a) **Anti-Muslim Populism Counter Narrative** — i.e., highlight the positive contribution of Muslims to country's livelihood, acknowledge prejudice but foster more open viewpoints and a less formulaic or rigid conception of Islam.
b) **Ethno-Nationalist Counter Narrative** — i.e., highlight zero-sum view of migration and positive economic benefits, acknowledge fears and grievances, work to de-escalate imminence of 'threat' frame and legitimacy of 'separate people groups' idea.
c) **Masculinist Counter Narrative** — i.e., create a new, inclusive definition of masculinity, in which feminists and LGBTI activists have empowered rather than emasculated society overall. Move beyond a reductive view of masculinity to a notion of social construction.
d) **Neo-Nazism and Nazi 'Revisionism' Narrative** — i.e., refer to the successful re-education and accounting for the past ("Vergangenheitsbewältigung") in postwar Germany by connecting (relative) economic success[152] and the establishment of a resilient democracy that offers more chances than any authoritarian form of ideocracy with different degrees of delimitation of freedom, i.e., "through governing", or *Durchherrschung*[153]). Stress the illegitimacy of a prerogative state in contrast to a normative state and the rule of law in

---

of Narrative & Life History, 7(1-4), 1997, 3-38, online at: http://dx.doi.org/10.1075/jnlh.7.02nar.

[152] The myth of the 'Miracle on the Rhine' was a successful framing, but not miraculous economic growth and increase of wealth that is often talked and written about. The myth has (not only) been deconstructed. See Ulrike Herrmann, 'Deutschland, ein Wirtschaftsmärchen. Warum es kein Wunder ist, dass wir reich geworden sind (Frankfurt: Westend Verlag, 2019).

[153] The term was coined by the German historians Jürgen Kocka and Alf Lüdtke. See (f.e.) Jürgen Kocka, 'Ein deutscher Sonderweg: Überlegungen zur Sozialgeschichte der DDR', Aus Politik und Zeitgeschichte 41 (40), 34-45.

a liberal democracy. Illustrate the cultural dullness and the unsuccessful oligarchic structure of National Socialism. Emphasise that Neo-Nazism represents a selective nostalgia about historical fascism and the Third Reich, whereby single issues might not have been awful, though the overall picture makes clear that democracy offers more net gains for people legally, culturally, and economically.

e) **Anti-Globalist Counter Narrative** — i.e., emphasise democratic legitimacy of international organisations and need to 'get involved' to change the 'system'. Talk of economic and political benefits as well as shared European values as basis for discussing difference.

f) **Victimhood Counter Narrative** — i.e., educate citizens regarding what they can and cannot expect from their governments, media and the state. Advise them about how they can get their voices heard through legitimate channels. Ask what perspectives aren't being listened to.

Turning from violent far-right narratives and counter narratives toward counter narrative campaigns, the UK and Germany have been at the forefront of global efforts to foster counter narrative best practice for some time now.[154][155] Added to this, there has been a concerted effort by the UK government to move beyond Islamist terrorism and tackle far-right extremism after the inception of the 2011 version of the Prevent Strategy,[156] but also a well-regarded and existing constitutional and law enforcement defence against far-right extremism in Germany. Below are some examples of cam-

---

[154] See Briggs, R. & Feve, S., 'Review of Programs to Counter Narratives of Violent Extremism,' (London: ISD, 2013); Tuck, H. & Silverman, H., 'The Counter Narrative Handbook', (London: ISD, 2016); Reynolds, L & Tuck H., 'The Counter Narrative Monitoring and Evaluation Handbook', (London: ISD, 2016) & Silverman, Stewart, Amanullah and Birdwell, 'The Impact of Counter Narratives', (London: ISD, 2016).

[155] See: https://redirectmethod.org.

[156] For more information on the impact of this shift, see McCann, C., The *Prevent Strategy and Right-wing Extremism: A Case Study of the English Defence League*, (London: Routledge, 2019).

paigns and methodologies that have been used by the UK and Germany toward far-right extremist groups that have become increasingly problematic (and indeed violent) in the past few years.

The most prominent, experienced and longest lasting organization in this area in Germany[157] is the non-governmental far-right de-radicalisation programme, Exit Germany. Exit's best-known campaign was "Operation Trojan T- Shirt" in 2011. Attending one of the largest "White Power" music festivals in Germany at the time, "Rock for Germany" [Rock für Deutschland] — organized by the NPD and hosting both Brutal Attack and Radikahl on stage — Exit Germany pretended to act as a supporter of the event by providing far-right merchandise in the form of free t-shirts. The shirts initially carried the slogan "Hardcore Rebels: National and Free" [Hardcore Rebellen: National und Frei] but when washed this was replaced by Exit Germany's intended message: "What your T-shirt can do, you also can do — We help you to free yourself from right-wing extremism. EXIT-Germany."[158] This innovative campaign quickly went viral. More than 300 newspapers reported, with dozens of TV stations airing reports around the world. Needless to say, page viewership also went through the roof. As a result, the projects original goal succeeded: neo-Nazis were (and still are) now aware of Exit Germany.[159] In the aftermath of this campaign, moreover, the "number of persons contacting EXIT and asking for help to leave the movement tripled".[160]

---

[157] Counter narrative campaigns here have been extracted from the Hedayah Radical Right Counter Narrative Project Germany Country Report, see the original here: https://www.hedayahcenter.org/resources/reports_and_publications/germany_radical_right_cve_narratives/.

[158] See Fabian Wichmann, 'Successfully Countering Hate and Far Right Propaganda: The Story of Exit Germany', Journal Exit-Deutschland. Zeitschrift für Deradikalisierung und demokratische Kultur 7, 2018, 64-67, here: 66-67 (The proper translation would be "If your T-shirt can do it, you can do it too").

[159] See Exit Deutschland, 'OPS // Trojan T-Shirt / EXIT-Deutschland', 30 March 2012, online at: https://www.youtube.com/watch?v=CSIbsHKEP-8&feature=youtu.be.

[160] See Fabian Wichmann, 'Successfully Countering Hate and Far Right Propaganda: The Story of Exit Germany', Journal Exit-Deutschland. Zeitschrift für Deradikalisierung und demokratische Kultur 7, 2018, 64-67, here: 67; Fabian

Figure 8: T-Shirt before and after washing[161]

(N.B: T-Shirt (L) "Hardcore Rebels: National and Free" & T-Shirt (R) "What your T-shirt can do, you also can do — We help you to free yourself from right-wing extremism")

On the other hand, some of the earliest, tentative formal interventions during the current period towards far-right extremist movements in the UK were used to disrupt and delegitimise narratives of the anti-Islamic English Defence League that reached its peak between 2009 and 2012. These were delivered by anti-fascist and anti-racism NGOs, Searchlight Educational Trust and Show Racism the Red Card, and included the former devising news-sheets and community events in four areas vulnerable to English Defence League activity to generate positive local identities as well as the latter delivering interactive seminars with young people between the ages of 11 and 18 to 'reject the narratives of groups like the English Defence League'.[162] Such campaigns therefore used a mixture of counter narratives and alternative narratives as well as targeted methodologies — aimed at a particular group and vulnerable age range at a specific time.

Wichmann, '4 Ways To Turn The Neo-Nazi Agenda On Its Head', Journal Exit-Deutschland. Zeitschrift für Deradikalisierung und demokratische Kultur 5, 2017, 93-98, here: 97-98.

[161] Taken from: Dafnos, A., 'Narratives as a Means of Countering the Radical Right; Looking into the Trojan T-shirt Project.', Journal EXIT Deutschland, 2014, online at: http://journals.sfu.ca/jed/index.php/jex/article/view/98. P. 174.

[162] HC Written Statement 154, 'Integration Update', 18 December 2014, online at: https://hansard.parliament.uk/commons/2014-12-18/debates/1412184300 0023/IntegrationUpdate.

Such tailoring should be brought forward for counter narrative best practice in the UK—depending on the far-right group in question and level of involvement within an extremist milieu.

Moving from more formal to informal attempts at counter the messages of the EDL, at the same time, there were more comedic efforts to counter the group's anti-Muslim populist narratives by the online antifascist collective—the English Disco Lover's. Formed in 2012, this counter campaign group was initially founded to satirise and eclipse coverage of the EDL. English Disco Lovers' most high-profile campaign, however, was a "Google bombing" attempt—hi-jacking the EDL acronym to outrank its far-right equivalent on search engines and social media.[163] The campaign was broadly successful on Facebook at least—in July 2017, the English Disco Lovers were found to have almost ten times as many likes on Facebook as the English Defence League.[164] The group's action also attracted widespread press attention[165] & led to copycat counter protest initiatives at EDL demonstrations in Brighton[166], Cambridge[167] and Birmingham.[168] The campaign's light-hearted framing gave it wide appeal—with many copycat iterations of its offline efforts appearing around the world. Such an easily replicable formula is ideal for a campaign that hopes to leverage its popularity against a fringe

---

[163] Counter Narrative Toolkit, 'English Disco Lovers', 2019, online at: http://www.counternarratives.org/html/case-studies-entry?id=12.

[164] As noted in Winter and Fürst (2018, Challenging Hate, 16), the English Disco Lovers had 63,834 likes, as compared with just 7,255 for the English Defence League. This has remained relatively stable for the former, with the latter being removed from Facebook in April 2019.

[165] Lynskey, D., 'How to Disco Dance the EDL off Google and Facebook', *The Guardian*, 1 February 2013, online at: https://www.theguardian.com/technology/shortcuts/2013/feb/01/disco-dance-edl-google-facebook.

[166] Jones, A., 'EDL (English Disco Lovers) Brighton 2013', 9 September 2013, online at: https://www.youtube.com/watch?v=AD0p07jzUGQ.

[167] Astro, S., 'Cambridge English Disco League Protest against EDL', YouTube, 23 February 2013, https://www.youtube.com/watch?v=zbRUoqKd4Mk.

[168] Nicholls, S., 'EDL rally and anti-fascist protesters in Birmingham', *Birmingham Live*, 20 July 2013, online at: https://www.birminghammail.co.uk/news/local-news/gallery/edl-rally-anti-fascist-protesters-birmingham-5164956.

extremist movement. Here, we can also see how more informal campaigns might gain more traction than formal interventions – as argued by Lee (2019).[169]

Figure 9:   Screenshot from English Disco Lover's Promotional Video[170]

Adding to this portfolio of informal UK-based counter narrative campaigns were those conducted against EDL successor group, Britain First. An attempt to counter Britain First's anti-Muslim populist and ultra-nationalist messages, 'Britain Furst' was founded in 2014 as a Facebook and then Twitter parody page. The campaign involved issuing memes reminiscent of those disseminated by Britain First but added a satirical twist – with posts that talked about 'Halal Sunglasses', 'Muslamic Timepieces' and likening Britain First's uniform to bin liners.[171] (Each of these campaigns received 39 retweets/14 likes/4 comments, 21 retweets/19 likes/2 com-

---

[169] Lee, B.J., 'Informal Countermessaging: The Potential and Perils of Informal Online Countermessaging', *Studies in Conflict & Terrorism*, 42(1-2), 2019, 161-177, online at: http://10.1080/1057610X.2018.1513697.

[170] Catch 21 Productions, ‚EDL (English Disco Lovers): VOTV', *Youtube*, online at: https://www.youtube.com/watch?v=16kV8BqhRxk.

[171] Walsh, J., 'Britain Furst: the halal Ray-ban-wearing far right Facebook mockers', *The Guardian*, 20 June 2014, online at: https://www.theguardian.com/media/2014/jun/20/britain-furst-the-halal-ray-ban-wearing-far-right-facebook-mockers.

ments and 65 retweets/24 likes/5 comments respectively) So successful was the campaign that Britain First took notice and reported the group to Facebook.[172] It was the subject of a number of national news articles—inspiring successor accounts and initiatives by other online activists, even beyond the main cycle of protest by the group itself.[173] Again, here we can also see how more informal campaigns might be more agile and gain more traction in comparison to formal interventions—despite being largely up to a committed activist community to maintain.

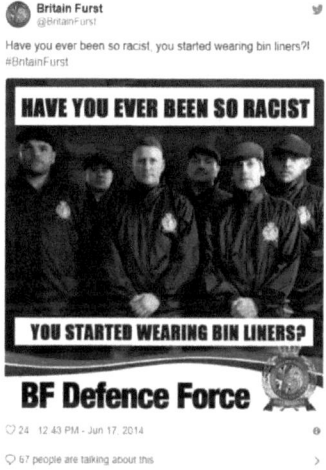

Figure 10: Screenshot of 'Britain Furst' Parody Tweet[174]

Moving back to the German scene, EXIT Germany was again at the forefront of constructions against far-right activism when it constructed a second innovative campaign called the "Right Against

---

[172] Ibid.

[173] Sommers, J., 'Britain First Parody Account 'British First' Goes Viral After Spoof Tweets Sent Amid Donald Trump Row', *Huffington Post*, 1 December 2017, online at: https://www.huffingtonpost.co.uk/entry/britain-first-parody-british-first_uk_5a2163ace4b03350e0b631fd.

[174] Britain Furst, 'Have you ever been so racist, you started wearing bin liners?! #BritainFurst', Twitter, 17 June 2014, online at: https://twitter.com/BritainFurst/status/478865477230690304.

Right" [*Rechts gegen Rechts*] campaign. Since 2001, the commemorative march for Hitler's' deputy, Rudolf Heß, has taken place in the Upper Franconian city of Wunsiedel where he was buried.[175] The city of Wunsiedel has thus become of site pilgrimage for neo-Nazis, even though they often face massive counter demonstrations. Exit Germany designed a campaign against these marches with the idea of adapting the charity run model. With every step made by the far-right participants of this commemorative march, they raised funds for the benefit of anti-fascist organisations and their activities. Far-right extremists attending the march were faced with the dilemma of marching and raising money against their cause, or not demonstrating to avoid the donations. The campaign started on 15 November 2014, and every metre walked raised 10 Euros.[176] Counter-march protesters updated marchers of how much they had raised throughout the march, posted "motivational" banners such as "Final Spurt instead of Final Victory" [Endspurt statt Endsieg] or "March and donate" [*Marschieren und spendieren*]; and finally, by offered bananas as marching rations. Since 2014, the number of participants in the march has drastically decreased, even without the

---

[175] From 1988 until 1990 the commemorative events respectively demonstrations took place in front of the administrative court of Bayreuth. From 1991 to 2000 the event was banned by regional courts and the commemorative events took place in Thuringia, Luxemburg or Denmark. In 2011, the tomb was removed with (belated) consent of the relatives. See Thomas Dörfler, Andreas Klärner, 'Der »Rudolf-Heß-Gedenkmarsch« in Wunsiedel. Rekonstruktion eines nationalistischen Phantasmas', Mittelweg 36 13 (4), 2004, 74-91; Hans Holzhaider, 'Grab von Rudolf Heß existiert nicht mehr', Süddeutsche Zeitung/SZ.de, 21 July 2011, online at: https://www.sueddeutsche.de/politik/wunsiedel-ende-einer-nazi-pilgerstaette-grab-von-rudolf-hess-existiert-nicht-mehr-1.1122689.

[176] The campaign was successfully transferred to other cities with the same problem of continuous Neo-Nazi demonstrations or commemorative events, as for example the city of Bad Nenndorf in Lower-Saxony where a commemorative march – announced annually until 2030 – for the "Victims of the Allied torture camp Wincklerbad" (Opfer des alliierten Folterlagers im Wincklerbad) takes place. See Angelika Henkel, Stefan Schölermann, 'Bad Nenndorf wehrt sich gegen rechts', Norddeutscher Rundfunk, 22 July 2012, online at: https://web.archive.org/web/20160119114435/https://www.ndr.de/nachrichten/dossiers/der_norden_schaut_hin/badnenndorf265.html.

campaign being present. To date it remains unclear if the commemorative march will take place in the future.[177]

Figure 11: Rudolf-Hess-Memorial March and Exit-Germany campaign banner "Donate The Hate"[178]

A third and last example from Exit Germany follows the same pattern as the "Right against Right" campaign, while transferring the charity run model online to counter hate speech.[179] For this campaign, "Donate the Hate" ["Hass hilft"], Exit Germany designed an app connected to various social sites dealing with the topic of migrants and refugees in Germany. Every hate speech comment detected resulted in a personal "Thank you for your donation"- comment, alongside and one Euro raised for charities. These donations were earmarked beforehand by media companies, a football club

---

[177] See Fabian Wichmann, 'Successfully Countering Hate and Far Right Propaganda: The Story of Exit Germany', Journal Exit-Deutschland. Zeitschrift für Deradikalisierung und demokratische Kultur 7, 2018, 64-67, here: 64-66; Fabian Wichmann, '4 Ways To Turn The Neo-Nazi Agenda On Its Head', Journal Exit-Deutschland. Zeitschrift für Deradikalisierung und demokratische Kultur 5, 2017, 93-98, here: pp.93-95.

[178] Europe Press, 'A German city tricks neo-Nazis, some Spaniards, into marching against themselves', Ideal.es, 20 November 2014, online at: https://www.ideal.es/sociedad/201411/20/ciudad-alemana-engana-unos-20141120091615.html.

[179] Among those described here, other campaigns of Exit Germany can be found here: https://www.exit-deutschland.de/projekte/.

(second division), and many individual donors. Once again, the target group — in this case hate speech purveyors — become trapped in a paradox: either cease engaging in hate speech or raise one Euro for each new comment. Additionally, the campaign site lists the Top 10 donor purveyors, using the data generated by hate speech comments.[180]

Figure 12: Donate the Hate campaign[181]

More recent examples of tailored, formal counter narrative campaigns in the UK include Exit UK's own recently launched website.[182] Using three stories of individuals that the organisation has

---

[180] See Fabian Wichmann, 'Successfully Countering Hate and Far Right Propaganda: The Story of Exit Germany', Journal Exit-Deutschland. Zeitschrift für Deradikalisierung und demokratische Kultur 7, 2018, 64-67, here: 66; Fabian Wichmann, '4 Ways To Turn The Neo-Nazi Agenda On Its Head', *Journal Exit-Deutschland*, 2017, 93-98, here: pp.96-97.

[181] Lake, H., ‚Donate the Hate turns hate comments into donation', UK Fundraising, 2 February 2016, online at: https://fundraising.co.uk/2016/02/02/donate-the-hate-turns-hates-comments-into-donations/

[182] EXIT UK 'Stories' Page, online at: https://exituk.org/stories.

helped in the past, they track a former gamer, football hooligan and soldier's journey of radicalisation and entry into UK-based far-right extremist movements. Each (short) video—receiving 116, 422, 17,080, and 4,496 views respectively—spells out the risks of becoming part of a far-right extremist organisation and the difficulties of exiting—demystifying and deglamourizing participation in such movements. Moreover, they explain how day-to-day deprivations and grievances—related to a weak sense of identity, economic prosperity, and political representation—can be compounded and preyed upon by the far-right extremist organisations—acting as a useful resource for educators also.

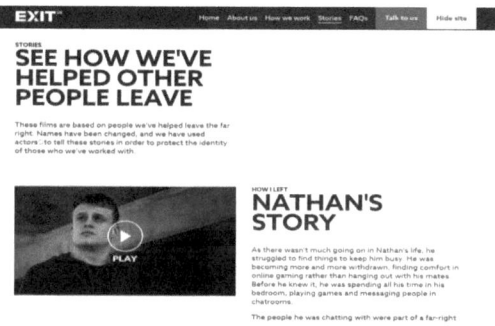

Figure 13: Exit UK 'Stories' Page[183]

Another UK example of a video campaign directed at educators is the London Grid for Learning's 'Counter-Extremism: Narratives and Conversations' resource.[184] Not so much a counter narrative campaign per se but a toolbox for teachers, this takes the user through a series of short tutorial videos with Professor of Politics at Kent University, Dr Matthew Goodwin, about the far-right in the UK but also counter narratives that can be deployed on the ground. In particular, the videos stress the importance of a non-argumentative approach that listens to grievances and stresses a 'no outsider' policy to conversations.

---

[183] Ibid.

[184] London Grid for Learning's, 'Counter-Extremism: Narratives and Conversations', 2015, online at: http://counterextremism.lgfl.org.uk/FR_values_counter_narrative.html.

Unfortunately, however, the only case example of a counter narrative that can be operationalised engages with the far-right's ethno-nationalist framing that 'immigrants are bad'.[185] Moreover, there is something to be said about the limitations of using experts to deliver dialogue-heavy videos rather than more interactive content.[186]

Figure 14: London Grid for Learning's 'Counter-Extremism' resource video[187]

Moving onto online targeted methodologies, there have been several innovative methodology experiments conducted by UK-based organisations (Moonshot CVE and the Institute for Strategic Dialogue) in this space — mainly looking at the more violent end of the extremist spectrum. The former organisation has found a technique of using algorithms and natural language processing to anonymously identify individuals who are searching for and accessing extremist content online, and then targeting them with counter narrative videos and one-to-one interventions in order to dissuade them from radicalising further. Such preventative interventions have been pioneered by Google and YouTube under the Redirect

---

[185] London Grid for Learning's, 'Counter-Extremism: Narratives and Conversations', 2015, online at: http://counterextremism.lgfl.org.uk/videos/FR/HD/vid_vcn_3.mp4.

[186] See (again) Lee, B.J., 'Informal Countermessaging: The Potential and Perils of Informal Online Countermessaging', *Studies in Conflict & Terrorism*, 42(1-2), 2019, 169.

[187] London Grid for Learning's 'Counter-Extremism' resource video, 2015, online at: http://counterextremism.lgfl.org.uk/videos/FR/HD/vid_vcn_3.mp4.

Method (Redirectmethod.org). Obvious ethical queries and caveats apply here surrounding anonymity and privacy but they do show how online, computational methodologies could be exploited to make sure that the above counter narratives get through to the right audience, and therefore overcoming pre-existing concerns about counter narrative effectiveness.[188] In the end, over 320,000 users were reached and the method saw an increase of up to 79% in engage with counter narrative content.

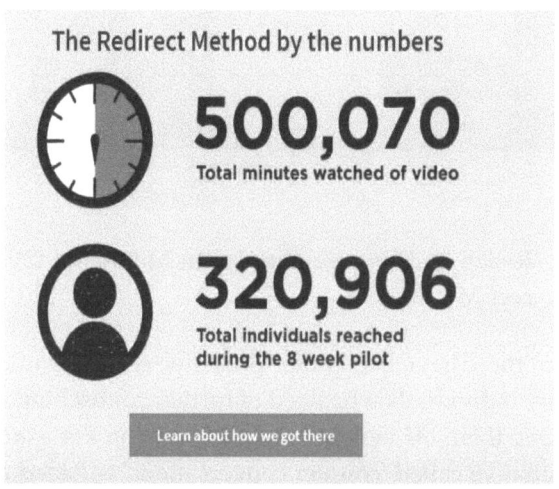

---

[188] See Ferguson, K., 'Countering violent extremism through media and communication strategies: A Review of the Evidence', (Partnership for Conflict, Crime and Security Research, University of East Anglia, 2016), pp.10-15, online at: https://www.paccsresearch.org.uk/wp-content/uploads/2016/03/Countering-Violent-Extremism-Through-Media-and-Communication-Strategies-.pdf.

102 MOVING BEYOND ISLAMIST EXTREMISM

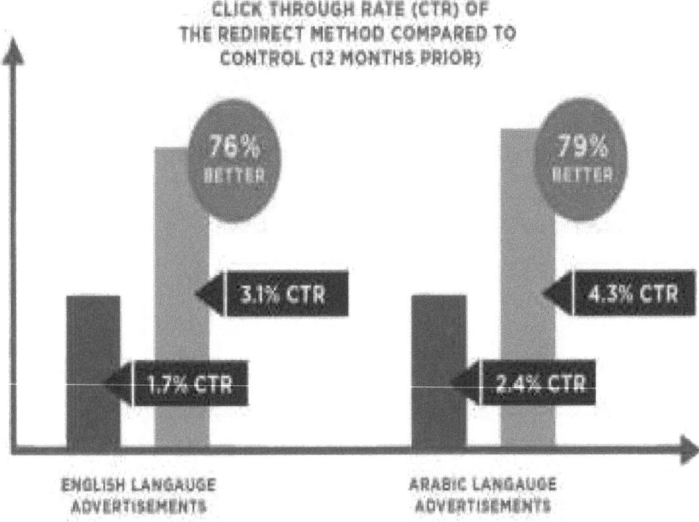

Figure 15: Reach and Engagements with Moonshot CVE's Redirect Method[189]

Moving on, there have been other proactive efforts to micro-target and identify individuals who need of further counselling and guidance to move them off violent extremist content. For example, one ISD-led initiative called 'counter conversations' engaged with individuals with both Islamist and far-right backgrounds. [190] This effectively is one-step on from counter narratives and posits an alternative by challenging extremist messages directly with online users one-to-one in order to help persuade individuals to exit online extremist milieus. Its results found that the approach was largely effective in sustaining conversations (64% of far-right extremist interactions) and providing a lasting positive impact on the trajectory of

---

[189] Moonshot CVE & Jigsaw, ,Redirect Method' Website, online at: http://redirectmethod.org/downloads/RedirectMethod-FullMethod-PDF.pdf

[190] Davey, J., Birdwell, J., and Skellett, R., 'Counter Conversations: A model for direct engagement with individuals showing signs of radicalisation online', (London: ISD, 2018).

individuals selected for the pilot (10% overall).[191] Whilst not a counter narrative per se, therefore, the 'counter conversations' method might be more targeted way of administering counter narratives as well as dealing with radicalising or radicalised far-right extremists who have a more hardened and rigid world view.

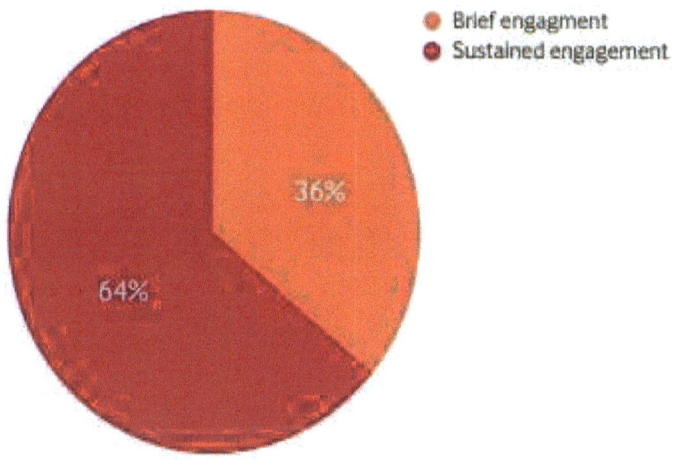

Figure 16: Response of Far-right Extremist to One-to-One Outreach[192]

---

[191] Ibid: 17 & 20.
[192] Ibid, P. 17.

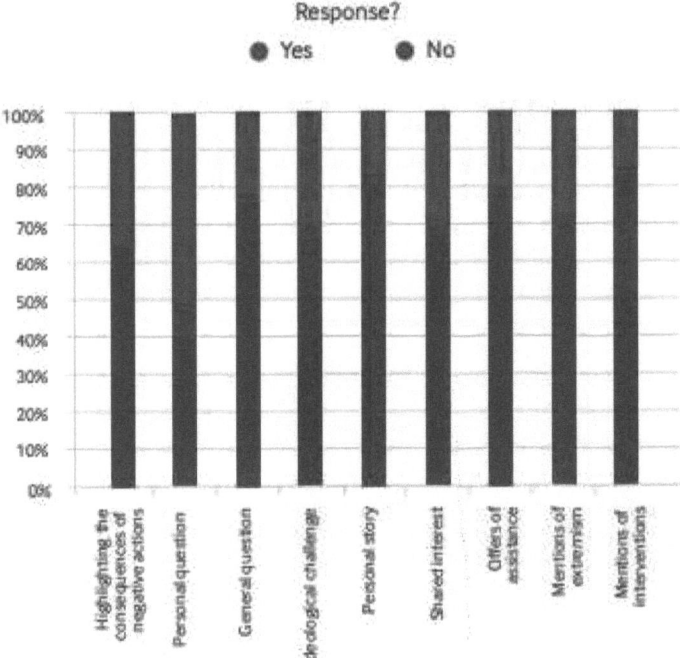

Figure 17: Message Content of One-to-One Outreach[193]

Recommendations and Conclusions

This chapter has tracked UK and German far-right extremist narratives and counter narratives at a time of transition for the far-right. Eschewing electoralism through street-based activism and into vigilantism and forms of terrorism, imminent, victimhood narratives around anti-Muslim hatred, the decline of a native in-group and masculine identity—as well as a rejection of globalist projects— have all come to a fore. These have become a rallying point for far-right extremist protest movements and (oftentimes violent, neo-Nazi) groupuscules who have attempted to popularise their discourse through wedge issues; both in the online and offline space. Such messages come at another, more violent crossroads for the UK

---

[193] Ibid, P. 18.

far-right and Britain as a nation—with the febrile atmosphere fostered by the Brexit process now allowing for new, more extreme and (as seen above) violent far-right narratives to gain traction in the public space.[194] Moreover, and since 2015 in Germany, there seems to be at least a minimum of common sense that right-wing extremism is the major problem to be tackled—with violent far-right ideologies permeating as far as actors within the German state itself.

In response to such challenging circumstances (and as demonstrated by several of EXIT Germany's counter-narrative campaigns), practitioners would be advised to find innovative and creative ways to deliver counter-narratives that de-escalate such imminence, the impact of trigger events and (rather pessimistically) the fallout of any future far-right extremist terror plot. Here, it is important to note that counter-narratives work best when they are able to delegitimise the reductive, simplified and conspiratorial elements of far-right extremist narratives. Moreover, and based on the overview of far-right counter narrative campaigns above, counter-narratives that take a non-argumentative approach and suggest an alternative narrative to grievances will work best here—diverting or 'offramping' individuals away from extremist propaganda and onto a different vision of where things are headed.

Finally, this report finds that the strongest far-right counter narrative campaign methodologies use informal actors, harness computational targeting and integrate process and impact statistics[195] into their campaign plans. As noted in the review of counter narrative campaigns above, the agility and reactivity of grassroots campaign organisations (such as Britain Furst and Exit Germany) is something to be harnessed—particularly when they come from

---

[194] Dearden, L., 'Brexit: Far-right groups threaten to riot at London protests as Boris Johnson warned over language', The Independent, 9 September 2019, online at: https://www.independent.co.uk/news/uk/home-news/brexit-protests-london-riots-unrest-far-right-boris-johnson-no-deal-a9095161.html

[195] For further discussion of MME statistics, see Helmus, T.C. & Klein, K., 'Assessing Outcomes of Online Campaigns Countering Violent Extremism: A Case Study of the Redirect Method', RAND Corp, 2018, online at: https://www.rand.org/pubs/research_reports/RR2813.html.

credible voices. Moreover, by analysing and targeting those engaging with extremist content separately from mainstream members of society, we might be more proactive in preventing those who distribute far-right extremist messages in the first place. Such an approach might therefore stop the contagion of narratives upstream before they have a destabilising effect on public conversations as a whole—or before they slip into something altogether more sinister. Finally, and added to this, publication of process and impact statistics by NGOs and think-tanks conducting far-right counter-narratives would make the assessment of effectiveness easier—promoting best practice and highlighting what is need to foster sustained attitudinal and behavioural change away from far-right sympathy and toward more mainstream forms of activism.

Chapter 3: Far-Right Extremist Narratives and Counter-Narratives in North America — The Cases of the US and Canada

Introduction

Over the past few years, North America has become a focal point for practitioners and researchers studying the far-right. Noted as a sizeable, growing threat and given the significant portion of far-right terrorist incidents and deaths (see Figure 17),[196] policymakers are more aware of the urgency of the threat posed by far-right violent extremism, as reflected in a shift in priorities away from overwhelming focus upon Islamist extremism. For example, in June 2019, Combat 18 was proscribed by the Canadian federal government and, in September of the same year, the US Department for Homeland Security (DHS) named white supremacist violent extremists as part of "an evolving domestic threat."[197] On 5 April 2020, the Russian Imperial Movement was also listed as a 'Specially Designated Global Terrorist' group by the US State Department,[198] the first time a white supremacist group was placed on this list.[199]

---

[196] Habib, J, 'Far-Right Extremist Groups and Hate Crime are Growing in Canada', *CBC News Network*, 13 July 2019, online at: https://www.cbc.ca/passionateeye/m_features/right-wing-extremist-groups-and-hate-crimes-are-growing-in-canada.

[197] *Department of Homeland Security*, 'Strategic Framework for Countering Terrorism and Targeted Violence', September 2019, online at: www.dhs.gov/sites/default/files/publications/19_0920_plcy_strategic-framework-countering-terrorism-targeted-violence.pdf.

[198] It should be noted that, while the US State Department is key in instigating such a listing, the US Treasury and Office of Foreign Assets Control are key at enforcing restriction related to this. All three leaders of the group are subject this as part to the ban.

[199] US State Department Press Release, 'United States Designates Russian Imperial Movement and Leaders as Global Terrorists', 7 April 2020, online at: https://www.state.gov/united-states-designates-russian-imperial-move-

108 MOVING BEYOND ISLAMIST EXTREMISM

In both cases, these policy shifts were compounded by the rise of a transnational, digitally-anchored, far- right 'white power' and 'accelerationist'[200] organisations, founded and operating on North American soil.[201]

---

ment-and-leaders-as-global-terrorists/; see also Robyn Dixon, 'Inside white-supremacist Russian Imperial Movement, designated foreign terrorist organization by U.S. State Department', *The Washington Post*, 13 April 2020, online at: www.washingtonpost.com/world/europe/russia-white-supremacist-terrorism-us/2020/04/11/255a9762-7a75-11ea-a311-adb1344719a9_story.html.

[200] Here, the doctrine of 'accelerationism' – defined as literally helping to accelerate a revolution, race war or even more apocalyptic scenarios — has been a notable theme amongst violent radical right extremist groups. Moreover, it has also taken the form of coded accelerationist terms, such as 'Big Luau', 'Boogaloo' or 'Cowabunga'. Even if the idea of a revolutionary right overthrow of 'the System' is an age old fascist and radical right trope, its renewed nihilistic emphasis among groups (like AtomWaffen Division, the Base and Brenton Tarrant further afield) has become a particular note of concern among security personnel and experts internationally.

[201] Anti-Defamation League, 'White Supremacists Embrace "Accelerationism"', 16 April 2019, online at: https://www.adl.org/blog/white-supremacists-embrace-accelerationism. See also Daniel De Simone et. al., 'Neo-Nazi Rinaldo Nazzaro running US militant group The Base from Russia', BBC News, 24 January 2020, online at: www.bbc.co.uk/news/world-51236915.

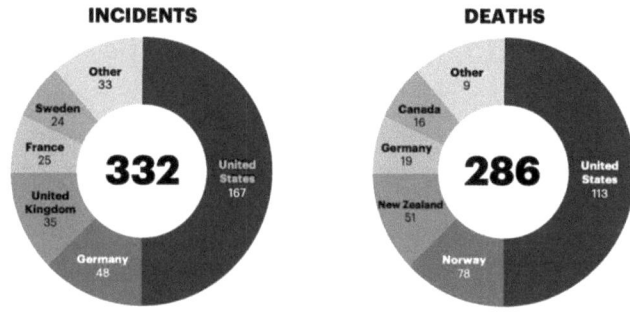

Figure 18: US Right-Wing Terror Incidents & Attacks vs. Other Western Nations, 2002–2019[202]

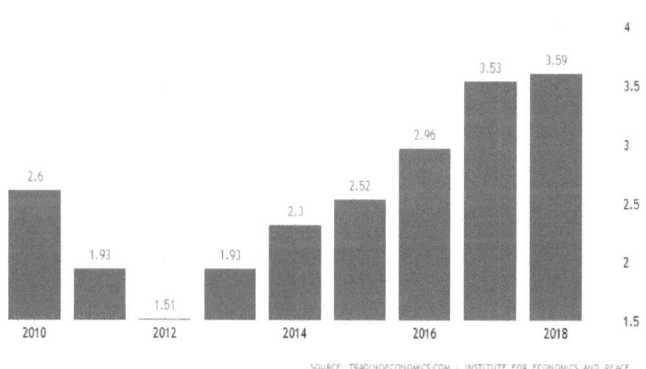

Figure 19: Canada's Global Terrorism Index Score, 2010–2018[203]

Yet it is the lone-actor nature of recent attacks of the North American far-right that have made them so unpredictable and concerning, often emerging from an unregulated online space where far-

---

[202] Institute for Economics & Peace, 'Global Terrorism Index 2019: Measuring the Impact of Terrorism', p. 47, online at: https://reliefweb.int/sites/reliefweb.int/files/resources/GTI-2019web.pdf.

[203] Trading Economics, 'Canada Terrorism Index', online at: https://tradingeconomics.com/canada/terrorism-index.

right militants are free to immerse themselves in extremist propaganda and consult fellow sympathisers before inflicting deadly attacks.[204] This chapter comes at a significant time for studying far-right extremist violence in the North America, as highlighted by recent attacks in Moncton, Toronto, Quebec City, Pittsburgh, Poway, El Paso and Tallahassee, and the influence of 'boogaloo' accelerationists on Black Lives Matter demonstrations (at the time of writing) in May and June of 2020.[205] Accordingly, the first part of this chapter surveys the activities of key US and Canadian far-right violent extremist groups and the narratives that they propagate at the present moment. Using these case study examples, the second part then suggests guidance for, as well as practical examples of, counter-narratives that can be posed in relation to North America-based far-right violent extremist narratives. A final section focusses on existing counter-narrative campaigns, concluding with recommendations for practitioners and policymakers interested in countering far-right-inspired violence.

---

[204] Macklin, G., 'The El Paso Terrorist Attack: The Chain Reaction of Global Right-Wing Terror', *CTC Sentinel*, December 2019, online at: https://ctc.usma.edu/app/uploads/2019/12/CTC-SENTINEL-112019.pdf.

[205] *BBC News*, 'Pittsburgh synagogue shooting: Suspect charged with murder', 28 October 2018, online at: www.bbc.co.uk/news/world-us-canada-46007707; *Times Staff*, 'Poway synagogue shooting captured on video, prosecutors say, as they describe attack', *Los Angeles Times*, 2 May 2019, online at: latimes.com/local/lanow/la-me-san-diego-synagogue-shooter-camera-explainer-john-earnest-20190502-story.html; *Staff & Agencies*, 'Texas man accused in El Paso mass shooting charged with federal hate crime', *The Guardian*, 6 February 2020, online at: www.theguardian.com/us-news/2020/feb/06/el-paso-walmart-shooting-hate-crime; Evans, R., & Wilson, J., 'The Boogaloo Movement Is Not What You Think', *Bellingcat*, 27 May 2020, online at: https://www.bellingcat.com/news/2020/05/27/the-boogaloo-movement-is-not-what-you-think/comment-page-4/; & Holcombe, M., Chavez, N., & Baldacci, M., 'Florida yoga studio shooter planned attack for months and had 'lifetime of misogynistic attitudes,' police say', *CNN US*, 13 February 2019, online at: https://edition.cnn.com/2019/02/13/us/tallahassee-yoga-studio-shooting/index.html.

Violent Far-Right Extremist Narratives in North America: Common Narratives of Ascendant Chauvinism & Accelerationism, added to Persistent White Supremacism and Anti-Government Extremism

With the decline of the alt-right (subscribing to more culturally ethno-nationalist & identitarian narratives) and the ebb of more traditional far-right movements (subscribing to older, more racially nationalist narratives, such as the Ku Klux Klan (KKK), Church of the Creator and Aryan Nations), the rise of accelerationist terror cells (such as Atomwaffen Division and the Base who subscribe to 'Siege' narratives of system destabilisation in order to animate revolution) and anti-government extremists have continued to animate violent forms of far- right extremist activism in North America over the past half-decade. Commonly focused around concerns of a loss of white supremacy, toxic expressions of masculinity and a deep distrust of their respective federal governments, North American far-right groups have been mobilising around a common set of white-nationalist, chauvinist, and anti-government narratives. Below is a breakdown of prominent far-right extremist groups, ranging from terror cells and violent protest movements to civil society organisations, categorised according to levels of violence as well as the radicalism of their ideology.

I. Violent Far-Right Extremist Groups in the US

a) The Base
Founder: Rinaldo Nazzaro
Membership: Unknown
Ideology: Neo-Nazism, Accelerationism, White Supremacism

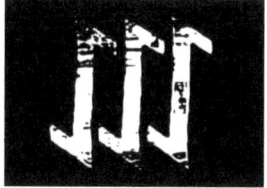

Description:
Formed in June 2018 by the American citizen based in Russia, Rinaldo Nazzaro, the Base have come to typify the recent accelerationist tendency of violent far-right extremist groups.[206] Aiming to destabilise Western democratic governments through racial "purification",[207] members of the Base have used encrypted messaging apps and the Russian meme website *iFunny*[208] to recruit new members and organise offline activism.[209] The Base drew particular attention in January 2020 after the group's private telegram channel was infiltrated by an antifascist whistle blower and the true identity of its leader, Rinaldo Nazzaro (who had previously acted under the pseudonym of 'Norman Spear' and 'Roman Wolf'), was revealed.[210] This accompanied a litany of other criminal activities related to the group's violent racist intent, ranging from the vandalism of synagogues in Racine, Wisconsin, and

---

[206] For a short overview of the Base's international ideological and strategic connections, see: De Simone, D., & Winston,L., 'Neo-Nazi militant group grooms teenagers', *BBC News*, 22 June 2020, online at: https://www.bbc.co.uk/news/uk-53128169

[207] See: Lamoureux, M & Makuch, B., 'Militant Neo-Nazi Group Actively Recruiting Ahead of Alleged Training Camp', *VICE News*, online at: https://www.vice.com/en_ca/article/bjwx55/militant-neo-nazi-group-actively-recruiting-ahead-of-alleged-training-camp; US State District Court for Maryland, 'Motion for Detention Pending Trial', online at: https://extremism.gwu.edu/sites/g/files/zaxdzs2191/f/Maryland%20Cell%20Motion%20for%20Detention%20Pending%20Trial.pdf; & US State District Court for Maryland, 'Three Alleged Members of the Violent Extremist Group "The Base" Facing Federal Firearms and Alien-Related Charges', 16 January 2020, online at: https://www.justice.gov/usao-md/pr/three-alleged-members-violent-extremist-group-base-facing-federal-firearms-and-alien.

[208] Broderick, R., 'iFunny Has Become A Hub For White Nationalism', *BuzzFeed News*, 15 August 2019, online at: https://www.buzzfeednews.com/article/ryanhatesthis/the-meme-app-ifunny-is-a-huge-hub-for-white-nationalists

[209] Wilson, J., Op Cit., 24 January 2020.

[210] Wilson, J., op. cit., 25 January 2020.

Hancock, Michigan (dubbed 'Operation Kristallnacht')[211] to their discussed transport of weapons to a pro-gun rally in Richmond, Virginia.[212]

Narrative Examples:

Neo-Nazism: "Yes, obviously. Focus on broad anti-white elements for now, though. N****r cars, Jew businesses etc."

- An excerpt from The Base's Telegram chat log.[213]

Accelerationism: "Our whole purpose is gradual escalation and we've done absolutely f*****g NOTHING."

- An excerpt from The Bases' Telegram chat log.[214]

White Supremacism: "Save Your Race, Join the Base."

- An excerpt from The Base flyer advertising the group as a Survivalism and Self-Defence Network.[215]

---

[211] Weill, K., 'Why Arrest of Richard Tobin Is Bad News for Neo-Nazi Group The Base', *The Daily Beast,* 18 November 2019, online at: www.thedailybeast.com/why-arrest-of-richard-tobin-is-bad-news-for-neo-nazi-group-the-base.

[212] Tyree, E., 'FBI arrests 3 white supremacists ahead of pro-gun rally', *ABC 13 News,* 16 January 2020, online at: https://wset.com/news/at-the-capitol/fbi-arrests-3-neo-nazi-suspects-with-weapons-planning-to-attend-gun-rally-in-richmond.

[213] Wilson, J., 'Prepping for a race war: documents reveal inner workings of neo-Nazi group', *The Guardian,* 25 January 2020, online at: www.theguardian.com/world/2020/jan/25/inside-the-base-neo-nazi-terror-group.

[214] Ibid.

[215] Wilson, J., 'Revealed: the true identity of the leader of an American neo-Nazi terror group', *The Guardian,* 24 January 2020, online at: www.theguardian.com/world/2020/jan/23/revealed-the-true-identity-of-the-leader-of-americas-neo-nazi-terror-group.

b) Atomwaffen Division
Founder: Brandon Russell
Membership: 80 (est.)[216]
Ideology: Neo-Nazism, Accelerationism, Satanism

Description:
First emerging in 2013 from US activists on the now-defunct Ironmarch forum, the Atomwaffen Division has become one of the most concerning international neo-Nazi networks in recent times. Structured as a series of regional cells, in the beginning the young group focused upon accelerationist violence as the only vehicle for apocalyptic, racial cleansing, and the imposition of an Aryan order in the US.[217] The Atomwaffen Division explicitly advocated neo-Nazism and drew a significant amount of inspiration from 'Siege', a 1980's newsletter published by the National Socialist Liberation Front under James Mason, and later compiled into a single volume now in its fourth edition.[218] The group also draw from Satanism and the occult. Links to a UK-founded Satanist neo-Nazi organisation led to a split forming within the group between the leadership and rank-and-file members in early 2018.[219] Since 2018, the organization has been linked to five killings[220] (including that of teenager Blaze Bernstein in late 2017[221])

---

[216] Thompson, A.C., Winston, A., & Hanrahan, J., 'California Murder Suspect Said to Have Trained With Extremist Hate Group.', *ProPublica*, 26 January 2018, online at: www.propublica.org/article/california-murder-suspect-atom-waffen-division-extremist-hate-group.

[217] Ibid.

[218] Counter Extremism Project, 'James Mason's Siege: Ties to Extremists', online at: www.counterextremism.com/james-masons-siege-ties-to-extremists.

[219] See: Weill, K. 'Satanism Drama is Tearing Apart the Murderous Neo-Nazi Group Atomwaffen', *The Daily Beast*, 21 March 2018, online at: https://www.thedailybeast.com/satanism-drama-is-tearing-apart-the-murderous-neo-nazi-group-atomwaffen.

[220] Mathias, C., '1 Neo-Nazi Group. 5 Murders In 8 Months.', *Huffington Post US*, 1 February 2018, online at: www.huffingtonpost.co.uk/entry/atomwaffen-nazi-murder-bomb-plot_n_5a70825ae4b00d0de2240328?ri18n=true

[221] Thompson, A.C., Winston, A., & Hanrahan, J., 'California Murder Suspect Said to Have Trained With Extremist Hate Group.', *ProPublica*, 26 January 2018,

and several arrests for threats of violence and the 'swatting' of offices of investigative journalists.[222] It has also produced spinoff groups in the UK, Australia, Canada, Germany, the Netherlands and beyond.[223]
Narrative Examples:
Neo-Nazism: "The frail whites will serve as prey to the Aryan predator".

- An excerpt from Atomwaffen Division homepage.[224]

---

online at: www.propublica.org/article/california-murder-suspect-atomwaffen-division-extremist-hate-group.

[222] Here, 'Swatting' is defined as the action of making a hoax call to the emergency services in order to lure them to a property, usually with a malicious intent. See: Eastern District of Virginia, 'Former Atomwaffen Division Leader Arrested for Swatting Conspiracy', 26 February 2020, online

at: https://www.justice.gov/usao-edva/pr/former-atomwaffen-division-leader-arrested-swatting-conspiracy & US District Court of Washington, 'United States of America v. Cameron Brandon Shea, Kaleb J. Cole, Taylor Ashley Parker-Dippe, & Johnny roman Garza', Complaint for Violation, 25 February 2020, online at: https://extreism.gwu.edu/sites/g/files/zaxdzs2191/f/Cole%20Shea%20Parker-Dipeppe%20Garza%20Complaint.pdf.

[223] See: Grierson, J., 'UK to ban neo-Nazi Sonnenkrieg Division as a terrorist group', *The Guardian*, 24 February 2020, online at: https://www.theguardian.com/uk-news/2020/feb/24/uk-ban-neo-nazi-sonnenkrieg-division-terrorist-group; Jackson, P.,' Transnational Neo-Nazism in the USA, United Kingdom and Australia', George Washington Programme on Extremism, February 2020, online at: https://extremism.gwu.edu/sites/g/files/zaxdzs2191/f/Jackson%20-%20Transnational%20neo%20Nazism%20in%20the%20USA%2C%20United%20Kingdom%20and%20Australia.pdf; Lamoureux, M., & Makuch, B., 'Atomwaffen, an American Neo-Nazi Terror Group, Is in Canada,' *VICE News*, 19 June 2018, online at: https://www.vice.com/en_us/article/a3a8ae/atomwaffen-an-american-neo-nazi-terror-group-is-in-canada; Lamoureux, M., & Makuch, B., 'An American Neo-Nazi Group Has Dark Plans for Canada', *VICE News*, 10 July 2018, online at: https://www.vice.com/en_us/article/ev847a/an-american-neo-nazi-group-has-dark-plans-for-canada; & Macklin, G., 'The Evolution of Extreme-Right Terrorism and Efforts to Counter It in the United Kingdom', *CTC Sentinel*, 12(1), online at: https://ctc.usma.edu/evolution-extreme-right-terrorism-efforts-counter-united-kingdom/.

[224] *Southern Poverty Law Centre*, 'Atomwaffen Division', online at: www.splcenter.org/fighting-hate/extremist-files/group/atomwaffen-division.

Accelerationism: "A New Order Will Rise from the Ashes of the Kike System". [225]

- An Atomwaffen Division poster.[226]

Satanism: "Satanism is alright. Depends on how you go about it. But then again, I'm more well read on the subject than most people. Most people get scared away and only go into the crust, rather than down to the core".

- An excerpt from a leaked conversation on Atomwaffen Division's Discord Server.[227]

c) Proud Boys
Founder: Gavin McInnes
Membership: Unknown
Ideology: Western Chauvinism, White Supremacism, Chauvinism

Description:
Established in September 2016 by Vice Media cofounder Gavin McInnes, the Proud Boys are self-described "western chauvinists" subscribing to an "anti-political correctness" and "anti-white guilt" agenda.[228] Emerging as part of the alt-right, McInnes distanced the group from the white-supremacist movement in 2017 (mainly to avert accusations of racism and obvi-

---

[225] Here, 'Kike' is used as a derogatory term for someone or something of supposed Jewish ethnic origin – often used by radical right extremists.

[226] Thompson, A.C., Winston, A., & Hanrahan, J., 'Inside Atomwaffen As It Celebrates a Member for Allegedly Killing a Gay Jewish College Student', *ProPublica*, 23 February 2018, online at: www.propublica.org/article/atomwaffen-division-inside-white-hate-group.

[227] *Southern Poverty Law Centre*, 'Atomwaffen Division', Op Cit.

[228] *Southern Poverty Law Centre*, 'Proud Boys', *Extremist Files*, online at: www.splcenter.org/fighting-hate/extremist-files/group/proud-boys.

ous controversies surrounding its involvement at the Charlottesville 'Unite the Right' rally in August 2017).[229] Yet this has not staved off controversy for a group once described by the Southern Poverty Law Centre as an "alt-right fight club".[230] For example, its propagation of white genocide conspiracy theories and involvement in violent activism have increasingly plagued the group over the past two years, which lead to McInnes' resignation in November 2018.[231] In particular, McInnes has previously talked about "white people" being "under siege", and blamed the media for "politicising" white men by constantly belittling them.[232] More concerning, several violent incidents, including targeted assaults on anti-fascist activists in New York[233] and fights with left-wing counter protestors in Oregon,[234] have led to the group being listed as an "extremist group with ties to white nationalism" by the FBI.[235]

---

[229] Woodhouse, L.A., 'After Charlottesville, the American Far Right is Tearing Itself Apart', *The Intercept*, 21 September 2017, online at: https://theintercept.com/2017/09/21/gavin-mcinnes-alt-right-proud-boys-richard-spencer-charlottesville/.

[230] Morlin, B., 'New "Fight Club" Ready for Street Violence', *Southern Poverty Law Centre*, online at: www.splcenter.org/hatewatch/2017/04/25/new-fight-club-ready-street-violence.

[231] Wilson, J., 'Proud Boys founder Gavin McInnes quits 'extremist' far-right group', *The Guardian*, 22 November 2018, online at: www.theguardian.com/world/2018/nov/22/proud-boys-founder-gavin-mcinnes-quits-far-right-group.

[232] Lam, S., 'Everything inside Gavin McInnes', *The Globe and Mail*, 18 August 2017, online at: www.theglobeandmail.com/arts/television/gavin-mcinnes-path-to-the-far-rightfrontier/article36024918/.

[233] Reinstein, J., 'Two Proud Boys Have Been Sentenced To Prison For Their Brutal New York City Assault', *BuzzFeed News*, 22 October 2019, online at: www.buzzfeednews.com/article/juliareinstein/proud-boys-sentenced-prison-new-york-city-assault-gavin.

[234] Wilson, J., 'Who are the Proud Boys, 'western chauvinists' involved in political violence?', *the Guardian*, 14 July 2018, online at: www.theguardian.com/world/2018/jul/14/proud-boys-far-right-portland-oregon.

[235] Wilson, J., 'FBI now classifies far-right Proud Boys as 'extremist group', documents say', *The Guardian*, 19 November 2018, online at: www.theguardian.com/world/2018/nov/19/proud-boys-fbi-classification-extremist-group-white-nationalism-report.

Narrative Examples:

Western Chauvinism: "all that is required to become a Proud Boy is that a man declare he is 'a Western chauvinist who refuses to apologize for creating the modern world.'"

- An excerpt from the Proud Boys "Who are they?" webpage.[236]

Anti-Immigration Sentiments: "This attitude [to abortion] + immigration = white genocide in the west (South Africa's version is much more intense)".

- A tweet by Gavin McInnes in June 2017 based on a spoof InfoWars article suggesting that a feminist magazine was demanding women abort pregnancies in an attempted effort at "white genocide" which was also compounded by Hispanic and Asian migration.[237]

Chauvinism: "So Proud Boys, this is a call to arms. You can choose to be a soft, weak, useless male. Or you can embrace the struggle and make yourself mentally and physically tough."

- An excerpt from "Proud Boys Weekly Workout #1" Blog.[238]

---

[236] The Elders, 'Proud Boys: Who are we?', *Proud Boys* website, online at: https://officialproudboys.com/proud-boys/whoaretheproudboys/.

[237] Hatewatch Staff,' Do You Want Bigots, Gavin? Because This Is How You Get Bigots', Southern Poverty Law Centre, 10 August 2017, online at: https://www.splcenter.org/hatewatch/2017/08/10/do-you-want-bigots-gavin-because-how-you-get-bigots.

[238] Judy, C., 'Proud Boys Weekly Workout #1', *Proud Boys* website, online at: https://officialproudboys.com/sports-talk/proud-boys-weekly-workout-1/.

d) Rise Above Movement (R.A.M.)
Founder: Robert Rundo
Membership: 50 (est.)[239]
Ideology: Identitarianism, Neo-Fascism, Anti-Muslim Populism

Description:
Founded in 2017 in Southern California, the Rise Above Movement (R.A.M.) rose to prominence amidst ongoing 'alt-right' protest around college campuses and the 'Unite the Right' rally in Charlottesville later that year. In particular, the group's notoriety for bloody confrontations with counter-protestors and fight-club style organisation mark the group out from others on the American white supremacist scene. For example, in March and April 2017, several of the movement's members deliberately engaged in violent confrontations with counter-protestors.[240] Moreover, in May 2019, Benjamin Daley and Michael Miselis pled guilty to conspiring to riot in Charlottesville, joining other Rise Above members who had done so earlier.[241] Three of the four were sentenced on July 19: Daley to 37 months, Gillen to 33 months, and Miselis to 27 months. In 2018, R.A.M. also launched a clothing line called 'Right Brand Clothing'.[242] Recent reports have also linked R.A.M. to the Ukraine-

---

[239] Thompson, A.C., Winston, A. and Bond Graham, D., 'Racist, Violent, Unpunished: A White Hate Group's Campaign of Menace', *ProPublica*, 19 October 2017, online at: www.propublica.org/article/white-hate-group-campaign-of-menace-rise-above-movement.

[240] Thomson, A.C., 'Federal Judge Dismisses Charges Against 3 White Supremacists', *ProPublica*, 4 June 2019, online at: www.propublica.org/article/federal-judge-dismisses-charges-against-3-white-supremacists.

[241] Thompson, A.C., 'Once Defiant, All Four White Supremacists Charged in Charlottesville Violence Plead Guilty', *ProPublica*, 6 May 2019, online at: www.propublica.org/article/all-four-white-supremacists-charged-in-charlottesville-violence-plead-guilty.

[242] Anti-Defamation League, 'Rise Above Movement', Hate Group Symbols/Logos, online at: www.adl.org/education/references/hate-symbols/rise-above-movement.

based neo-Nazi group Azov Battalion.[243] With the potential to cause additional violent disorder, the group is likely to continue to animate the white nationalist scene in Southern California, especially Orange County, into the future. As of May 2020, R.A.M has 936 followers on its Gab.ai account.[244]

Narrative Examples:

Identitarianism: "The main task of The Rise Above Movement is to revive the spirit of a warrior and to see the rebirth of values of Western Civilization's forefathers."

- An excerpt from 18 December 2017 Rise Above Movement Gab post.[245]

Neo-Fascism: "We want to rise above all of today's destructive culture and see the rebirth of our people, strong in mental and physical capacities as our forefathers were."

- An excerpt from a 12 June 2017 R.A.M. Instagram post.[246]

Anti-Muslim Populism: "Defend America Islamists out! RAPEFUGEES stay away NOT WELCOME [Sic]."

---

[243] See: Colborne, M., 'There's One Far-Right Movement That Hates the Kremlin', *Foreign Policy,* 17 April 2091, online at: https://foreignpolicy.com/2019/04/17/theres-one-far-right-movement-that-hates-the-kremlin-azov-ukraine-biletsky-nouvelle-droite-venner/; Colborne, M., 'Friday Night Fights With Ukraine's Far Right', *The New Republic,* 9 July 2019, online at: https://newrepublic.com/article/154434/friday-night-fights-ukraines-far-right; & Miller,C., 'Azov, Ukraine's Most Prominent Ultranationalist Group, Sets Its Sights On U.S., Europe', *Radio Free Europe,* 14 November 2018, online at: https://www.rferl.org/a/azov-ukraine-s-most-prominent-ultranationalist-group-sets-its-sights-on-u-s-europe/29600564.html.

[244] This figure was collected in February 2020. It is also a note of concern that other US groups, like the Base and Atomwaffen, have had high numbers of followers on Telegram and other more clandestine online platforms.

[245] Anti-Defamation League, 'Rise Above Movement (R.A.M.)', online at: www.adl.org/resources/backgrounders/rise-above-movement-ram.

[246] Ibid.

- Signs used by R.A.M. members at an anti-Sharia law rally in San Bernardino, California in June 2017.

e) Patriot Prayer
Founder: Joey Gibson
Membership: 15 (est).[247]
Ideology: Anti-Muslim Populism, Anti-Government Sentiments, Christianism

Description:
Founded in 2016 by the self-described "Conservative libertarian" Joey Gibson,[248] Patriot Prayer has grown notorious for its rallies and protests, attracting white supremacists and engaging in violent confrontations.[249] Joined by the Proud Boys and Hell Shaking Street Preachers, confrontations with counter protestors and antifascist activists have become a frequent part of Patriot Prayer's demonstrations, with physical clashes and incidents of serious violent escalation both evident.[250] With its activist base mainly concentrated in

---

[247] This is based on an insiders account of core membership, but wider membership most likely to be at least one hundred times this – given average demonstration attendance figures. See for former figure: Zielinkski, A., 'Undercover in Patriot Prayer: Insights From a Vancouver Democrat Who's Been Working Against the Far-Right Group from the Inside', *Portland Mercury*, 26 August 2019, online at: www.portlandmercury.com/blogtown/2019/08/26/27039560/undercover-in-patriot-prayer-insights-from-a-vancouver-democrat-whos-been-working-against-the-far-right-group-from-the-inside.

[248] Ibid.

[249] May, P., 'Who's behind this weekend's right-wing rally at Crissy Field?', *The Mercury News*, 23 August 2017, online at: www.mercurynews.com/2017/08/23/whos-behind-this-weekends-right-wing-rally-at-crissy-field/.

[250] Bivins, M., 'Alt-right rally draws protests in Portland, Oregon', *Al-Jazeera*, 5 June 2017, online at: www.aljazeera.com/news/2017/06/alt-rally-draws-protests-portland-oregon-170605081719281.html & Sheperd, K., 'Police in Vancouver Detain Man for Nearly Running Down Antifa Protesters With His Truck', *Wilamette Week*, online at: www.wweek.com/news/2017/09/10/police-in-vancouver-arrest-man-for-nearly-running-down-antifa-protesters-with-his-truck/.

the Pacific Northwest, activism has largely been confined to Portland, Seattle, and San Francisco. Yet there have also been signs of the group extending its reach to Vancouver.[251] Arguably not ideologically far-right, Patriot Prayer does nevertheless rally on similar issues to the far-right, such as gun rights and free speech, as well as more regional concerns surrounding the "liberat[ion of ...] conservatives on the West Coast".[252] Its Christianist ethos is, likewise, reminiscent of other anti-Islam groups. The group currently has a sizeable online following: 48,700 on YouTube', 7,986 on Twitter, and 2,667 Facebook followers.[253]

Narrative Examples:

Anti-Muslim Populism: "To have a problem with Islam is not racist. That's having an issue with someone's ideology, not race."

- An excerpt from an August 2017 interview with Patriot Prayer leader, Joey Gibson.[254]

Anti-Government Sentiments: "I'm brown so I'm definitely not a white supremacist, definitely not a white nationalist, definitely not a Nazi because I want limited government."

- Patriot Prayer leader, Joey Gibson, commenting on Patriot Prayer's (cancelled) August 2017 San Francisco rally.[255]

---

[251] Matarrese, A. 'Protesters clash in Patriot Prayer demonstration on Vancouver waterfront', *The Columbian*, 10 September 2017, online at: www.columbian.com/news/2017/sep/10/protesters-clash-in-patriot-prayer-demonstration-on-vancouver-waterfront/.

[252] Matarrese, A., and Drake, L., 2 July 2017, Op. Cit.

[253] These figures were collected from Patriot Prayer official social media accounts in February 2020. They do not include the accounts of the group's leader, Joey Gibson.

[254] Fowler, L., 'Patriot Prayer leader dislikes racists, but they seem to hear a whistle', *Crosscut*, 24 August 2017, online at: https://crosscut.com/2017/08/patriot-prayer-joey-gibson-white-supremacists-rally.

[255] Westervelt, E., 'Bay Area Braces For Protests: 'Charlottesville Has Raised The Stakes',' *NPR*, 25 August 2017, online at: https://www.npr.org/2017/08/25/546007440/bay-area-braces-for-protests-charlottesville-has-raised-the-stakes.

Christianism: "I truly believed God wanted me to have the rally. I do believe the scheduling, the way it was scheduled, happened for a reason."

- Patriot Prayer leader, Joey Gibson, commenting on Patriot Prayer's (almost cancelled) 4 June 2017 rally.[256]

---

[256] Matarrese, A., and Drake, L., 2 July 2017, Op. Cit.

f) Oath Keepers
Founder: Stewart Rhodes
Membership: 30,000 (est.)[257]
Ideology: Anti-Government extremism, Anti-Government Violence, Agenda 21 Conspiracy Theory

Description:
Started in 2009 by Yale Law School graduate and former U.S. Army paratrooper, Stewart Rhodes, the Oath Keepers are one of the US's largest sovereign citizen's movements. Oath Keepers count present and former law enforcement officials and military veterans among its ranks.[258] Like other US sovereign citizen groups, in claiming to defend the US Constitution, it also encourages members to not obey orders that they believe would violate it, including "orders to disarm the American people, to conduct warrantless searches, or to detain Americans as 'enemy combatants'".[259] It also subscribes to the Agenda 21 conspiracy theory that the US risks being forced into a one-world socialist government, or so-called "New World Order". Perhaps the most concerning element of the Oath Keepers' activism is their ability to mobilise and organise militia-like vigilante groups against government and law enforcement officials in Montana, Oregon, and Nevada. In April 2014, for example, Stewart Rhodes and several other Oath Keepers went to the Nevada ranch of Cliven Bundy to protect him from an imagined plot to attack his property with drones.[260] Four months later, when rioting broke out in Ferguson, Missouri, Oath Keeper members patrolled the city

---

[257] This is a 2016 figure that's improbably high, see: www.splcenter.org/fighting-hate/extremist-files/group/oath-keepers.

[258] Anti-Defamation League, 'The Oath Keepers' Profile, online at: www.adl.org/resources/profiles/the-oath-keepers.

[259] *Oath Keepers* website, 'About Oath Keepers' Page, online at: https://oathkeepers.org/about/.

[260] Dickinson, T., 'Judge Rules Against 'Delusional' Bundy Clan Leader' *Rolling Stone Magazine*, 10 April 2019, online at: www.rollingstone.com/politics/politics-news/bundy-standoff-oregon-nevada-judge-ruling-820410/.

with rifles.[261] Such patrols continued into the subsequent May and June 2020 Black Lives Matter demonstrations after the death of George Floyd.[262]

Narrative Examples:

Anti-Government Extremism: "Below is our declaration of orders we will NOT obey because we will consider them unconstitutional (and thus unlawful) and immoral violations of the natural rights of the people. Such orders would be acts of war against the American people by their own government, and thus acts of treason."

- An excerpt from Oath Keeper's "Declaration Of Orders We Will Not Obey" Page. [263]

Anti-Government Violence: "John [Mc]Cain is a traitor to the Constitution ... He would deny you the right for trial to jury, but we would give him a trial by jury. Then after we convict him, he should be hung by the neck until dead."

- An excerpt from a Speech by Oath Keepers founder, Stewart Rhodes, in May 2015.[264]

Agenda 21 Conspiracy Theory: "The battle lines have been drawn, and the fight is engaged between the Globalist New World Order versus the Populist Nationalist Traditionalists."

---

[261] Laughland, O., Swaine, J., & Walters, J., 'White militiamen roam Ferguson with rifles while black men wrongly arrested', *The Guardian*, 12 August 2015, online at: https://www.theguardian.com/us-news/2015/aug/11/oath-keepers-ferguson-automatic-rifles.

[262] KABC News, 'Video shows Orange County deputy wearing militia symbols during protest', 5 June 2020, online at: https://abc7.com/orange-county-sheriffs-deputy-sheriffs-department-oathkeepers-and-three-percenters-militia/6230637/.

[263] *Oath Keepers* website, 'Declaration Of Orders We Will Not Obey' Page, online at: https://oathkeepers.org/declaration-of-orders-we-will-not-obey/.

[264] *Southern Poverty Law Centre*, 'Oath Keepers', *Extremist Files*, online at: https://www.splcenter.org/fighting-hate/extremist-files/group/oath-keepers.

- An excerpt from an Oath Keepers blog concerning Donald Trump and Vladimir Putin press conference in July 2018.[265]

g) III%ers (Three Percenters)
Founder: Michael Graham
Leader: Michael "Mike" Brian Vanderboegh
Membership: Unknown
Ideology: Anti-Government Extremism, Sovereign Citizens Conspiracy Theory, Violence

Description:
Part of a broader "Pacific Patriots Network" alongside the Oath Keeper and other anti-government groups, the Three Percenters have emerged as a transnational threat after the formation of a Canadian chapter in March 2016.[266] Formed in 2008 and named after the (erroneous) belief that only 3% of colonists fought against the British during the US Revolutionary War of 1776, Three Percenters view themselves as modern day versions of those revolutionaries, fighting against a tyrannical U.S. government.[267] Often heavily armed, the group's local chapters engage in paramilitary activities (such as marksmanship training) as well as protest rallies. In 2015, for example, a Three Percenter group protested the resettlement of refugees in the state[268] whilst in 2017 the group provided security

---

[265] Dawkins, S., 'Trump-Putin Summit and the Death of the New World Order!!!', *Oath Keepers* website, 17 July 2018, online at: https://oathkeepers.org/2018/07/trump-putin-summit-and-the-death-of-the-new-world-order/.

[266] *Southern Poverty Law Centre*, 'Oath Keepers', Op Cit.

[267] Anti-Defamation League, 'Three Percenters' Glossary Entry, online at: https://www.adl.org/resources/glossary-terms/three-percenters.

[268] Hafner, J, 'Three Percenters: What is the gun-toting group? And what do its supporters want?', *USA Today*, 15 December 2019, online at: https://eu.usatoday.com/story/news/nation-now/2018/03/01/three-percenters-what-gun-

for a Patriot Prayer 'Rally for Trump and Freedom' protest[269] as well as for far-right activists at the August 2017 'Unite the Right' rally in Charlottesville, Virginia.[270] The group's most recent actions have been to protect three Republican lawmakers in Oregon who fled the capitol in June 2019 in an attempt to block the passage of landmark climate-change legislation.[271]

Narrative Examples:

Anti-Government Extremism: "Our goal is to utilize the failsafes put in place by our founders to rein in an overreaching government and push back against tyranny."

- An excerpt from Three Percenter's "About Us" webpage.[272]

Sovereign Citizens Conspiracy Theory: "I will NOT obey orders to disarm the American people."

- One of ten oaths taken by Three Percenter members, and common among US sovereign citizens groups.[273]

Violence: "We do not seek to incite a revolution. However, we will defend ourselves when necessary."

---

toting-group-and-what-do-its-supporters-want/38 5463002/.

[269] Brown, D., 'Photos & Video: Protesters Arrested at a Donald Trump Rally in Vancouver', *Portland Mercury*, 2 April 2017, online at: https://www.portlandmercury.com/blogtown/2017/04/02/18926966/photos-and-video-protesters-arrested-at-a-donald-trump-rally-in-vancouver/.

[270] Michel, C., 'How Militias Became the Private Police for White Supremacist', *Politico Magazine*, 17 August 2017, online at: https://www.politico.com/magazine/story/2017/08/17/white-supremacists-militias-private-police-215498.

[271] Einbinder, N., 'Here's what you need to know about the Three Percenters, the militia group protecting GOP lawmakers in Oregon', *Insider*, 25 June 2019, online at: https://www.insider.com/the-three-percenters-militia-group-protecting-gop-lawmakers-in-oregon-2019-6.

[272] *Three Percenters* website, 'About Us' Page, online at: https://www.thethreepercenters.org/about-us.

[273] *Three Percenters*, 'National By-Laws' Document, online at: https://c18b93ab-8f43-4864-87fb-d705a72ea68d.filesusr.com/ugd/6ecfe6_8ccf0db741614cce809bcdfd496863cf.pdf.

- An excerpt from Three Percenter's "About Us" webpage.²⁷⁴

II. Violent Far-Right Extremist Groups in Canada

a) *Atalante-Quebec*
Founder: Raphaël Lévesque
Membership: Unknown
Ideology: Ultra-nationalism, Neo-Fascism, Autochonism

Description:
Formed in Quebec in 2016, Atalante says it advocates an "identity policy for community, sports, cultural and intellectual purposes". Its members parade regularly in the streets of Quebec, in particular to call for the "remigration" of Quebec's cultural communities, that is, the return of immigrants to their countries of origin.²⁷⁵ Their activities include but are not limited to 'flyering', banner drops, participating in anti-immigrant rallies (alongside SoO Quebec), and providing food to the homeless in Quebec.²⁷⁶ Perhaps of most concern are Atalante's links to intimidation and violent forms of activism. In May 2018, for example, Atalante activists stormed the Montréal offices of VICE magazine and cited unfavourable coverage by one of its journalists, tossing leaflets and clown noses around the online news magazines offices.²⁷⁷ Moreover, Atalante Montréal organizer Shawn Beauvais-MacDonald was among a number of Canadian far-right extremists involved in violence at the 2017 Charlottesville

---

²⁷⁴ *Three Percenters* website, 'About Us' Page, Op Cit.

²⁷⁵ Coutu, S, 'The far right and the antifas promise an eventful summer', *VICE News*, 18 May 2018, Online at: https://www.vice.com/fr_ca/article/zm8xay/lextreme-droite-et-les-antifas-se-promettent-un-ete-mouvemente.

²⁷⁶ Anti-Racist Canada, 'Who Are Atalante? A Deep Dive Into A Quebec Hate Group', 5 December 2019, online at: http://anti-racistcanada.blogspot.com/2019/12/who-are-atalante-deep-dive-into-quebec.html.

²⁷⁷ Coutu, S, 'Far-Right Extremists Stormed the VICE Office in Montréal', *VICE News*, 24 March 2018, online at: https://www.vice.com/en_us/article/nekzpk/far-right-extremists-stormed-the-vice-office-in-montreal.

'Unite the Right' rally[278], to an extent to which some Quebec-based anti-fascist groups allege a connection between his presence and the death of counter-protestor Heather Heyer.[279] At the time of writing in January 2020, Atalante Quebec has 6,725 Facebook, 180 Twitter, and 57 Instagram followers.

Narrative Examples:

Ultra-nationalism: "Only the Nation can synthesize between a territory, a people, its culture, its history and its national conscience."

- An excerpt from Atalante's Home Page.[280]

Neo-Fascism: "What we want is to create the new Nation, the new society. In short, a new social order which would not be based on material gains, but on the sense of sacrifice, heroism, honor and the common good."

- An excerpt from Atalante's Mission Statement.[281]

Autochonism: "We believe in the self-determination of peoples, in their independence and their right to be in the majority on their lands."

- An excerpt from Atalante's website Home Page.[282]

---

[278] Coutu, S, 'We talked to a Quebecer who joined the white supremacist rally in Charlottesville', *VICE News*, 18 August 2017, online at: https://www.vice.com/en_ca/article/8xmknk/we-talked-to-a-quebecer-who-joined-the-white-supremacist-rally-in-charlottesville.

[279] Anti-Racist Canada, 'Who Are Atalante? A Deep Dive Into A Quebec Hate Group', 5 December 2019, online at: http://anti-racistcanada.blogspot.com/2019/12/who-are-atalante-deep-dive-into-quebec.html.

[280] *Atalante* Website, 'Acceuil' Home Page, online at: http://www.atalantequebec.com/?fbclid=IwAR1ZivCkBxt76903G2dZLC8FfJEj2HsRzPuEU0Pk2faHd32NvGWRvOzSK80.

[281] *Atalante* Website, 'Mission' Page, online at: http://www.atalantequebec.com/a-propos/mission/.

[282] *Atalante* Website, 'Acceuil' Home Page, Op Cit.

b) Aryan Guard
Founder: Kyle McKee
Membership: Unknown
Ideology: Neo-Nazism, Antisemitism, White Supremacist

Description:
Founded in 2006 in Calgary by a young neo-Nazi, Kyle McKee, protests in 2007, 2008, and 2009 as well as an accusation of pipe bombing have firmly placed the Aryan Guard on Canada's far- right extremist map. Coming to prominence initially for its anti-immigration 'flyering' campaign in early 2007,[283] the group quickly became the most notorious neo-Nazi group in Canada following their first White Pride March that took place in downtown Calgary in August of that year.[284] Using White Pride CDs to recruit youth and becoming more visible through their public marches, more than 40 Aryan Guard supporters turned up again with flags in downtown Calgary proclaiming "White Pride Worldwide".[285] Finally, on 21st March 2009, the group held its last publicly recorded rally in Calgary, at which 60 Aryan Guard members violently confronted a group of 400 counter protestors.[286] After a pipe bomb was planted outside the home of a rival gang member, an arrest warrant for Kyle Mckee was issued and he was later deemed guilty of the possession of

---

[283] *Street Church*, 'City officials let neo-Nazis march without a permit', 3rd April 2009, online at: https://www.streetchurch.ca/news/press-coverage/city-officials-let-neo-nazis-march-without-a-permit/.

[284] Gundlock, B, 'A New Look at Calgary's Neo-Nazi Movement', *VICE News*, 12th March 201, online at: https://www.vice.com/en_ca/article/exkmvz/a-new-look-at-calgarys-neo-nazi-movement.

[285] Komarrnicki, J, 'Anti-racists clash with Aryan Guard', *The Gazette*, 21st March 2008, online at: https://web.archive.org/web/20080323050210/http://www.canada.com/montrealgazette/news/story.html?id=d80a966a-c835-456a-8021-ed04c1ebedd3&k=5402.

[286] Aryan Guard, 'March 21st – Aryan Guard Hosts White Pride March', 2007, online at: https://web.archive.org/web/20070929082946/http://www.aryanguard.org/.

bomb marking materials (though not of planting the bomb itself). After this accusation and subsequent legal action, the group later renamed itself 'Blood and Honour' before ultimate proscription in June 2019.[287]

Narrative Examples:

Neo-Nazism: "We are Guardians of the White Aryan Race, and as guardians we focus our lives and efforts towards fighting for the freedoms, future and survival of our children and beautiful people."

- An excerpt from Aryan Guard Canada's 'Mission Statement' Page.[288]

Antisemitism: "Kill Jews".

- Words tattooed on the shins of Aryan Guard Canada's leader, Kyle McKee.[289]

White Supremacism: "Our agenda is simple—the 14 Words: 'We must secure the existence of our people and a future for White children.'"

- An excerpt from Aryan Guard Canada's 'Mission Statement' Page, which quotes a phrase that is popular among white supremacists globally.[290]

---

[287] *Canadian Association for Security and Intelligence Studies*, 'Aryan Guard', 2018, online at: https://casisvancouver.ca/1_19_fifth-generation-warfare.html/rwe-group-database/aryan-guard/.

[288] *Aryan Guard* Website, 'Mission Statement' Page, September 2007, online at: https://web.archive.org/web/20070929082946/http:/www.aryan-guard.org/.

[289] *Southern Poverty Law Centre*, 'Aryan Guard Marches on Calgary', Intelligence Report, Summer Issue, 29 May 2009, online at: https://www.splcenter.org/fighting-hate/intelligence-report/2009/aryan-guard-marches-calgary.

[290] *Aryan Guard* Website, 'Mission Statement' Page, September 2007, Op Cit.

c) *Church of the Creator*
Founder: George Burdi
Membership: Unknown
Ideology: Neo-Nazism, Neo-Paganism, White Supremacism

Description:
Founded in the US among white supremacists in 1973 by Ben Klassen, the Canadian branch of the Church of the Creator has seen a fusion with the white power music scene in the country. Formed by the founder of the white supremacist band, RaHoWa, George Burdi became the leader of the Canadian chapter, and he in turn pushed the white power scene across the country as a critique of Christianity.[291] Moreover, in the early 1990's Burdi organized Church of the Creator paramilitary training with a former member of the Canadian Forces Airborne regiment. In 1993 six homes belonging to members of the Church of the Creator were raided, guns seized and three members of the group were arrested.[292] Such violent potential was typified in the same year after the (same) three Church of the Creator members violently kidnaped a young activist from rival Canadian neo-Nazi group, Heritage Front on suspicion of stealing the group's computer containing lists of activists and names of other neo-Nazis in the Canadian military.[293] Arrested in 1997 for non-payment of taxes, Burdi exited the movement.[294] Today, the Creativity Movement still exists in Canada but on a smaller scale,

---

[291] Perry, B. & Scrivens, R, *Right-Wing Extremism in Canada*, London: Palgrave Macmillan, 2019, PP. 26 & 174.

[292] Ibid, P. 188.

[293] Ibid.

[294] Michael, G., 'RAHOWA! A History of the World Church of the Creator', *Terrorism and Political Violence*, 18(4), 2007, 561-583.

where its Toronto chapter features links to a number of international far-right extremist groups, including the British Nationalist Party (BNP), and American Creativity groups.[295]

Narrative examples:

Neo-Nazism: "... might was right when German troops, Poured down through Paris way, It's the gospel of the ancient world. And the logic of today."

- Lyrics from RaHoWA song, named 'Might is Right'.[296]

Neo-Paganism: "I pluck the beard of your Christian "god", And hack open his worm-eaten skull..."

- Lyrics from RaHoWA song, named 'God is Dead'.[297]

White Supremacism: "Our race is our religion, it's our reason and our creed; No cowards linger in our ranks, no weaklings make us bleed."

- Lyrics from RaHoWA song, named 'RaHoWa'.[298]

d) Heritage Front
Founders: Wolfgang Droege, Gerry Lincoln, Grant Bristow and James Scott Dawson
Membership: Less than 10 (est.)
Ideology: Neo-Nazism, Antisemitism, White Supremacism

---

[295] Barbara Perry & Ryan Scrivens, 'Uneasy Alliances: A Look at the Right-Wing Extremist Movement in Canada', *Studies in Conflict & Terrorism*, 39:9, 2016, 827, DOI: 10.1080/1057610X.2016.1139375.

[296] RaHoWa, 'Might is Right', Cult of the Holy War Album, 1995, lyrics online at: http://www.darklyrics.com/lyrics/rahowa/cultoftheholywar.html#9.

[297] RaHoWa, 'Might is Right', Cult of the Holy War Album, 1995, lyrics online at: http://www.darklyrics.com/lyrics/rahowa/cultoftheholywar.html#11.

[298] RaHoWa, 'RoHoWa', Cult of the Holy War Album, 1995, lyrics online at: http://www.darklyrics.com/lyrics/rahowa/cultoftheholywar.html#10.

Description:
Founded in 1989 by four former members of the neo-Nazi Nationalist Party of Canada, Heritage Front was a key part of Canada's white nationalist subcultural milieu until it was disbanded in 2005. Engaged in maintaining a telephone propaganda line, organising white power music concerts and other white supremacist cultural events, the group offered a platform for prominent far-right extremist ideologues and Holocaust Deniers in Canada, including Thomas Metzger and David Irving.[299] More worrying for law enforcement and public officials, however, was the trail of violence left behind by the organisation, with riots and violent assaults frequently following its music events. In 1993, for example, a riot broke out on Parliament Hill in Ottawa after a concert by George Burdi's rock band, RaHoWa (code for "Racial Holy War").[300] In the same year, a Heritage Front 'hanger on', attacked a 45-year-old Tamil refugee in Toronto, which left the victim brain damaged and partially paralysed.[301] After an attack on an Anti-Racist Action headquarters in 1993 and the ensuing legal action,[302] the group's founding leader was forced to step down and subsequently entered into abeyance after the largely unsuccessful leadership of fellow neo-Nazi, Marc Lemire.[303]

---

[299] Romney, L., 'Metzger Seized by Canadian Authorities After Speech', *Los Angeles Times,* 30 June 1992, online at: https://www.latimes.com/archives/la-xpm-1992-06-30-me-1437-story.html. & FPP, 'Witness Statement of Warren Kinsella', 21 January 1999, online at: http://www.fpp.co.uk/Legal/Penguin/witness/KinsellaPrivileged.html.

[300] Farnsworth, C.H., 'Head of Detroit White Supremacist Group Faces Trial in Canada', *New York Times,* 24 March 1995, online at: https://www.nytimes.com/1995/03/24/us/head-of-detroit-white-supremacist-group-faces-trial-in-canada.html.

[301] Perry, B. & Scrivens, R., *Right-Wing Extremism in Canada,* London: Palgrave MacMillan, 2019, P. 189.

[302] *Security Intelligence Committee Review,* 'The Heritage Front Affair: Report to the Solicitor General of Canada', 9 December 1994, online at: https://www.publicsafety.gc.ca/lbrr/archives/jl%2086.s4%20s43%201994-eng.pdf, P.22.

[303] Brean, J, 'Scrutinizing the human rights machine', *National Post,* 22 March 2008, online at: https://archive.is/20080324231719/http://www.nationalpost.com/news/story.html?id=391873.

Narrative examples:
Neo-Nazism: "I remember as a child, my one brother David showing me books on the topic of the Third Reich. I saw a strong, loyal and faithful country, built with strong, loyal and faithful families."

- An excerpt from Heritage Front's December 1997 Newsletter.[304]

Antisemitism: "We do not consider Jewish people to be Euro-Canadians, because they are not descended from Europe"

- An excerpt from Heritage Front website 'FAQs' page.[305]

White Supremacism: "No longer will we be silent as the Canadian government treats Whites as second class citizens. The Heritage Front opposes anti-White Employment 'Equity'"

- An excerpt from Heritage Front website homepage.[306]

e) Blood and Honour (Club 28)
Founder: Kyle McKee
Membership: Unknown (100 est.)
Ideology: Neo-Nazism, Antisemitism, Ultra-nationalism

Description:
Formed in late 2009 after the collapse of Aryan Guard, Blood and Honour (B&H) emerged onto Canada's far-right extremist scene

---

[304] Lemke, S.L., 'The Whole Rotten Stinking Story that I Never had the Chance to Tell', *The HF Report*, December 1997, online at: https://wayback.archive-it.org/227/20060324205049/http://www.heritagefront.com/reports/hf_report_dec97.html.

[305] *Heritage Front* Website, 'Frequently Asked Questions' Page, online at: https://wayback.archive-it.org/227/20060324204632/http://www.heritagefront.com/faq/index.html.

[306] *Heritage Front* Website, 'Home' Page, online at: https://wayback.archive-it.org/227/20060324204426/http://www.heritagefront.com/.

around the time of the imprisonment of its leader, Kyle McKee. Performing several rallies and white power rock concerts during the late 2000s and early 2010s, it was famed for its violent activities whilst taking to the streets, putting up pro-white flyers, fighting with antiracists, and attempting to intimidate minorities.[307] Indeed, police referred to McKee as a "micro-führer" with the group organising an annual white pride march in its native Calgary.[308] Despite a relatively large attendance at such marches (100 in 2011), its activities started to tail off in the mid-2010s as a result of increasing arrests and police clampdowns on the movement.[309] The final major setback for the group was the Canadian Government's decision to place the group on a list of proscribed terrorist entities in June 2019, the government citing the group's involvement in domestic violent actions and murders (as well as other such acts in countries outside of North America) as key determinants for the decision.[310] Disputing the effectiveness of such bans, several agencies pointed out at the time that the group still had an online presence with its own website and profile on VK, a Russian social media site popular among far-right extremists.[311] In addition, practitioners in Canada have noted a displacement effect, post-ban, which has seen a shift

---

[307] Lamoureux, M, 'Canada Adds Far-Right Groups to Terror Watch List for First Time', *VICE News*, 26 June 2019, online at: https://www.vice.com/en_ca/article/8xz77k/canada-adds-far-right-groups-to-terror-watch-list-for-first-time.

[308] Wingrove, J, 'Calgary's in-your-face neo-Nazis take to the streets', *The Globe and Mail*, 18 March 2011, online at: https://www.theglobeandmail.com/news/national/calgarys-in-your-face-neo-nazis-take-to-the-streets/article573162/.

[309] See a facsimile version of Canada's Blood & Honour blog for more details of events: http://canadianbloodandhonour.blogspot.com/.

[310] Bell, S, 'Canada adds neo-Nazi groups Blood & Honour, Combat 18 to list of terror organizations.' *Global News*, 26 June 2019, online at: https://globalnews.ca/news/5432851/canada-adds-neo-nazi-groups-blood-honour-and-combat-18-to-list-of-terror-organizations/.

[311] Counter Extremism Project, 'Extremist Content Online: Blood & Honour and Combat 18 Maintain Online Presence', 1 July 2019, online at: https://www.counterextremism.com/press/extremist-content-online-blood-honour-and-combat-18-maintain-online-presence & 'White Pride World Wide' VK Group, online at: https://vk.com/wpww14880.

of activists from B&H to various neo-völkisch and racist skinhead groups, including Asatru Folk Assembly and Canadian Hammerskins (who have a page on the international Hammerskins website).[312]

Narrative examples:

Neo-Nazism: "NSDAP [Swastika]' & 'Waffen SS"

- Slogans written on Christmas stockings owned by Kyle McKee, Blood and Honour Canada's former leader.[313]

Antisemitism: "Kill Jews".

- Words tattooed on the shins of Aryan Guard Canada's leader, Kyle McKee.[314]

Ultra-Nationalism: "It is also the goal of the Blood and Honour movement to unite those people with a legitimate interest in securing the future of our European cultural identity under one common banner."

- An excerpt of statement on Blood & Honour Canada's Home page.[315]

Summary

Given the above survey of North America-based violent far-right extremist groups and actors, it is apparent that the key narratives centre around: white supremacism; anti-migrant sentiments; neo-Nazism/Fascism; antisemitism; anti-Muslim populism; anti-government extremism; chauvinism. Notwithstanding the more culturally nationalist (e.g., anti-Islam, identitarian and so-called "alt-lite" groups) and anti-government extremist groups, more violent

---

[312] Galloway, B. (February 2020) Op Cit.
[313] Wingrove, J, Op Cit.
[314] *Southern Poverty Law Centre*, 29 May 2009, Op Cit.
[315] *Blood and Honour Canada Website*, 'Home' Page, February 2011, online at: https://web.archive.org/web/20110213043345/http:/www.28canada.org/indexx.html.

tendencies tend to lie with groups that take a more racially nationalist stance (usually preaching a form of white endangerment and acceleration towards a racial holy war).[316] When compared with other contexts, what is so fascinating about the North American case, then, is simply the breadth and volume of far-right extremist groups and their narratives.[317] A key challenge for practitioners in this context is to prioritise more violent groups and narratives that are only the tip of the iceberg when it comes to the broader radical-right extremist ecosystem.

Drawing upon the above North American far-right extremist actor profiles, these narratives can be simplified to the following positions:

1. **White Supremacist Narratives**: i.e., Majority ethnic identities are under threat from indigenous populations and African-Americans as well as Asian & Hispanic migration; elites are complicit in a 'white genocide' that will invariably end in a 'race war' (or for cultural nationalists, a 'great replacement' of US-born whites). Key Term: **White Genocide Conspiracy Theory & Great Replacement Conspiracy Theory.**
2. **Neo-Nazi/Neo-Fascist Narratives**: i.e., the decadent and morally corrupt liberal democratic system in the North America needs to be replaced through a process of agitation and revolution, only then (through sovereign ethno-states) can a morally 'pure' new nation be born. Key Terms: **Accelerationism & Palingenetic Nationalism.**[318]

---

[316] For more information about this distinction between culturally and ethnically nationalist radical right groups, see: Ravndal, J.A. & Bjørgo, T., 'Extreme-Right Violence and Terrorism: Concepts, Patterns, and Responses', The Hague: ICCT Policy Brief, September 2019, online at: https://icct.nl/wp-content/uploads/2019/09/Extreme-Right-Violence-and-Terrorism-Concepts-Patterns-and-Responses.pdf.

[317] Fadel, L., 'U.S. Hate Groups Rose 30 Percent In Recent Years, Watchdog Group Reports', NPR, 20 February 2019, online at: www.npr.org/2019/02/20/696217158/u-s-hate-groups-rose-sharply-in-recent-years-watchdog-group-reports.

[318] According to noted scholar of historical fascism, Roger Griffin, Palingenetic Nationalism (or the rebirth of the nation) is a key component of fascism, and is

3. **Anti-Immigration Narratives:** i.e., Antipathy towards immigrants, asylum seekers, and refugees, expressed as culturally or racially inferior, also leading to white marginalisation or 'genocide' (as stated in narrative 1 above). Key Terms: **Islamophobia, Sinophobia & Asylophobia.**
4. **Antisemitic Narratives**: i.e., Jewish interests are part of a globalist conspiracy to create a one-world, Zionist-occupied government; US & Canadian elites are being controlled and manipulated by the Jewish population and aided by cultural Marxists, they look out for Jewish interests whilst letting non-Jewish US whites suffer. Key Terms: **Agenda 21 Conspiracy Theory & Zionist Occupied Government Conspiracy Theory.**[319]
5. **Anti-Muslim Narratives:** i.e., national & cultural identities are under threat because of Islam, elites are complicit in the erasure of a strong, traditionally western 'American' identity, this will inevitably end in a clash of civilisations. Key Terms: **Anti-Muslim Populism & Clash of Civilisations Thesis.**
6. **Chauvinist Narratives:** i.e., Societies are under threat because men cannot live 'according to their nature'; feminists and the LGBT community are considered race traitors; and in response, North American-based whites must return to the heteronormative past. In response, we need to train and prepare 'whites only' enclaves in the Pacific North West. Key Terms: **Anti-Feminism, Misogyny, & Pacific Northwest Imperative.**
7. **Anti-Government Narratives**: i.e., the modern US and Canadian federal government has outgrown its remit; since their role is to keep 'the people' down, there is a need to form well-armed militias in order to rise up against the Government should it be needed. Key Terms: **Sovereign Citizens Conspiracy Theory & Q-Anon Conspiracy Theory.**

---

often seen among such groups a coming after a time of so-called 'moral decadence' (Griffin, *The Nature of Fascism*, 1991).

[319] Here, 'Zionist Occupied Government Conspiracy Theory' is the belief that the state has be captured by Jewish elites and interests and no longer represents the interests of white people (Daniels, *White Lies: Race, Class, Gender and Sexuality in White Supremacist Discourse*, 1997).

Violent Far-Right Counter-Narratives in North America: Tapping into White Supremacist, Neo-Nazi/Fascist, Anti-Immigration, Antisemitic, Anti-Muslim, Chauvinist and Anti-Government Narratives

North America presents one of the largest far-right extremist scenes and set of violent milieus known to researchers globally. The methodology of constructing counter-narratives towards these groups does however remain fairly similar, if with a more local inflection (e.g., hatred aimed at native residents, Hispanic/Latino groups, African-Americans and the orientalised Asian 'foreigner') in order to better resonate with sympathetic, local audiences. If attempting to construct counter-narratives in order to disrupt, delegitimise and/or devalue the appeal of the above narratives, it is useful to identify what we can call 'entry points' within the structure of extremist narratives in order to unpick their veracity, authenticity and believability. Such a process can be begun by breaking down such narratives into their orientation (e.g., who, what, where, how & when), action (i.e., evaluation of orientation) and resolution (i.e., prescribed course of action). Whilst it might be unprofitable to contest the factual veracity of the orientation statement, both the action and solution sections of the narrative might be more profitably contested. The rationale behind such a technique is that far-right extremists tend to do most harm in how they interpret and offer solutions to what is happening 'out there', and how they frame reality. Opinions are also a softer target than facts, and this maps onto how extremists use grievances to add their own ideological 'twist' on real world events. Therefore, disputing the action and resolution statement are more profitable as it means practitioners are disputing the ideological interpretation of the truth (or factual reality) presented, rather than the reality itself. Examples that could deployed by practitioners in North American context include:

1. **White Supremacist Counter-Narrative**: i.e., highlight the positive contribution of native Americans, African-American, Asian and Hispanic migrants to the US's livelihood and past; show examples of cooperation between different races as part of the US and Canadian cultural heritage; acknowledge legitimate concerns of white supremacists, but try to foster more open viewpoints and a less formulaic or rigid conceptions of migrants and other minority populations.
2. **Anti-Migrant Counter-Narratives**: Highlighting the positive contribution of Asian and Hispanic migrants to the country's livelihood and past; acknowledging prejudice but fostering more open viewpoints and a less formulaic or rigid conception of American national identity, refugees and migrants.
3. **Neo-Nazi/Fascist Counter-Narrative**: i.e., highlight the rational inconsistencies of accelerationism and violent revolution (i.e., that it might actually lead to national decline rather than rebirth) and the inevitable risks to so-called 'indigenous, white' populations associated with this course of action; try to foster trust through examples of politicians acting with integrity; and, ultimately, divert inveterate activists to safer forms of non-racist political activism (i.e., political party or peaceful protest) over time.
4. **Antisemitic Counter-Narrative**: i.e., point out that scapegoating others for our problems is a very easy thing to do and distracts us from our own problems, point out that as a minority it is more likely for the Jewish population to be oppressed than vice versa, ultimately try to move adherents away from a sense of ethnic and cultural endangerment and towards the positive contribution of Jewish intellectuals and luminaries in the life of US and Canada as a nation (e.g., Albert Einstein and Milton Friedman).
5. **Anti-Muslim Populism Counter-Narrative**: i.e., highlight the positive contribution of Muslims to the country's physical and intellectual livelihood (e.g., Syrian doctors and Ayaan Hirsh Ali), acknowledge prejudice but foster more

open viewpoints and a less formulaic or rigid conception of Islam.
6. **Chauvinist Counter-Narrative:** i.e., stress positive contribution by women (e.g., Hannah Arendt) and the LGBT+ community (e.g., Harvey Milk) to the life of the nation in order to humanise. Reduce threat perception by stressing allegiances in thought and not division. Again, try to reduce threat perception and fill the 'void' with alternatives (e.g., more inclusive and positive conceptions of masculinity).
7. **Anti-Government Counter-Narrative:** i.e., emphasise positive modes of activism instead of militia-based violence. Talk of efficiencies, benefits and successes of the current representative system as well as risks of paramilitary activism (e.g., misdirected attacks, retaliation and burnout). Try to unpick anti-government conspiracies (especially around the notion of a 'deep state' or 'hidden powers'), with examples of transparency and accountability.

Turning from far-right narratives and counter-narratives toward counter-narrative campaigns, there have been several attempts to foster best practice when challenging far-right narratives, in both the online and offline spaces. These attempts have been as a result of (some recently aborted)[320] government funded initiatives but also were due to a vibrant NGO and thinktank sector, both in the US and Canada, which paid greater attention to far-right and far-right sympathetic audiences.[321] Below is a snapshot of some notable recent North America-based counter-narrative initiatives that targeted far-right extremists and potential recruits.

The first tentative attempt at targeting the basis of far- right extremism upstream through counter-narrative campaigns came through a US State Department strategic communications initiative

---

[320] Beinart, P., 'Trump Shut Programs to Counter Violent Extremism', *The Atlantic*, 29 October 2018, online at: www.theatlantic.com/ideas/archive/2018/10/trump-shut-countering-violent-extremism-program/574237/.

[321] Examples here including tech-based companies and think tanks (such as Moonshot CVE and the Institute for Strategic Dialogue) but also non-government actors in the radical right de-radicalisation sector (such as EXIT USA, Life After Hate, & Free Radicals).

in 2011, called "2011 Hours Against Hate". Spearheaded by the Secretary of State, the Special Representative to Muslim Communities and the Special Envoy to Monitor and Combat Antisemitism, the campaign was designed as a call to action for young people to engage in offline activism and pledge an hour to help someone different to them.[322] In addition to posting a picture of their pledge and posting it online, young people were asked to help at a women's shelter, religious charity or homeless shelter.[323] Though the original website and Facebook page for the initiative no longer exist, it appears that, according to its YouTube engagement and viewership statistics (see screenshot in figure 19 below), uptake of the initiative was fairly low; it received only 2,585 views across all four launch videos for the campaign (as well as a few likes and comments).[324] Such is a cautionary tale of taking a top-down approach to counter-narrative campaigns that feature less effective messengers at reaching the target audience, elite speakers (e.g., government officials as opposed to a well-known and trusted celebrity or sports figure), and found a low organic reach. Despite this, however, the science of a 'call to action' as part of the campaign and tackling prejudice through intergroup contact is sound,[325] and could be replicated in initiatives that incorporate different messengers.

---

[322] Counter Narrative Toolkit, 'Hours Against Hate' Case Study, online at: www.counternarratives.org/html/case-studies-entry?id=19.

[323] US State Department, '2011 Hours Against Hate', 10 February 2011, online at: https://2009-2017.state.gov/s/srmc/156531.htm.

[324] US State Department, 'Special Representative Pandith Introduces 2011 Hours Against Hate', *YouTube*, 11 February 2011, online at: www.youtube.com/watch?v=bCrr8XyR5vY; US State Department, 'Special Envoy Rosenthal Introduces 2011 Hours Against Hate', *YouTube*, 11 February 2011, online at: www.youtube.com/watch?v=tHK3jDYRQdM; US State Department, 'Special Representative Pandith, Special Envoy Rosenthal Highlight 2011 Hours Against Hate (Short)', *YouTube*, 14 February 2011, online at: www.youtube.com/watch?v=jzYumnqoER8; & US State Department, 'Secretary Clinton Underscores 2011 Hours Against Hate Campaign', *YouTube*, 8 April 2011, online at: www.youtube.com/watch?v=Q-4XlLis7CA.

[325] See: Pettigrew, T. F., & Tropp, L. R., ,A meta-analytic test of intergroup contact theory', *Journal of Personality and Social Psychology*, 90(5), 2006, 751–783, online at: https://doi.org/10.1037/0022-3514.90.5.751 & RAN, 'How can online communications drive offline interventions?', *Ex Post Paper*, 22-23 November 2018, online at: https://ec.europa.eu/home-affairs/sites/homeaffairs/files/what-we-do/networks/radicalisation_aw

Figure 20: Screen Grab from 2011 Hours Against Hate Campaign 'Launch' Video[326]

Moving on to counter-narrative projects per se, the second project of note in recent times was Against Violent Extremism (AVE) network's 'Communitas' project. Started in 2014, the goal of Communitas was to strengthen individual and community resilience through social interdependence, active citizenship, dialogue, and youth leadership.[327] The project spotlighted the needs of various communities and had presences in the Canadian cities of Montréal, Ottawa, the Greater Toronto Area, London, Calgary, Edmonton and Vancouver. Perhaps most notable was the project's focus on dialogue in areas affected by far-right extremism. For example, it developed inter-religious and inter-community initiatives with

---

areness_network/about-ran/ran-c-and-n/docs/ran_c-n_amsterdam_ca
ll_to_action_20181123_22_en.pdf

[326] US State Department, 'Special Representative Pandith, Special Envoy Rosenthal Highlight 2011 Hours Against Hate (Short)', *Youtube*, 14 February 2011, online at: www.youtube.com/watch?v=jzYumnqoER8.

[327] Communitas Website, 'Project Concept', 30 June 2014, online at: http://communitas.ccmw.com/about/.

among 300+ diverse youth (18-30) from across Canada.[328] Unfortunately, an assessment of this project cannot be facilitated at the present time due to the inaccessibility of the project's reports.[329]

A second project of note was Extreme Dialogue, a counter-narrative project launched in 2015 by the Institute for Strategic Dialogue. Combining multimedia educational resources with short documentary films, the aim of the project was to develop students' critical thinking skills and resilience to radicalisation, explore shared values, and challenge various types of extremist propaganda and ideologies. The films told the personal stories of people who have been affected by violent extremism and include testimony from former members of extreme groups as well as survivors. Extreme Dialogue began in Canada in 2015, and was also launched in the UK, Germany, and Hungary in 2016 with new films and resources featuring the stories of people from those three countries.

One independent assessment of the initiative showed (whilst extensive press and online dissemination saw successful exposure and coverage) the project was less successful in converting this exposure and coverage into continuing levels of engagement beyond the one-week launch period.[330] Indeed, once paid-for advertising had worn off, the impact was not sustained, as unpaid and organic reach and engagement dropped off. In fairness, however, some of this misfortune was attributable to the platforms selected for the launch of the project videos themselves. As the same report argues, some platforms prohibited targeting advertisements at under 18's.[331] Such an obstacle emphasises the need for those conducting these campaigns to take advantage of technical advertising support offered by technology platforms as well as the need for informal

---

[328] Canadian Council of Muslim Women, 'Project Communitas', online at: https://ccmw.com/project-communitas//

[329] Communitas Website, 'Project Reports', 3rd September 2014, online at: http://communitas.ccmw.com/project-reports/.

[330] SecDev Foundation, 'Extreme Dialogue: Social Media Target Audience Analysis and Impact Assessments in Support of Countering Violent Extremism', March 2016, online at: https://bit.ly/37zacr3.

[331] Ibid, P.13.

actors to be involved in the organisation of counter-narrative initiatives.

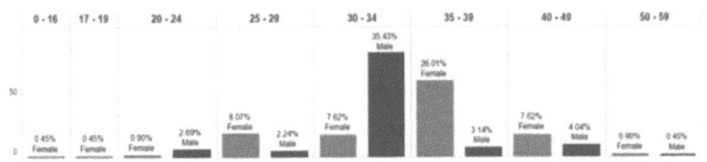

Figure 21: Age Range of Twitter Users from the Extreme Dialogue Dashboard[332]

The third counter narrative intervention to note in the North American context was EXIT USA's (2015) video campaign consisting of four videos that used EXIT USA and Against Violent Extremism (AVE) network former extremist testimonies to highlight personal stories and falsities propagated by far-right extremist groups.[333] Using short and emotionally-charged messages tailored for social media to sit alongside its day-to-day offline intervention work, the videos (see figure 21 below for examples) were targeted at violent white supremacists across the broadest geographical area—cognizant of the wide spread of white supremacist groups across the entirety of the country, and using key words and hashtags in order to capture a large cross-section of the extremist scene. The aim of the campaign was not just to garner views but to also encourage engagement through comments.

---

[332] SecDev Foundation, 'Extreme Dialogue: Social Media Target Audience Analysis and Impact Assessments in Support of Countering Violent Extremism', March 2016, online at: https://bit.ly/37zacr3, P. 23.

[333] Counter Narrative Toolkit, 'Exit USA' Case Study, online at: www.counternarratives.org/html/case-studies-entry?id=17.

ExitUSA VIDEO TITLES AND DESCRIPTION

NO JUDGEMENT JUST HELP

The video explains that since 9/11 home-grown white supremacists have killed more Americans on US soil than ISIS, Al-Qaeda and the Taliban combined and continues to offer a way out to those involved in white supremacist movements. This video has a reflective tone and presents an ideological challenge and an offer of assistance.

THERE IS LIFE AFTER HATE

Tim Zaal spent half of his life thinking that he had killed a man one night when he was out looking for a fight. It wasn't until he came face to face with his victim many years later that he realised the power of forgiveness. This video has a reflective and sentimental tone, and presents a personal story.

OAK CREEK

This video tackles the same issues as *No Judgement Just Help* but is presented in a different format.

THE FORMERS

The Formers in this video begin by provocatively telling the viewer the 'truths' they believed whilst still in their violent extremist movements. At the end of the video they reveal that these were 'lies' that they fell for, highlighting the realities of hateful ideologies. This video has a reflective tone and presents an ideological challenge and personal story.

Figure 22: Overview of EXIT USA (2015) Counter Narrative Videos[334]

An independent assessment of EXIT USA's (2015) counter narrative campaign suggests it was broadly successful in its objectives, engaging over 212,000 users on Facebook alone.[335] Moreover, and when compared to other similar violent Islamist counter narrative

---

[334] Silverman, T., Stewart, C.J., Amanullah, Z., & Birdwell, J., 'The Impact of Counter-Narratives', London: ISD Global, 2016, online at: www.isdglobal.org/wp-content/uploads/2016/08/Impact-of-Counter-Narratives_ONLINE_1.pdf, P.17.

[335] Ibid., p. 24.

campaigns, EXIT USA's videos had the highest retention rates, suggesting that the short and emotionally-charged nature of the videos worked.[336] The EXIT USA campaign also received high (and largely positive) comment traffic, with 32% of comments being supportive and 18% negative.[337] This might be due to EXIT USA's deliberate strategy of fostering discussion and the accessibility of its staff throughout the campaign, with several users reaching out to them via direct message function of certain platforms (see example in figure 23 below). Moreover, we can see how such campaigns might be beneficial for future communications campaigns (EXIT USA seeing its YouTube subscriber base double, its Twitter Followership treble and the reach of its Facebook content also nearly trebling (see figure 22 for detailed statistics)).[338] Whilst specific in scope, such a campaign tells us of the need for short, emotionally charged videos when deploying counter narratives online and the need for responsiveness by skilled intervention providers when using the comment or direct message function.

---

[336] Ibid., p. 25.
[337] Ibid., pp. 33-34.
[338] Ibid., p.31.

[EXIT Former 1]: **Hey guys I am a former white supremacist**

[ExitUSA]: Hi [former]. **Thank you for reaching out. How can we help you?**

[EXIT Former 1]: **I have been away from it for a few months but I still get old feelings an thoughts**

Figure 23: Example of Direct Message from Exit USA Campaign[339]

TABLE 4: BEFORE AND AFTER ENGAGEMENT STATISTICS FOR ALL ORGANISATIONS						
		FACEBOOK		TWITTER	YOUTUBE
CAMPAIGN	CAMPAIGN PERIOD	PAGE LIKES	ORGANIC REACH/DAY	FOLLOWERS	SUBSCRIBERS
ExitUSA	Before	192	1 to 34	50	16
	Gained	94	956 to 2,779	105	16
	Total at end	*286*	*0 to 32*	*155*	*32*

Figure 24: Before and After Engagement Statistics for EXIT USA Campaign[340]

Building on EXIT USA's success in generating sustained engagements, a third notable initiative launched in the same year in the USA, UK and Canada was the Institute for Strategic Dialogue's (ISD) One-on-One programme. A small-scale pilot programme in collaboration with Curtin University, the project used ten former extremists (including five former far-right extremists from North America) to send a direct message to try and start a dialogue and sow initial 'seeds of doubt' around the validity of extremist groups

---

[339] Silverman, T., Stewart, C.J., Amanullah, Z., & Birdwell, J., 'The Impact of Counter-Narratives', London: ISD Global, 2016, online at: www.isdglobal.org/wp-content/uploads/2016/08/Impact-of-Counter-Narratives_ONLINE_1.pdf, p. 38.

[340] Ibid., p. 31.

and narratives with 160 individuals considered at-risk or already expressing sympathies for extremist organisations.[341] Besides using former extremists, one of the innovations of the project was using highly tailored matching of intervention providers with recipients, focusing on the age, ideology and gender of recipients. A prototype of a larger Counter Conversations project by ISD, it was also highly successful in engaging individuals compared with standard email marketing campaigns, with over 60% of messages leading to contact and discussion of their extremist beliefs.[342] Again, the main barrier to successful contact and intervention were technological difficulties, with 42 of the 154 profiles identified taken down by Facebook through the course of the project.[343] This again stresses the need for counter narrative campaign providers to work closely with online platforms when designing and executing their interventions in order to make sure that unintended consequences don't lead to counter-productive outcomes.

Moving to a more grassroots form of counter-narrative initiative, the end of 2015 also saw the creation of the University of New Mexico's "Know Extremism" campaign. Put together by undergraduate Marketing students at the University as part of the US State Department's Peer to Peer (P2P): Challenging Extremism initiative, the "Know Extremism" campaign used its own website, online adverts, as well as social media channels to share a set of counter-narrative videos, infographics (see an example in figure 24), relevant news stories and the #ChallengeExtremism hashtag. The aim of the campaign was to encourage young people to educate themselves about violent extremism and to "speak out against it."[344] Whilst not far-right specific in its focus, its focus on victims in

---

[341] Counter Narrative Toolkit, 'One-to-One: Institute for Strategic Dialogue' Case Study, online at: www.counternarratives.org/html/case-studies-entry?id=25.

[342] Frenett, R. & Dow, M, 'One to One Online Interventions: A Pilot CVE Methodology', London & Perth: ISD & Curtin University, 2016, p. 14, online at: https://ec.europa.eu/home-affairs/node/7493_en.pdf; and www.isdglobal.org/wp-content/uploads/2016/04/One2One_Web_v9.

[343] Ibid., p. 21.

[344] See Counter Narrative Toolkit, 'Know Extremism' Campaign, online at: www.counternarratives.org/html/case-studies-entry?id=23.

response to terror attacks[345] and blogs focusing on other forms of extremism[346] suggest at least a nod to the far-right. For such a small-scale programme, awareness and engagement was reasonably impressive, with a combined followership on Facebook, Twitter, Instagram, and YouTube of 3,343 users and a peak viewership of 435 on its counter-narrative explainer-type videos.[347] Comparing awareness then with the 2011 US State campaign above, this shows the strength of using informal (i.e., citizens), tech-savvy individuals (i.e., students) backed by the state to conduct higher impact campaigns, with a far greater organic reach.[348]

---

[345] *'Know Extremism' Campaign*, 'Stand with Paris' Post, *Instagram*, 14 November 2015, online at: https://www.instagram.com/p/-E2pq1uIJc/.

[346] *'Know Extremism' Campaign*, 'The latest developments in the Planned Parenthood Colorado Springs shooting' Post, *Twitter*, 28 November 2015, online at: https://twitter.com/knowcampaign/status/670415932775231488.

[347] See: *'Know Extremism' Campaign*, YouTube Channel, online at: www.youtube.com/channel/UCMLL5buyK5uqnddxfpZRg9g.

[348] See more here: Lee, B.J., 'Informal Countermessaging: The Potential and Perils of Informal Online Countermessaging', *Studies in Conflict & Terrorism*, 42(1-2), 2019, 161-177, online at: http://10.1080/1057610X.2018.1513697.

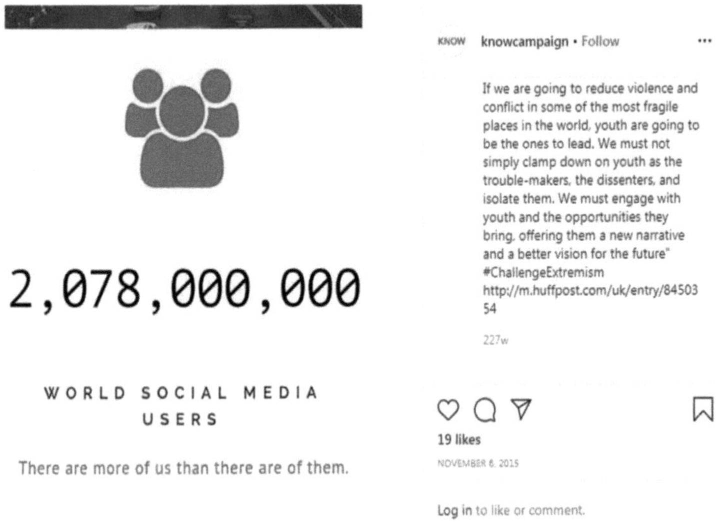

Figure 25: Example Infographic from the 'Know Extremism' Instagram Account[349]

The fourth reported counter-narrative interventions that we can report on in North America was a community-based initiative started by students at Canada's Simon Fraser University, called Voices Against Extremism (VAE). Launched in September 2016 and backed by the Organization for Security and Co-operation in Europe (OSCE), the VAE counter narrative campaign was aimed at challenging extremist beliefs while simultaneously promoting awareness and education about how issues of extremism impact the community.[350] To this end, the students responsible for VAE decided to build their counter narrative campaign around the four key pillars of humanization, education, respect, and empowerment.[351] As

---

[349] *'Know Extremism' Campaign,* 'World Social Media Users' Post, *Instagram,* 6 November 2015, online at: https://www.instagram.com/p/9uSI_GuIEV/.

[350] Macnair, L. & Frank, R, 'Voices Against Extremism: A case study of a community-based CVE counter-narrative campaign', *Journal for Deradicalization,* (10), 2017, P.155.

[351] Ibid. P.156

part of their intervention, students embarked on a video campaign (titled 'Stories of Resistance') that interviewed a wide profile of individuals (e.g., refugees, immigrants, law enforcement officials and formers) who had been affected by extremism and solicited their thoughts on community and Canadian identity. During the 14 weeks that it took to design and implement the VAE campaign, the videos relating to the campaign gained significant reach with over 160,000 individuals exposed to the campaign's content. Moreover, VAE students engaged with nearly 100 elementary school students and 300 members of the public at an art gallery event.[352]

Figure 26: Screen Grab from OSCE video reviewing the Voices Against Extremism Project[353]

Despite this reach, a number of limitations can be noted about this intervention, which targeted both far-right and extreme Islamist ideologies. Firstly, and due to the condensed period of implementation, little is known about the empirical impact of the campaign upon those who engaged with the videos and the extent to which it changed recipients' attitudes or behaviours. Secondly, it should be

---

[352] Ibid. P.158

[353] OSCE, 'Peer-2-Peer: Voices Against Extremism', 30 December 2016, online at: https://www.osce.org/secretariat/291681.

noted that reports at the time of the initiative suggested that a majority of individuals involved in offline engagements for the project tended to be people already knowledgeable about the problematic nature of extremism and to some degree active in stopping it. For example, a 2017 article by Logan Macnair and Richard Frank found that attendees at the art gallery event were from law-enforcement, academic, and community-leader backgrounds.[354] Finally, and relatedly, there was also little attempt to measure how the concepts of humanization, education, respect, and empowerment might manifest in those encountering campaign materials, perhaps pointing to a lost measurement opportunity on the part of its creators. All this being said, however, the group of students did remarkably well to reach a wider audience given the time and budget restraints imposed on them, using everyday experiences in an effective way to authentically express how extremism affects individuals, professionals, and wider communities.

Another student-led counter narrative initiative used to combat far-right extremism in the wake of a terror attack in Edmonton, Alberta in 2017 was provided by students at the University of Alberta. Targeting those vulnerable to far-right propaganda, the six-minute video (entered into Facebook's 2017 'Peer-to-Peer: Global Digital Challenge' project) takes the viewer through the process of an individual being groomed into radicalisation as a result of the attack and their realisation of the simplistic and binary narratives of far-right extremists. It then leaves the viewer with the question of "Who do you want to be?". Using such a question allowed the viewer to make up their mind after sowing a seed of doubt.[355] Providing an example of an alternative narrative, it shows the positive response of minority communities to the attack and their support by mainstream actors. While no independent evaluation has been done of the video and its impact, the overall reach and engagement metrics are promising, with combined views for the short and

---

[354] Ibid. P. 159

[355] McMaster, G., 'Class project questions racist assumptions that can lead to violence', Organisation for the Prevention of Violence, 5 December 2017, online at: https://preventviolence.ca/publication/racist-assumptions/.

long form versions of the video pegged at 13,600 along with a number of shares, likes, and comments for the videos posted on 'Our Alberta['s]' Facebook page.[356] Despite this traction, it has had a mixed reaction, with the majority of comments on the videos voicing scepticism towards the video's core message.[357]

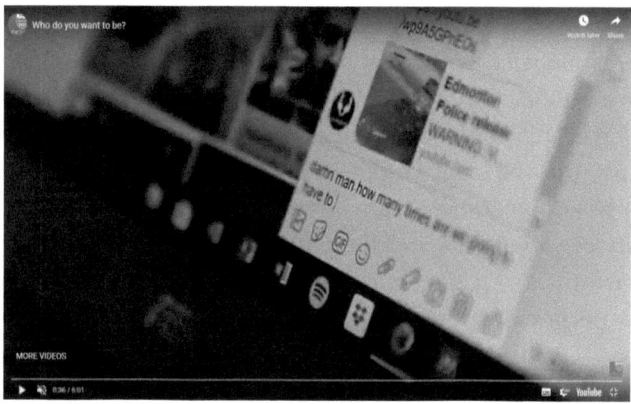

Figure 27:   Screen Grab from 'Peer-to-Peer: Facebook Global Digital Challenge' Video, "Who do you want to be?"[358]

Another community-based project that has tried to take a more creative arts-based and research-led approach to counter narratives is Concordia University's SOMEONE (SOcial Media EducatiON Every day) initiative. Launched in April 2016, it is a web-based portal of multimedia materials aimed at preventing hate speech against ethnic minorities and building resilience towards extremism.[359] The materials are targeted at youth, school and community members, policy officials, as well as the broader Canadian public by focusing

---

[356] *Our Alberta* Facebook Community Page, online at: https://www.facebook.com/OurAlberta/.

[357] *Our Alberta* Facebook Community Page, 'It's Not That Simple' Video, online at: https://www.facebook.com/OurAlberta/videos/155430945072753/.

[358] University of Alberta, 'Wo do you want to be?', *Youtube*, 28 November 2017, online at: https://www.youtube.com/watch?v=V3mekPXGY1Q.

[359] Project Someone Website, 'About' Page, online at: https://projectsomeone.ca/about.

on the development of critical thinking and information literacy skills, and encouraging dialogue about how hatred towards minorities is developed in everyday life through social media. One project that has gained particular traction is the 'Landscape of Hate' Project that aims to promote a dialogue about how to deal with anti-minority hatred through panel discussions, debates, live art expositions and performance.[360] Since its launch in 2017, the project has put on six events globally, with a wide mixture of artists, researchers, and former extremists taking part. Whilst not specifically focused towards far-right groups themselves, the 'Landscape of Hate' Project does spell out the creative potential of using multiple messengers when presenting ethno-nationalist counter narratives, presenting a plurality of viewpoints and therefore breaking down simplistic binary narratives of 'Us' versus 'Them' that far- right extremists frequently perpetuate.

Figure 28: Picture of 'Landscape of Hate' Project in Action[361]

Two final examples of a recent online counter narrative campaign directed at far- right extremists in the North American context are Free Radical's 2018 "We are Free Radicals: Finding Our Way

---

[360] Project Someone Website, 'Landscape of Hate' Project, online at: https://projectsomeone.ca/landscapeofhate.

[361] Project Someone Website, 'Landscape of Hate' Project, online at: https://projectsomeone.ca/landscapeofhate.

Again" website and Light Upon Light's 'Ctrl+Alt+Del-Hate' (2019) magazine.[362] Turning to the former, this scrollable resource (see example in figure 28 below) starts by engaging users at a social level by talking about the essential need for "belonging" and "identity", before presenting real-life case studies (e.g., Dylann Roof, William Atchison, & Elliot Rodgers) and statistics showing how far-right ideology leads to violence (See figure 28). It then points out the narratives that far-right groups use to ensnare new members (e.g., "fear" of the other, "familiarity" through the enforcement of online echo chambers and the labelling of contradictory viewpoints as "fake news") before linking the user to the Free Radical's homepage, which includes a form available for extremists or associates to request help. Like in other international examples of far-right counter narrative campaign best practice,[363] this therefore provides a counter narrative that delegitimises violent activism (e.g., the statistics and the identification "fear", "familiarity" and "fake news" narratives) combined with an alternative narrative (e.g., offering an alternative route out by stressing "There's an Exit in Sight"). Despite being mainly targeted at far- right activists, then, the use of an alternative narrative layered onto a counter narrative emulates best practice in this case, filling the mental void left after the rejection of the extremist worldview.[364]

---

[362] The actual website is now offline, but it can still be accessed on the Internet Archive. See: https://web.archive.org/web/20190809043606/http://wearefreeradicals.net/index.html.

[363] See: European Commission Home Affairs website, 'Exit Germany — Trojan T-Shirt', online at: https://ec.europa.eu/home-affairs/node/7493_en.

[364] See: Cook, J. & Lewandowsky, S., 'The Debunking Handbook' St. Lucia, Australia: University of Queensland, 2011, online at: http://sks.to/debunk & Lewandowsky, S., 'Misinformation and Its Correction: Continued Influence and Successful Debiasing.' *Psychological Science in the Public Interest*, 13(3), 106-131, 2012.

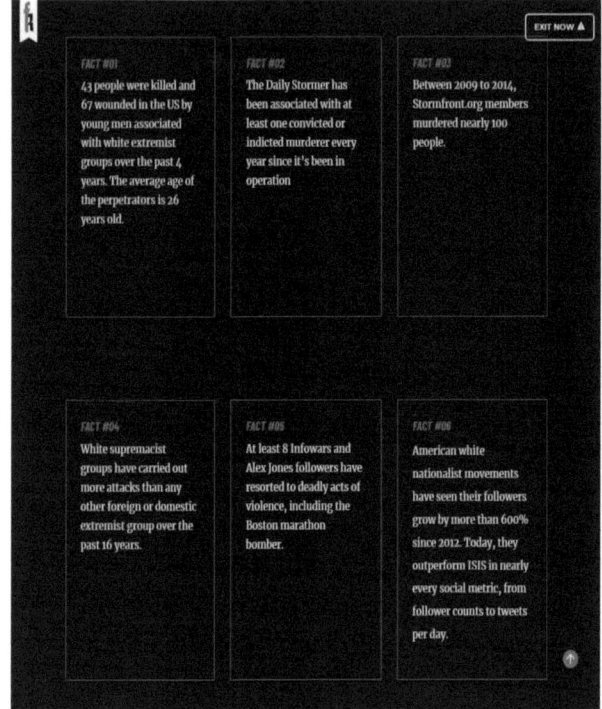

Figure 29: Statistics and Facts used on "We are Free Radicals: Finding Our Way Again" website[365]

Turning to the similar initiative performed by Light upon Light, the 'Ctrl+Alt+Del-Hate' (2019) online magazines are designed to "provide positive alternatives for those susceptible to or engaged in radical movements."[366] Including testimonies of former violent extremists, survivors of extremist violence and researchers, the magazine also attempts to "prevent interest in extremist ideologies and movements and to provide positive alternatives for those susceptible to or engaged

---

[365] *Free Radicals*, ,We Are Free Radicals', 9 August 2019, online at: https://web.archive.org/web/20190809043606/http://wearefreeradicals.net/index.html.

[366] *Light Upon Light*, 'Ctrl+Alt+Del-Hate E-Magazine Issue 01', 1 November 2019, online at: https://www.scribd.com/document/433021364/Ctrl-Alt-Del-Hate-E-Magazine-Issue-01.

in radical movements". In its first issue of November 2019, for example, the magazine included features with American, Canadian and UK based former far- right extremists (including Brad Galloway of Volksfront and Jeff Schoep of the National Socialist Movement) as well as a hate crime survivor, Hope Hyder. A largely textual outfit, it will be interesting to see how far the reach of the campaign stretches, considering the virality of video-based content on the internet.

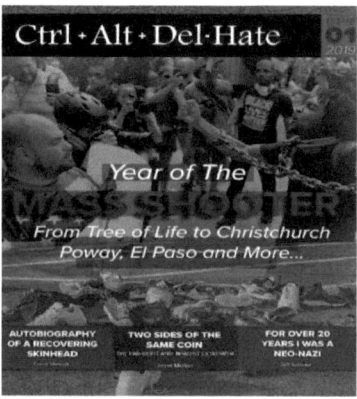

Figure 30: Front Cover of the November 2019 Edition of 'Ctrl+Alt+Del-Hate'[367]

Conclusions and Recommendations

This chapter has tracked North American far-right narratives and counter narratives at a heightened time of far-right extremist solo-actor violence. Moving from cell-based neo-Nazis through mass protest and into anti-government militias, this chapter has uncovered the concerning overlaps between ideologically distinct groups when it comes to narratives of white genocide and demographic replacement in the continent. It has also highlighted the existence of several cell and 'fight club'-type groups (e.g., the Base and Proud Boys), the chauvinistic and accelerationist narratives of which paint

---

[367] *Light Upon Light*, 'Ctrl+Alt+Del-Hate E-Magazine Issue 01', 1 November 2019, online at: https://www.scribd.com/document/433021364/Ctrl-Alt-Del-Hate-E-Magazine-Issue-01.

a concerning threat picture, with the potential for more violence going forward. Added to this, we have found several US groups that have a strong bearing on the far-right's international cultural milieu, with more historic organisations like the National Alliance and Creativity Movement transmitting fictional and neo-paganist imaginaries of white supremacist, 'racially pure' futures, across borders.

In response to the emergent lone-actor threat specifically, North American-based practitioners would be advised to conduct counter narrative campaigns that interlace debunking online conspiracy theories, but also importantly fill that space with an alternative vision. Here, it is important to note that there have already been a number of programmes that have attempted to do this. In particular, the approach taken by EXIT USA, the Institute for Strategic Dialogue, the University of Alberta and Free Radical's Project suggest a way forward when dealing with the violent lone-actor threat in conjunction with counter narrative videos and infographics that refer individuals to de-radicalisation experts. In particular, it is recommended that more is done to fund such grassroots projects, as well as recruiting intervention providers to interact with sympathetic individuals and layering alternative narratives on top of counter narratives as a way of diverting individuals away from extremist content. According to independent assessments, such approaches are likely to yield the highest level of sustained impact on cell-based and self-radicalising individuals at the hard end of violent far-right extremist movements.[368]

Going forward, therefore, such campaigns need to be placed on a more sustained and wide-scale footing. This can be done

---

[368] See: Cook, J. & Lewandowsky, S., 'The Debunking Handbook' St. Lucia, Australia: University of Queensland, 2011, online at: http://sks.to/debunk; Dafnos, A., 'Narratives as a Means of Countering the Radical Right; Looking into the Trojan T-shirt Project.', *Journal EXIT Deutschland*, 2014, online at: http://journals.sfu.ca/jed/index.php/jex/article/view/98; Lewandowsky, S., 'Misinformation and Its Correction: Continued Influence and Successful Debiasing.' *Psychological Science in the Public Interest*, 13(3), 2012, 106-131; & Silverman, T., Stewart, C.J., Amanullah, Z., & Birdwell, J., 'The Impact of Counter Narratives', London: ISD Global, 2016.

through extending already-established funding cycles and increasing the number of individuals trained as intervention providers. It can also be done through harnessing the ability of algorithms to identify and target individuals in the process of radicalising with counter narrative content. At a broader societal level, campaigns like the US State Department backed "2011 Hours Against Hate", Extreme Dialogue, Project SOMEONE and "Know Extremism" programmes will also serve a role in inoculating individuals[369] with carefully targeted and honed messages tailored for a broad-based as opposed to an extremist audience. When it comes to these broader-based counternarratives themselves, therefore, it will involve: 1) using the right elite messengers with mass appeal (e.g., celebrities and sports figures) in order to cut through to non-far-right aligned audiences and 2) using informal (i.e., citizens), tech-savvy individuals (i.e., students) backed by the state to conduct higher impact campaigns, with a far greater organic reach as a result.

By building the extra capacity needed to deliver alternative narratives directly to individuals in the process of radicalisation and using trusted individuals and informal civil-society actors to further embed broader-based societal counter narratives, North American practitioners will do better in inhibiting the spread of violence within the far-right extremist scene and inoculating citizens from engaging in such activism in the first place, acting to reduce the social harms of extremism from above and below in a pincer-like movement.

---

[369] See: Braddock, K., 'Vaccinating Against Hate: Using Attitudinal Inoculation to Confer Resistance to Persuasion by Extremist Propaganda', *Terrorism and Political Violence*, 2019, https://doi.org/10.1080/09546553.2019.1693370.

Chapter 4: Far-Right Extremist Narratives and Counter Narratives in Australasia — The Cases of Australia and New Zealand

The spectre of Australasian far-right violence has come to prominence over the past ten years. It is now considered a notable security threat. Host to a fairly striking array of white skinhead gangs and anti-Islam protest groups, far-right violence reached its apotheosis in both countries in March 2020 when Australian born citizen Brenton Tarrant killed 51 people and wounded another 50 in cold blood. The Christchurch incident has led policymakers, politicians and civil society groups to highlight the potential for far-right extremist violence in Australia and New Zealand, with Australia's Security and Intelligence Organisation (ASIO) issuing warnings of a heightened far-right threat over the last year[370] and security practitioners in New Zealand ominously displaying their concern about a small bloc of white supremacist extremist individuals were "fervent firearms owners" with "high capability" to carry out an attack.[371]

Before this, there were several (isolated signs) of the far-right violence in both South Pacific countries. In Australia, violent far-right manifestations and rhetoric tended to originate from neo-Nazi groupuscules — such as Antipodean Resistance, Blood and Honour, the Southern Cross Hammerskins and Combat 18 — and such groups showed their intentions towards violence — with Combat 18 activists conducting a shooting at a Mosque at the start of the 2010s,

---

[370] Karp, P., 'Threat from extreme rightwing terrorism in Australia has increased, Asio says' *The Guardian*, 16 October 2019, online at:www.theguardian.com/australia-news/2019/oct/16/threat-from-extreme-rightwing-terrorism-in-australia-has-increased-asio-says.

[371] Battersby, J. & Ball, R., 'Christchurch in the context of New Zealand terrorism and right-wing extremism', *Journal of Policing, Intelligence and Counter Terrorism*, 14:3, 2019, 191-207, cited p.198.

and one Reclaim Australia activist convicted of plotting an attack on left-wing activists at the end of 2019.[372] Indeed, in New Zealand, the (now defunct) neo-Nazi 'Fourth Reich' group (originally formed by inmates inside Christchurch prison in early 1993) went on a killing spree in the late 1990s to early 2000s murdering a Māori sportsman, a gay man, a Korean tourist and a white female between 1997 and 2010.[373] In addition, a decade earlier a neo-Nazi activist murdered the son of New Zealand cricketer Richard Motz in Christchurch.[374]

This chapter focuses on small-cell forms of far-right extremism in Australia and New Zealand in the contemporary era. To do so, the next section surveys the activities of nine key far-right extremist groups in Australasia, coupled with key narratives propagated by them. Drawing upon these case studies, the report's second part will then suggest counter narratives in relation to Australasian-based far-right extremism. A third section focuses on the dearth of existing counter narrative campaigns, before the report concludes with further recommendations and initiatives that could be conducted going forward for counteracting these hateful messages in this South Pacific context.

---

[372] *WA Today*, 'Mosque shooter fined more than $9000', 23 August 2010, online at: www.watoday.com.au/national/western-australia/mosque-shooter-fined-more-than-9000-20100823-13fid.html; and *Australian Associated Press*, 'Far-right extremist Phillip Galea found guilty of plotting terror attacks in Melbourne', *The Guardian*, 5 December 2019, www.theguardian.com/australia-news/2019/dec/05/far-right-extremist-phillip-galea-found-guilty-of-plotting-terror-attacks-in-melbourne.

[373] Battersby, J. & Ball, R., 'Christchurch in the context of New Zealand terrorism and right-wing extremism', *Journal of Policing, Intelligence and Counter Terrorism*, 14:3, 2019, 191-207, cited p.198.

[374] Leask, A., 'Christchurch triple fatal: Dead teens' link to high-profile murder-suicide', New Zealand Herald, 17 January 2019, online at: https://www.nzherald.co.nz/nz/news/article.cfm?c_id=1&objectid=12191435.

Violent Far-Right Extremist Groups and Narratives in Australasia: Ascendant Anti-Muslim Populism, Ethno-Nationalism, White Supremacism and Chauvinism

With electoral success only occurring in the past few years, the predominant actor on Australia and New Zealand's far-right extremist scene have been anti-Islam protest movements, white skinhead gangs and neo-Nazi cells. With online links now established between Australian far-right extremist actors and the Christchurch shooter,[375] it is increasingly clear that far-right extremism in Australasia form a cohesive milieu that mobilises around a common set of anti-Muslim populist, ethno-nationalist, white supremacist and chauvinist narratives. Below is a list of violent far-right extremist groups and organisations that represent what scholars have variously characterised as Australasia's "undulating", "diverse" and "complex" far-right extremist scene (broken down according to organisation type, ideology and narrative structure).[376][377] These profiles include examples of key narratives that violent far-right extremists in Australia and New Zealand are using at the present moment.

---

[375] Begley, P., 'Threats from white extremist group that 'tried to recruit Tarrant'', *The Sydney Moring Herald*, 2 May 2019, online at: https://www.smh.com.au/national/threats-from-white-extremist-group-that-tried-to-recruit-tarrant-20190501-p51j5w.html; Mann, A., Nguyen, K., & Gregory, K., 'Christchurch shooting accused Brenton Tarrant supports Australian far-right figure Blair Cottrell', *ABC News*, 23 March 2019, online at: https://www.abc.net.au/news/2019-03-23/christchurch-shooting-accused-praised-blair-cottrell/10930632; & Begley, P., 'Alleged Mosque Shooters Meme Popular with Australian Far Right Group', *The Sydney Morning Herald*, 15 March 2019, online at: https://www.smh.com.au/national/nsw/alleged-mosque-shooter-s-meme-popular-with-australian-far-right-group-20190315-p514ns.html.

[376] Peucker, M. & Smith, D., 'Far Right Groups in Australia: An Introduction', in Peucker, M. & Smith, D. (eds.) *The Far-Right in Contemporary Australia* (London, Palgrave Macmillan: 2019), p. 7.

[377] Battersby & Ball (2019), Op Cit., pp. 201.

I. Violent Far-Right Extremist Groups in Australia

a) United Patriots Front (UPF)
Founders: Shermon Burgess, Blair Cottrell and Neil Erikson
Membership: Unknown
Ideology: Anti-Muslim Populism, Anti-Semitism, Neo-Nazism

Description:
After a split with Reclaim Australia organiser Monika Evers in May 2015, several activists with alleged neo-Nazi pasts decided to form their own anti-Islam street protest movement, the United Patriots Front (UPF). Starting with a demonstration against an anti-racism protest in Melbourne, the group quickly rose to notoriety through its anti-Islam rhetoric and publicity stunts. The most notable of such stunts was the mock beheading of a black dummy in October 2015 outside council buildings in Bendigo, Victoria (a key site of protest for the group due to a putative Mosque building application from 2014).[378] With two of its leaders (Cottrell and Erikson) becoming increasingly associated with neo-Nazi rhetoric, the group reportedly disbanded in 2017, after which several former members formed a new white supremacist group, the Lads Society, setting up clubhouses in Melbourne and Sydney. Online comments dating back to April 2016 by the Christchurch attacker, Brenton Tarrant, suggest that he was a vocal supporter of then UPF-leader Blair Cottrell.[379]
Narrative Examples:
Anti-Muslim Populism: "It is in the public interest in a democratic society to be aware of the dangers of Islam."

---

[378] Worrall, A., 'Anti-Islam group beheads dummy in protest of Bendigo Mosque', *The AGE*, 4 October 2015, online at: https://www.theage.com.au/national/victoria/antiislam-group-beheads-dummy-in-protest-of-bendigo-mosque-20151004-gk0zmi.html.

[379] Mann, A., Nguyen, K., & Gregory, K., 'Christchurch shooting accused Brenton Tarrant supports Australian far-right figure Blair Cottrell', *ABC News*, 23 March 2019, online at: https://www.abc.net.au/news/2019-03-23/christchurch-shooting-accused-praised-blair-cottrell/10930632.

- Blair Cottrell, defending himself after being found guilty of contempt and ridicule of Muslims.[380]

Anti-Semitism: "The Jews are as small physically as they are degenerate in character [... They] infiltrate and subvert entire generations of other nations in a bid for world power [and are] a much deadlier enemy than the violent Islamic pillagers, who just kill and maim openly."

- Cottrell's comments on his (now defunct) Facebook page.[381]

Neo-Nazism: "My personal opinion is stick to the Muslim shit and Cultural Marxism for max support do Jews later you don't need to show your full hand."

- Neil Erikson, discussing UPF tactics in a Facebook conversation after Cottrell's elevation to UPF leader.[382]

b) Lads Society
Founder: Tom Sewell
Membership: Unknown
Ideology: White Supremacism, Neo-Nazism, Chauvinism

---

[380] *Australian Associated Press*, 'United Patriots Front trio found guilty of inciting serious contempt of Muslims', *The Guardian*, 5 September 2017, online at: https://www.theguardian.com/australia-news/2017/sep/05/united-patriots-front-trio-say-beheading-stunt-during-bendigo-mosque-protest-an-act-of-free-speech.

[381] Bachelard, M. & McMahon, L., 'Blair Cottrell, rising anti-Islam movement leader, wanted Hitler in the classroom', *Sydney Morning Herald*, 17 October 2015, online at: https://www.smh.com.au/national/blair-cottrell-leader-of-aussie-patriots-upf-wanted-hitler-in-the-classroom-20151016-gkbbvz.html.

[382] Kolowski, M., 'How Australia's far-right were divided and conquered — by themselves', *The Sydney Morning Herald*, 11 January 2011, online at: https://www.smh.com.au/politics/federal/how-australia-s-far-right-were-divided-and-conquered-by-themselves-20190108-p50qcb.html.

Description:
Founded in 2017 from the disbanded anti-Islam protest movement, the United Patriots Front (UPF), Lads Society is a white supremacist group with men's-only clubhouses in Sydney and Melbourne. In 2018, Lads Society launched a covert infiltration strategy for Australian right-wing political parties.[383] Lads Society members and allies joined the Young Nationals in NSW. They also engaged in branch stacking at the May 2018 conference, trying to push an alt-right agenda by infiltrating local branches. It would appear that the Lads Society was joined in this by the violent far-right groupuscule affiliated with the Atomwaffen Division in the US, Antipodean Resistance (see below). In January 2019, the Lads Society joined other far- right extremist groups at a rally in St. Kilda against so-called African gangs, making Sieg Heil salutes and brandishing SS helmets. Their activity was highly publicised in social media, with former UPF leaders Cottrell and Erikson (see below) calling for a Cronulla-style race riot.[384] With potential for social unrest emerging from, amongst other violent undertakings,[385] the organisation of underground fight clubs, Lads Society presents a significant violent extremist threat. The group's first leader and founder, Tom Sewell, also claims to have tried in 2017 to recruit the Christchurch Attacker, Brenton Tarrant. Sewell alleges he discussed the creation of a white ethno-state with Tarrant. He has more recently warned the Lads Society of an impending race war, in which his group aims to encourage the "speed and ferocity of the decay" of society.[386] The

---

[383] Such covert infiltration replicates the same attempts by the Australian League of Rights in the 1960s.

[384] Molloy, S., 'The new extremist threat in Australia: Right-wing groups who have ASIO's attention.' *News.Com.UA*, 4 January 2019, online at: https://www.news.com.au/national/the-new-extremist-threat-in-australia-rightwing-groups-who-have-asios-attention/news-story/44ae06be0aaa765c862fd6d20426fe9.

[385] Graham, B.,' Secret location of Aussie underground fight club leaks', *News.Au.Com*, 30 November 2018, online at: https://www.news.com.au/national/nsw-act/news/secret-location-of-aussie-underground-fight-club-leaks/news-story/16f5b680a7ab4cc5de0078cb2a37ccc9.

[386] Begley, P., 'Threats from white extremist group that 'tried to recruit Tarrant'', *The Sydney Moring Herald*, 2nd May 2019, online at:

group's founder, Blair Cottrell, has been convicted of violent assault and arson.[387]

Narrative Examples:

White Supremacism: "As Europeans, we come from a line of explorers, inventors, great leaders and warriors. It's time that we take back the freedom that is rightfully ours".

- Blog on Lads Society website about "Freedom".[388]

Neo-Nazism: "National Socialism is the worldview of Truth. Another word for Truth is Nature. By Truth or Nature, we are referring to the Natural laws of the universe."

- Blog on Lads Society website about "Why National Socialism?"[389]

Chauvinism: "[National Socialism] represents men coming together to form one nation stronger than any of men alone."

- Blog on Lads Society website about "Why National Socialism?"[390]

---

https://www.smh.com.au/national/threats-from-white-extremist-group-that-tried-to-recruit-tarrant-20190501-p51j5w.html & McGowan, M., 'Australian white nationalists reveal plans to recruit 'disgruntled, white male population'.' *The Guardian*, 11 November 2019, online at: https://www.theguardian.com/australia-news/2019/nov/12/australian-white-nationalists-reveal-plans-to-recruit-disgruntled-white-male-pop ulation.

[387] O'Rourke, G. & Thompson, A. "United Patriots Front Leader Blair Cottrell Details Violent Criminal Past in Video," Herald Sun, 11 June 2016, online at: http://www.heraldsun.com.au/news/victoria/united-patriots-front-leader-blair-cottrell-details-violent-criminal-past-in-video/news-story/d107bccff2d3b305788e17d881ccec27.

[388] Forbes, J., 'Freedom', *Lads Society* Website, online at: https://www.ladssociety.com/single-post/2019/09/09/Freedom

[389] Hersant, J., 'Why National Socialism?', *Lads Society* Website, online at: https://www.ladssociety.com/single-post/2019/09/19/Why-National-Socialism.

[390] Ibid.

c) Combat 18 (Australia)
Founders: Charlie Sargent and Harold Covington[391]
Membership: Less than 30.
Ideology: Neo-Nazism, Ethno-Nationalism, Anti-Immigration Sentiment.

Description:
Australia's branch of the global neo-Nazi group Combat 18 has lacked coverage in news reporting, making it hard to track down its continuity and development as a groupuscule.[392] However, this lack of publicly accessible information is not to downplay the violent and racist activism of the group. The aforementioned Perth Mosque attack in late 2010 was perpetrated by Bradley Neil Trappitt and three accomplices from the Combat 18 group.[393] Five years later, there were further reports that the group had been distributing material at a Melbourne playground claiming that there should be "No Islamic Takeover" and that people should "Support your local skinheads".[394] More recently, after the Christchurch attacks, Combat 18 Australia's Facebook page was found to be still active in 2019, where the group were complaining that "media and leftists would carry on for months" about far-right extremism.[395]

---

[391] These are the original co-founders of the UK progeny of Combat 18. It's Australian leaders at the time of writing in June 2020 are Jacob Marshall Hort and Bradley Neil Trappitt.

[392] Here, 'Groupuscules' are defined as tiny, often neo-Nazi, groups of far-right extremists that establish a milieu with reference points that stretch out internationally as well as into the past as well (Jackson 2014, National Action and National Socialism for the 21st Century, p.101).

[393] *WA Today*, 'Mosque shooter fined more than $9000', 23 August 2010, online at: https://www.watoday.com.au/national/western-australia/mosque-shooter-fined-more-than-9000-20100823-13fid.html.

[394] Hall, B., Op Cit.

[395] Dearden, L., 'Neo-Nazi groups allowed to stay on Facebook because they 'do not violate community standards", *The Independent*, 24 March 2019, online at: https://www.independent.co.uk/news/uk/home-news/facebook-new-zealand-neo-nazis-white-supremacists-a8837886.html.

Whilst not involved in regular activism, the subcultural and transnational element of this neo-Nazi group nevertheless remains of concern, especially given its recent proscription in Canada (2019) and Germany (2020).[396]

Narrative Examples:

Neo-Nazism: "Combat 18 advocates covert action as the only constructive form of action which should be undertaken at this moment in time by individuals committed to the National Socialist cause."

- An excerpt from Combat 18's "National Socialist Vanguardisms Handbook".[397]

Ethno-Nationalism: "In this magazine we are going to tell the truth about the modern day-nightmare that the white Race is being plunged into, we will expose traitors and infiltrators that have plagued nationalism for decades, we will urge our supporters to intimidate and attack the enemies of our people just as they have intimidated us."

- An excerpt from Combat 18's official magazine.[398]

Anti-Immigration Sentiment: "To ship all non-whites back to Africa, Asia, Arabia, alive or in body bags, the choice is theirs."

---

[396] Bell, S., 'Canada adds neo-Nazi groups Blood & Honour, Combat 18 to list of terror organizations', 26 June 2019, online at: https://globalnews.ca/news/5432851/canada-adds-neo-nazi-groups-blood-honour-and-combat-18-to-list-of-terror-organizations/ & *BBC News*, 'Germany bans Combat 18 as police raid neo-Nazi group', 23 January 2020, online at: https://www.bbc.com/news/world-europe-51219274.

[397] Counter Extremism Project, 'Combat 18', online at: https://www.counterextremism.com/supremacy/combat-18.

[398] *Combat 18*, 'The Aims of C18', online at: https://ia600104.us.archive.org/15/items/Combat18/Combat%2018/Ef3824e2beb9985f682e99fd133515b22cfa03ef4_Q20647_R331396_D1942757.pdf.

- An excerpt from "The Aims of C18" in Combat 18's official magazine. [399]

d) True Blue Crew (TBC)
Founder: Kane Miller
Membership: Unknown
Ideology: Anti-Muslim Populism, Ultra-Nationalism

Description:
Like UPF, True Blue Crew (TBC) emerged in early 2015 from activists involved in the 2014 "Voices of Bendigo" and "Stop the Mosques" Bendigo protests. The group rose to prominence in May 2016 when joining a protest in Melton, along with members of the United Patriots Front and the Love Australia or Leave Party, against a so-called 'Muslim housing development'.[400] This came off the back of another anti-Mosque protest in the area by the group in November 2015. From 2016 on, TBC has become increasingly violent in its anti-Islam activism, such as an August 2016 protest resulting in scuffles with anti-Muslim street patrol group the Sons of Odin.[401] In June 2016 a knife and a knuckleduster were confiscated from TBC activists at Melbourne's annual "Australian Pride" rally.[402] Later that year former Reclaim Australia and TBC activist Phillip Galea was convicted of terrorism-related offences, including collecting or making documents to prepare for terrorist acts, and

---

[399] *Combat 18*, 'The Aims of C18', online at: https://ia600104.us.archive.org/15/items/Combat18/Combat%2018/Ef3824e2beb9985f682e99fd133515b22cfa03ef4_Q20647_R331396_D1942757.pdf.

[400] Choahan, N., 'Anti-Islam protest: Far-right groups rally in Melton against 'Muslim' housing estate', *The AGE*, 28 August 2016, online at: https://www.theage.com.au/national/victoria/antiislam-protest-farright-groups-rally-against-melton-south-housing-estate-20160828-gr2umo.html/.

[401] Allaoui, T., Op Cit.

[402] Hill, J., 'Weapons Found At 'Australian Pride' And Anti-Racism Protests In Melbourne,' *The Huffington Post*, 25 July 2017, online at: https://bit.ly/2NKS6tf.

carrying out acts in preparation for a terrorist act against Australian-based left-wing groups.[403] In January 2018 it was reported that the UPF and TBC were planning vigilante patrols in the wake of gang violence allegedly committed by young African men in Melbourne.[404] In keeping with its provocative demonstrations, the group was banned from Facebook in March 2019 after posting Islamophobic messages in the wake of the Christchurch massacre.[405] Like with the UPF leadership, an online trail also links TBC with Brenton Tarrant, Tarrant having left comments on their (now defunct) Facebook page.[406] However, it is important to note that TBC became inactive before the Christchurch massacre, and even before the aforementioned January 2019 St Kilda rally, they had largely fallen silent online and appear not to exist any longer as a formal group.

Narrative Examples:

Anti-Muslim Populism: "Islam killed 270 million in 1400 years. No. Islam Sharia Law Against Mankind."

---

[403] Australian Associated Press, 'Victorian extremist Phillip Galea planned to bomb leftwing premises, police say', *The Guardian*, 31 October 2016, online at: https://www.theguardian.com/australia-news/2016/oct/31/victorian-extremist-phillip-galea-planned-to-bomb-leftwing-premises-police-say.

[404] It seems that this was an idle boast. See: Brook, B., 'Channel 7 accused of going soft on racism by airing interview with far-right leader', *News.Au.Com*, 15 January 2018, online at: https://www.news.com.au/entertainment/tv/current-affairs/channel-7-accused-of-going-soft-on-racism-by-airing-interview-with-farright-leader/news-story/5aec26e0e445a49557da274ce386c027.

[405] Begley, P., 'One Nation candidate attended extremist event, used volunteer member', *The Sydney Morning Herald*, 5 May 2019, online at: https://www.smh.com.au/national/one-nation-candidate-attended-extremist-event-used-volunteer-member-20190504-p51k3p.html.

[406] Mann, A., Nguyen, K., and Gregory, K., 'Christchurch shooting accused Brenton Tarrant supports Australian far-right figure Blair Cottrell', *ABC News*, 23 March 2019, online at:: https://www.abc.net.au/news/2019-03-23/christchurch-shooting-accused-praised-blair-cottrell/10930632.

- Banner at Melton anti-'Muslim housing development' protest.[407]

Ultra-Nationalism: "It's a wake-up call. If you want to be in Australia, you should have to live like an Australian."

- True Blue Crew, Kane Miller, speaking at the Melton anti-'Muslim housing development' protest.[408]

e) *The Dingoes*
Founders: Unknown
Membership: Unknown
Online Presence: The Convict Report Podcast & #DingoTwitter Hashtag
Ideology: Alt-Right, White Supremacism, Homophobia

Description:
The Dingoes are an Australian online-based alt-right group responsible for constructing localised memes as well as for the podcast Convict Report. Commencing its online activity in 2015, this collective has described themselves as "politically incorrect larrikins" against "the premise of universal humanism", and in favour of "white identity".[409] The former Labour leader turned One Nation

---

[407] Engineer, C., 'More than 200 people attend anti-Islam protest against 'Muslim' housing estate', *Daily Express*, 30 August 2016, online at: https://www.express.co.uk/news/world/704861/True-Blue-Crew-Melbourne-anti-Islam.

[408] Allaoui, T., 'Anti-Muslim protesters even turn on each other in Melbourne's west', *Herald Sun*, 28 August 2016, online at: https://www.heraldsun.com.au/news/law-order/antiislam-rally-in-melton-victoria-police-issues-warning-to-protesters/news-story/957ee082924f82c69028465789bfdcd0.

[409] Craw, V., 'The Dingoes claim to be 'growing' part of Australian alternativeright political scene', *News.Com.Au*, 5 December 2016, online at: https://www.news.com.au/technology/online/the-dingoes-claim-to-be-growing-part-of-australian-alternativeright-political-scene/news-story/d6ae348e0e1c6a3189dac86914d538d3.

candidate, Mark Latham, as well as National MP George Christensen, have both appeared on the group's podcast.[410] In May 2017, the group organised a convention in Sydney which they called "DingoCon". In attendance were *The Right Stuff* founder, noted neo-Nazi activist Mike Enoch, with tickets costing $88 (the numerical code-phrase for the Nazi slogan "Heil Hitler").[411] Perhaps the group's main claim to infamy are its links to the Christchurch attacker, Brenton Tarrant, who used jokes and phrases popularised by the group (including a "Hold still while I glass you" meme (above) on 8chan in a post when writing of the (then) forthcoming Mosque attack).[412]

Narrative Examples:

Alt-Right: "The alt-right is effective, efficient. We deliver results that the nominal right can only dream of. This is an attractive feature for a lot of ex-libertarians."

- Comments by Dingoes activist, Kev Renner, in an interview with News.Aus.Com.[413]

White Supremacism: "White Man: Tired of Anti-White Propaganda. You're Not Alone."

- Meme retweeted by Dingoes Twitter Account.[414]

Homophobia: "Get in faggot, we're making America great again."

---

[410] Begley, P., 'Alleged Mosque Shooters Meme Popular with Australian Far Right Group', *The Sydney Morning Herald*, 15 March 2019, online at: https://www.smh.com.au/national/nsw/alleged-mosque-shooter-s-meme-popular-with-australian-far-right-group-20190315-p514ns.html.

[411] Iggulden, T., 'George Christensen tries to stop visit from neo-Nazi Mike Enoch for DingoCon convention.' *ABC News*, 14th May 2017, online at: https://www.abc.net.au/news/2017-05-15/george-christensen-tries-to-stop-visit-from-neo-nazi-mike-enoch/8525672.

[412] Begley, P., Op Cit, 15 March 2019.

[413] Craw, V., Op Cit, 5 December 2016.

[414] Ibid.

- Tweet by Dingoes activist, Kev Renner, in an interview with News.Aus.Com.[415]

II. Violent Far-Right Extremist Groups in New Zealand

a) New Zealand National Front
Founder: Colin Ansell
Membership: Under 30 (est.)
Ideology: White Supremacism, Ethno-Nationalism, Neo-Fascism, Anti-Māori Sentiment

Description:
Formed as a replica of Britain's National Front in 1967, the New Zealand branch eventually emerged in 1977 proper from a local group of activists who opposed the biculturalism associated with Māori communities on one hand, and the multiculturalism associated with immigration on the other.[416] Initially encouraging its members to infiltrate mainstream parties, the New Zealand National Front has historically struggled to mobilise on the street and at the ballot box (gaining 1.9% of the vote at Christchurch's 2004 Mayoral Contest[417]), and only mustering 45 supporters at a rally in Wellington to protest changes to the New Zealand flag in the same year.[418] In October 2017, a rally of National Front and Right Wing Resistance (see below) members protesting outside Parliament was

---

[415] Ibid.

[416] For more information about its formation and for the other activities of similar groups at this time, see: Spoonley, P., *The Politics of Nostalgia: Racism and the Extreme Right in New Zealand*, (Palmerston North: Dunmore Press, 1987), p. 149

[417] Christ Church City Council, 'Declaration of Results of Elections', 9 October 2014, online at: https://web.archive.org/web/20131022152155/http://www1.ccc.govt.nz/council/proceedings/2004/october/Clause1Attachment.pdf.

[418] Chapman, K., 'Two groups poles apart to rally at Parliament,' *NZ Herald*, 23 October 2004, online at: https://www.nzherald.co.nz/nz/news/article.cfm?c_id=1&objectid=3603497.

disrupted by a counter protest, despite this the protest itself passed off fairly peacefully compared with previous iterations of the same event nine years earlier.[419] Whilst the New Zealand National Front is not itself influential, it is instead the white supremacist and white nationalist narratives which are of greatest concern. Above all, it is important to take note of the notion of 'white genocide' used to make multiculturalism and diversity a wedge issue. In the wake of the Christchurch attacks, however, the New Zealand National Front attempted to distance itself from the massacre, suggesting that it did not "condone or agree" with the attacker's beliefs or the "wanton murder of innocent people."[420]

Narrative examples:
White Supremacism: "Diversity = White Genocide."

- A placard used at the New Zealand National Front's October 2017 protest.[421]

Ethno-Nationalism: "You have taken the first step towards becoming a member of the leading organisation in New Zealand concerned with the preservation and advancement of unique New Zealand European culture."

- An excerpt from the New Zealand National Front's (now defunct) website homepage.[422]

Neo-Fascism: "'Culture' as a life-form is bequeathed through the generations and is built upon in each generation (or is eroded in periods of decadence). Hence, every member of the cultural organism by virtue of his birthright is entitled to fully

---

[419] Ibid & Nightingale, M. 'Clashes outside parliament as protesters face National Front,' *NZ Herald*, 28 October 2017, https://www.nzherald.co.nz/politics/news/article.cfm?c_id=280&objectid=11937772 7.

[420] Radio New Zealand, 'Christchurch terror attack: Anti-immigration websites taken down after shootings', RNZ.co.nz, 16 March 2019, online at: https://www.rnz.co.nz/news/chch-terror/384867/christchurch-terror-attack-anti-immigration-websites-taken-down-after-shootings.

[421] Nightingale, M. Op Cit, 2017.

[422] *New Zealand National Front*, 'Home Page', online at: https://web.archive.org/web/20041027022438/http:/www.nationalfront.org.nz/.

appreciate his cultural heritage, regardless of his income or social background."

- An excerpt from the New Zealand National Front's (now defunct) 'Policies' webpage.[423]

Anti-Māori Sentiment: "While Euro-New Zealanders are brainwashed into believing they are collectively guilty for colonialism; the historic reality is that the forefathers of most of us came to this land from Britain to escape an unjust economic system"

- An excerpt from the New Zealand National Front's (now defunct) 'Policies' webpage.[424]

b) Right Wing Resistance
Founder: Kyle Chapman
Membership: 50-100 (est.)[425]
Ideology: White Supremacism, Ethno-Nationalism, Neo-Nazism
Description:
Founded in June 2009 by the former leader of the New Zealand National Front, Kyle Chapman, Right Wing Resistance (RWR) rose to notoriety due to street patrols in New Brighton, South Island, and was directed at Polynesian youths and Asian migrants.[426] In October of that year, around 30 RWR and NZNF activists joined the New Zealand National Front for a 'flag day' celebration.[427] Two years

---

[423] *New Zealand National Front*, 'Principles of Policy' Page, online at: https://web.archive.org/web/20041110010458/http://www.nationalfront.org.nz/policy.php

[424] Ibid

[425] Spoonley, P, Comments to Author Via Email, March 2020, Leeds, UK.

[426] *New Zealand National Front*, 'Principles of Policy' Page, Op Cit.

[427] Hume, T., 'Far-right leader Kyle Chapman returns', *Stuff.co.nz*, 25 October 2009, online at: http://www.stuff.co.nz/national/politics/2998598/Far-right-leader-Kyle-Chapman-returns.

later, reports suggested that the group was responsible for distributing anti-immigrant flyers in Christchurch and Auckland. Despite posing the question 'Immigration or Invasion?' and trying to recruit new members through a phone number and email address, Chapman defended the action merely as a recruitment drive.[428] More worryingly, in November of the same year a dozen balaclava-clad RWR members forced themselves into a candidate meeting in Christchurch. They threatened to disrupt nationwide polling booths and claimed that the publicity stunt was designed to draw attention to how the government was "running the country into the ground".[429] Added to this stunt a year later, however, was an incidence of violence, with a stabbing taking place at RWR's annual 2016 flag day march.[430] Whilst now limited to small-scale forms of activism, RWR's heavily militaristic dress and direct-action style of activism caused great concern and demonstrated signs of violent intent. Also, of concern is the transnational reach of the group's activism, which inspires similar formations in the USA, Scandinavia and the UK. It is important to note the significant online profile of the group that has led to its proliferation outside of the New Zealand context.[431]

Narrative examples:

White Supremacism: "If current trends continue, whites will soon be a minority in this country."

---

[428] Lynch, K., Op Cit., 12 January 2011.

[429] Lynch, K. "'Guerrillas' in camo gear 'spoil' meeting', *Press.Co.Nz*, 23 November 2011, online at: http://www.stuff.co.nz/the-press/news/election-2011/6015012/Guerrillas-in-camo-gear-spoil-meeting.

[430] Sherwood, S., 'Man stabbed at Right Wing Resistance party in Christchurch', *Stuff.Co.Nz*, 24 October 2016, online at: https://www.stuff.co.nz/national/crime/85672679/man-stabbed-at-right-wing-resistance-party-in-christchurch.

[431] Spoonley, P. (2019) Comments to Author Via Email. Leeds, UK.

- An excerpt from RWR's 2011 'Asian Invasion' Posters.[432]

Ethno-Nationalism: "We're not about going around bashing up Polynesians or Asians. We'd probably say 'Hey, what are you doing? That's not really the white way'."
- Member of RWR talking to a reporter at its October 2009 vigilante patrols.[433]

Neo-Nazism: "We must secure the existence of our people and a future for white children."
- Phrase modified from Mein Kampf, relating to the 14 words displayed on RWR's logo.

c) Unit 88
Founder: Colin Ansell
Membership: 30-40 (est.)
Ideology: Neo-Nazism, White Supremacism, Violence

Description:
Formed in the late 1990s in Auckland, the 88 group were seen as one of the most violent neo-Nazi skinhead groups at the time (training in fighting and self-defence as well as conducting attacks on Somali refugee families)[434]. Using the numerology of 88 to signify

---

[432] Lynch, K., 'White supremacist flyers offend,' *Stuff.co.nz*, 12 January 2011, online at: https://web.archive.org/web/20110113100908/http://www.stuff.co.nz/the-press/news/christchurch/4532423/White-supremacist-flyers-offend.

[433] Steward, I. 'Right-wing vigilantes on patrol in Christchurch', *Stuff.co.nz*, 29 October 2009, http://www.stuff.co.nz/national/2999197/Right-wing-vigilantes-on-patrol-in-Christchurch.

[434] Harmer, B., 'WYSIWYG New Zealand News', 22 November 1997, online at: https://web.archive.org/web/20081119155233/http://wysiwygnews.com/1997_News/1997November22.html.

'HH', or "Heil Hitler", the group also distributed pro-Nazi literature, which was investigated by New Zealand's Race Relations office in 1997.[435] After plans for a large National Meeting for White Nationalists from around New Zealand in their Auckland base was discovered in 1998, the group disbanded and tried to form their own chapters of the Texas-based Hammerskins Nations movement. Victims of poor organisation and an improving economy,[436] ex-Unit 88 members have since formed other groups like the Frontline Skinheads, while others have joined the Psycho Skins (also now defunct). Though largely inactive, Unit 88 is a cautionary lesson in far-right violent activism, with police reports suggesting that white supremacist gangs would regularly roam and recruit new members on New Zealand's streets.[437]

Narrative Examples:
Neo-Nazism: "The Celtic cross is probably the most popular symbol among (seemingly not only) European Neo-Nazis"

- Description of Celtic cross used by Unit 88 as its emblem on a website dedicated to interrogating far-right extremist iconography.[438]

White Supremacism: "'We have a youth division. We want to teach them to keep their blood pure, to keep ancestral lines pure. This is not racist—this is purist."

- Pamphlet distributed by Unit 88 in 1997.[439]

---

[435] Ibid.

[436] Gilbert, J., *Patched: The History of Gangs in New Zealand*. Auckland, NZ: Auckland University Press, 2013.

[437] Ibid.

[438] CWR Flags, 'Neo-Nazi Flag Symbolism', online at: https://www.crw flags.com/fotw/flags/qt-z_sym.html#cac.

[439] Barber, D., 'Upsurge in racism worries authorities', New Zealand Herald, 29 November 1997, online at: http://www.hartford-hwp.com/archives/24/053.html.

Violence: "Police said the gang, which reportedly has bases in several cities on both islands, was circulating literature urging members to 'waste' non-whites."

- An excerpt from news report at the time suggesting more violent motives by Unit 88 and other racist skinhead groups.[440]

d) Wargus Christi
Founder: Daniel Waring
Membership: Unknown
Ideology: Christianism, Antisemitism, Misogyny, Islamophobia

Description:
Describing itself as a "martial-monastic Christian brotherhood" and founded by the neo-Nazi Daniel Waring, Wargus Christi formed in 2018 and became a key point of concern among experts and policymakers. Principally a far-right bodybuilding club, in mid-December 2019 it was discovered that one of its activists was a New Zealand Defense Forces weapons specialist. He was taken into military custody for his involvement in the group.[441] Launched in September 2019, Wargus Christi's Facebook page has become a source of homophobic, antisemitic, misogynist and Islamophobic rhetoric.[442] Moreover, it was also discovered that members of the group's Discord channel could be found as far afield as the US, UK and Europe.[443] Most concerning is the violent imagery and background of the group's leader, Daniel Waring. In a December 2019

---

[440] Ibid.

[441] Daadler, M., 'Soldier with far-right ties in military custody', *Newsroom*, 18 December 2019, online at: https://www.newsroom.co.nz/2019/12/18/952975/soldier-with-far-right-ties-in-military-custody.

[442] Ibid.

[443] *Unicorn Riot*, Twitter Post, 19 December 2019, online at: https://twitter.com/UR_Ninja/status/1207555074743926784.

Facebook post, the group published a meme threatening violence on "fornicators" and advocates of "premarital sex".[444] In 2010, Waring was convicted of vandalising a church in Feilding, a town in the Manawatū District of North Island.[445]

Narrative Examples:

Christianism: "Would be initiates must possess a knowledge of Christian religion, a commitment to athleticism, and the fanaticism to improve themselves by these things to the glory of God."

- A Comment by a member of Wargus Christi's Discord Server.[446]

Antisemitism: "[Jews] killed the son of God and [are] the child of Satan."

- A Wargus Christi Telegram Post.[447]

Misogyny: "Satan simply works through the jews (and women+gays)."

- A Wargus Christi Telegram Post.[448]

Islamophobia: "like Islam, Judaism is a diametrical enemy of Christ."

- A Wargus Christi October 2019 Facebook Post.[449]

---

[444] Alexander Reid Ross, Twitter Post, 17 December 2019, online at: https://twitter.com/areidross/status/1207061282894925824/photo/1.

[445] Sutton, J., 'Neo-Nazi in attack on church,' *Stuff.co.nz*, 14 July 2010, online at: http://www.stuff.co.nz/manawatu-standard/news/3914200/Neo-Nazi-in-attack-on-church.

[446] *Unicorn Riot*, 'Discord Leaks', online at: https://discordleaks.unicornriot.ninja/discord/search?q=christian&s=181.

[447] Daadler, M., 'Soldier with far-right ties arrested at Linton Military Camp', *Stuff.Co.Nz*, 18 December 2019, online at: https://www.stuff.co.nz/national/crime/118280866/soldier-with-farright-ties-arrested-at-linton-military-camp.

[448] Ibid.

[449] Ibid.

Summary

The above survey of Australian-based far-right actors reveals a constellation of anti-Muslim populist, ethno-nationalist, white supremacist and ultra-nationalist narratives. The potential for violence has been demonstrated not just by the actions of individuals affiliated the aforementioned groups, but through the inspiration and cross-dissemination of extremist narratives to far-right terrorist actors, including most notoriously Brenton Tarrant, but also Bradley Neil Trappitt (Combat 18) and Phillip Galea (Reclaim Australia and other groups). The graphic below (Figure 30) illustrates some of the lines of influence between far-right extremist actors in Australia and the New Zealand murderer of 51 innocent worshippers on 15 March 2019.

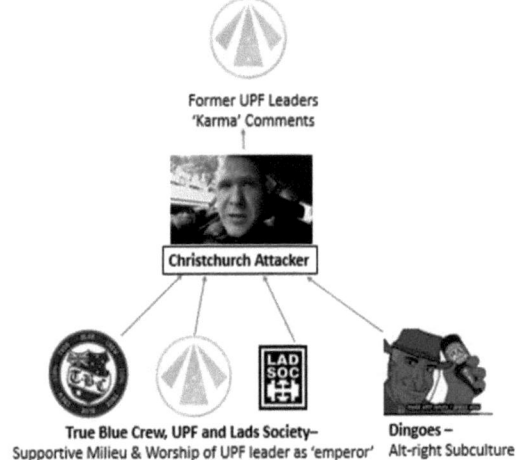

Figure 31: Linkages between Australia Far-Right and Christchurch Attacker[450]

---

[450] For more on these links, see the Christchurch Commission Report at: https://christchurchattack.royalcommission.nz/.

Drawing upon recent academic research into the Australian far-right,[451] narratives from the above groups and activists can be summarised as the following:

1. **Anti-Migrant Narratives**: Antipathy towards non-white immigrants, asylum seekers and refugees, with people harbouring prejudice towards non-white immigrants, asylum seekers and refugees suggesting special treatment vis-à-vis 'indigenous white' populations, leading to so-called 'white marginalisation' or even 'white genocide'. Key Terms: **Sinophobia & Islamophobia**.
2. **Cultural Protectionist Narratives:** Western values are under threat, mandating a so-called 'defence' of Australia and New Zealand's citizens from political correctness and multiculturalism. Such defence can be undertaken through ensuring free speech and giving so-called 'ordinary Australians and New Zelanders' priority access to housing, welfare and state resources. Key Term: **Nativism**.
3. **Accelerationist[452] Narratives:** The system is degenerate and corrupt; we must therefore engage in violent socio-political and economic conflict in order to bring about the revolution and race war that will hasten in a new 'pure' & 'white' system or world order. Key Terms: **White Genocide Conspiracy Theory**.

---

[451] Dean, G., Bell, P. & Vakhitova, Z., 'Right-wing extremism in Australia: the rise of the new radical right', *Journal of Policing, Intelligence and Counter Terrorism*, 11(2), 2016, 121-142.

[452] In addition to information about accelerationism contained in footnote 3, it is important to note that accelerationism has its origins in anti-democratic neo-reactionary doctrine from the 1990s in Nick Land's *Dark Enlightenment* and has since been massaged and adopted by a number of radical right extremist groups, including neo-Nazi solo actor terrorists and groupuscules. Inspired more specifically by US neo-Nazi ideologue, James Mason, the doctrine of 'accelerationism' — literally helping to accelerate revolution, race war or even more apocalyptic scenarios — has been a notable theme amongst violent radical right solo-actors and groups – including the Australian-born Christchurch shooter. (See: Beauchamp, Z., 'Accelerationism: the obscure idea inspiring white supremacist killers around the world', *Vox*, 18 November 2019, online at: https://www.vox.com/the-highlight/2019/11/11/20882005/accelerationism-white-supremacy-christchurch).

4. **'Traditional Values' Narratives:** Feminism promotes the destruction of traditional gender norms; feminists and LGBT are so-called 'traitors' to the nation, and are responsible for low birth-rates among the native (white) population; it is essential to return to an imagined heteronormative past. Key Terms: **Anti-Feminism and Chauvinism**.
5. **Anti-establishment Narratives:** Elites contribute to systemic corruption. They do this through their collaboration with migrants/outsiders. Radical renewal is needed through strong political leadership, populist participation and restricted representation. Key Terms: **Sovereignty and Populism**.
6. **'Strong State' Narratives:** State is weak on migrant crime/terrorism; an empowered and strengthened Australian state is urgently needed to preserve a white Anglo-Saxon form of national identity through authoritarian law-and-order measures and security policy. Key Term: **Authoritarianism**.

Violent Far-Right Counter Narratives & Counter Narrative Campaigns in Australasia: Tapping into Anti-Muslim, Populist, Ethno-Nationalist, White Supremacist and Ultra-Nationalist Narratives

If attempting to construct counter narratives in order to disrupt, delegitimise and/or devalue the appeal of the above narratives, it is useful to identify what we can call 'entry points' within the structure of extremist narratives in order to unpick their veracity, authenticity and believability. Such far-right counter narratives can be done by breaking down such narratives into their orientation (i.e., who, what, where, how & when), action (i.e., evaluation of orientation) and resolution (i.e., prescribed course of action).[453] Whilst it

---

[453] This is a simplified version of a similar schema, laid out in: Labov, W., & Waletzky, J., 'Narrative analysis: Oral versions of personal experience', *Journal of Narrative & Life History*, 7(1-4), 1997, 3-38, online at: http://dx.doi.org/10.1075/jnlh.7.02nar.

might be unprofitable to contest the factual veracity of the orientation statement, both the action and solution sections of the narrative might be more profitably contested. The rationale behind such a technique is that far-right extremists tend to do most harm in how they interpret and offer solutions to what is happening 'out there', and how they frame reality. Opinions are also a softer target than facts, and this maps onto how extremists use grievances to add their own ideological 'twist' on real world events. Therefore, disputing the action and resolution statement are more profitable as it means practitioners are disputing the ideological interpretation of the truth (or factual reality) presented, rather than the reality itself. Below are some key counter narratives that could deployed by practitioners to respond to the Australian far-right extremist messages identified above, and could include:

1. **Anti-Migrant Counter Narratives**: Highlighting the positive contribution of Asian migrants to a country's livelihood and past, acknowledging prejudice but fostering more open viewpoints and a less formulaic or rigid conception of Islam, refugees and migrants.
2. **Cultural Protectionist Counter Narratives:** Advance a new, inclusive definition of cultural and national identity, one which champions the achievements of multicultural society.[454] Contest the definition of Australian and New Zealand 'culture' on which so-called 'cultural protectionism' rests and move beyond a reductive view of essentialised cultures and towards an embrace of working together towards a positive and inclusive Australian and New Zealander national identity.
3. **Accelerationist Counter Narratives:** Emphasise democratic legitimacy of domestic institutions. Engage critically with the nihilistic nature of accelerationism and

---

[454] As national official narratives have been promoting this for decades, and the Scanlon Survey continues to show very high support amongst mainstream Australians for multiculturalism, this might be less fruitful than combating the notion of 'culture' instrumentalised by cultural protectionists.

how it leads to the erosion of moral values. Try to emphasise the causal inconsistencies between violence and a return to a stable social order.

4. **'Traditional Values' Counter Narratives:** Openness to a new, inclusive definition of masculinity as well as masculinity's destructive elements (e.g., violent masculinity and male forms of gender-based murder and domestic violence).[455] Stress the positive contribution by feminists and LGBT movement to the life of the nation (including greater equality, tolerance and inclusion of diverse viewpoints). Reduce threat perception by stressing allegiances in thought and shared interests.

5. **Anti-Establishment Counter Narratives:** Again, emphasise democratic legitimacy of domestic institutions. Talk of efficiencies and benefits of the current representative system as well as the benefits of non-violent extra-parliamentary activism.

6. **'Strong State' Counter Narratives:** Educate citizens regarding what they can and cannot expect from their governments, media and the state (including limitations on (hate) speech). Be transparent about steps the government is taking to teach Australian and New Zealand national values. Ask what perspectives are not listened to and need to be included in any national conversation.

Moving on from looking at counter narratives themselves to counter narrative campaigns, Australia is notable due to its lack of countering violent extremism initiatives targeted at far-right extremist groups. To date, there has been only one systematic, large-scale programme, which started as Community Action for Preventing Extremism's (CAPE) 'Exit White Power' project and one notable strategic communication came in response to a far-right extremist terror attack. Such a lacuna is obviously related to the low threat picture posed by far-right extremism and terrorism in general in New Zealand prior to the tragic events of 15 March 2019. It is therefore a

---

[455] The latter forms of identity-based violence have been notable in Australia during recent years and might tackle more society-based drivers for violent far-right extremism.

propitious time for police, government and civil society to redouble their efforts in thinking about how to prevent another similar attack through developing a far-right counter narrative campaign.

Starting in Australia, the most innovative Australian-based Countering Violent Extremism (CVE) sector organisations countering far-right extremist narratives in Australia has been the CAPE programme at All Together Now. Its website acts as a useful resource for those wishing to learn more about white supremacist narratives in Australia, as well as drivers of national involvement in extremist organisations.[456] Broken down into sections on "Am I in the right place?"; "Am I right to be concerned?"; "What are the signs to be looking for?"; and "What Steps can I take to help?", the site guides users through key far-right narratives, alongside advice on how to provide alternative narratives for those involved in these movements.[457] The All Together Now website also provides "Responding to Far-Right Extremism" training days for front-line public officials who may increasingly encounter individuals vulnerable to extremism.[458]

Unfortunately, to date counter narratives are limited to one pulldown box, the minimalist nature of such a resource is in contrast to previous counter narrative and CVE programmes made available by CAPE (presented in Figure 31 below). The website rectifies this lack in its "FAQs", however.[459] Answers here directly tie into far-right extremist narratives, such as "Why shouldn't I expect people who come here to 'FIT IN' also?"; "Why are only 'WHITE' nations like Australia expected to open their borders?"; and "Is Discriminating Against Muslims Racist?" This section of the website addresses difficult and challenging tropes in a way that should be emulated in far-right extremist

---

[456] CAPE Project, 'Home Page', 2019, online at: https://cape.alltogethernow.org.au/.

[457] CAPE Project, 'What steps can I take to help?', 2019, online at: https://cape.alltogethernow.org.au/how-can-i-help/.

[458] CAPE Project, 'Responding to Far Right Extremism', 2019, online at: https://cape.alltogethernow.org.au/wp-content/uploads/2017/03/CAPE-Training-Program-2.jpg.

[459] All Together Now, 'FAQs' Page, 2019, online at: https://alltogethernow.org.au/racism/faq/.

counter narrative work elsewhere, not least in order to foster debate and dialogue without legitimising the core narratives themselves.

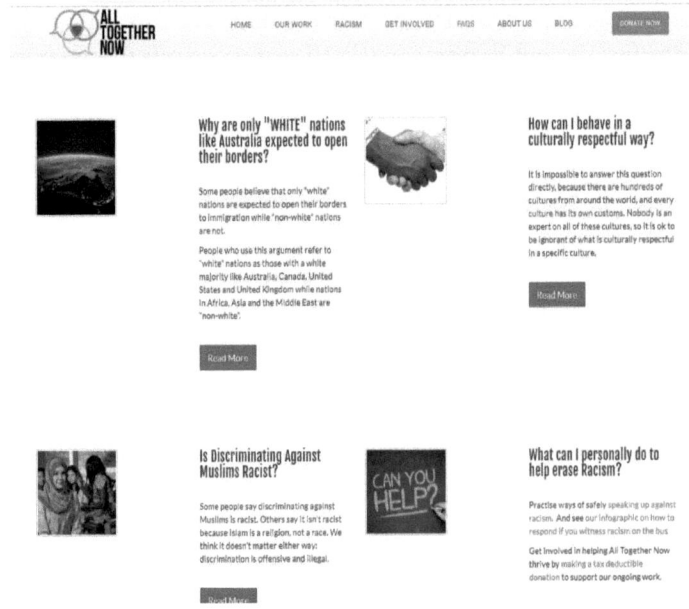

Figure 32: All Together Now (2019) "FAQs" Page.[460]

Another ground-breaking counter narrative intervention provided by CAPE and All Together Now was an exitwhitepower.com website, with a related Facebook forum established ("White Power? Discussion Page") for those tempted by far-right extremist movements. According to the programme's manager, Stevie Voogt, the number of Australians engaging with CAPE's website and forum "significantly exceeded" numbers originally anticipated: there were 22,000 unique views of its website between 2013-2015 and 2000 "likes" of its Facebook page in the first year alone. Moreover, of the (small) number of users who filled out evaluation questionnaires linked to the main website, a majority claimed that they were

---

[460] All Together Now, 'FAQs' Page, 2019, online at: https://alltogether-now.org.au/racism/faq/.

yet to be involved in a white supremacist group due to the intervention. Moreover, of a subset already active, around half have reassessed their involvement with extremist movements as a result of the intervention.[461]

Looking beyond the evaluation questionnaires, one of the key innovations and successes of the CAPE initiative was the tailored nature of the online discussions, alongside CAPE's openness to incorporating feedback from police, academics and former far-right extremists. For example, CAPE volunteers were able to use the Facebook page to post questions relating to far-right involvement (such as "Do you share your opinions about white nationalism with your friends and family?" and "Do you get a hard time for what you believe?"). They were also able to differentiate responses for users with a limited vocabulary as opposed to those who link their extremist beliefs to more intellectual arguments about race, migration and multiculturalism. The addition of the online forum, furthermore, came in direct response to practitioners at a Radicalisation Awareness Network meeting.[462] This is obviously less reliable than polling a wider pool of users, but the results nonetheless reveal the importance of professional feedback and tailoring in the ongoing development of online counter narrative projects.

Another 2015 article by Sara Zeiger (Hedayah) and Anne Aly (Curtin University) focused in on the specific messaging and background characteristics that best described users of CAPE's "White Power?" Facebook discussion page. Interestingly, this independent analysis finds that the Australian page had a reach of 19,529 users (that is, those who saw the page) and that it engaged 10,266 users (those

---

[461] Stevie Voogt, 'Countering far-right recruitment online: CAPE's practitioner experience', *Journal of Policing, Intelligence and Counter Terrorism*, 12:1 (2017), 34–46, cited p. 39.

[462] Ibid., p. 38.

who liked, commented on or shared posts) over the lifetime of the project.[463] Buttressing CAPE's own figures, Zeiger and Aly also found that there were 24,323 visits to the page, and a total of 3,086 comments in response to the 24 discussion starters.

Most pertinent for far-right counter narrative work in general, Zeiger and Aly's analysis found that, overall, discussion starters that were aimed at ideological beliefs relating to white supremacy attracted more comments than those focusing on the social or personal reasons for their involvement in a far-right group (p.84). This gently pushes back at the view that belonging and brotherhood are the overriding factors in far-right extremist participation (rather than ideological affinity)[464] and suggests that looking both at narratives and personal circumstances when constructing far-right counter narratives is crucial.

---

[463] Aly, A. and Zeiger, S., 'Countering Violent Extremism Online in Australia: Research and Preliminary Findings', in Aly, A. and Zeiger, S., eds., *Countering Violent Extremism: Developing an Evidence-base for Policy and Practice* (Hedayah and Curtin University, 2015), pp. 81–89.

[464] For examples, see: Bjørgo, T., Grunenberg, S. & Van Donselaar, J., 'Exit from right-wing extremist groups: Lessons from disengagement programmes in Norway, Sweden and Germany', In: Bjørgo, T. & Horgan, J., *Leaving Terrorism Behind: Individual and Collective Disengagement*, London: Routledge, 2009 & Dechesne, M., 'Deradicalization: Not Soft but Strategic', *Crime, Law, and Social Change*, 2011, PP. 287–292.

#	Discussion Starter	Type	Likes	Comments
1	Is multiculturalism the death of White Australia?	IB	74	149
2	Do you share your opinions about white nationalism with your friends and family? Do you get a hard time for what you believe?	GI	23	51
3	There's a fair few passages in the Bible promoting violence against infidels (or non-believers) - so why are people more worried about similar quotes from the Qu'ran?	IB	36	149
4	Should white nationalists in Australia try to hold themselves to higher personal standards e.g. no drinking or drugs, not engaging in violence? Do white nationalists you know achieve this?	GI	30	136
5	https://www.youtube.com/watch?v=KDAQ4zHiqvo Did anybody catch this show? What do you make of his story?	GI	7	39
6	How often do you question what you read? How do you know which sources to trust?	GI	171	63
7	Rock music has its roots in Africa. Beer was first made in Ancient Egypt. The surfboard was first developed in Polynesia. The list goes on. Can we say that multiculturalism doesn't benefit us if some of our most cherished cultural icons first came from other, non-White countries?	IB	48	106
8	Do you think white nationalism has a good image in Australia? Is it something you can feel proud to be part of?	GI	136	222
9	Of the many people who have left white power groups, a decent amount used to be quite senior within them. Also interesting is that since leaving, these very people said that they see the error of their beliefs, and that they only joined because of things missing in their personal lives. How much confidence does that give you about the leaders in these organisations and whether they actually believe what they're telling you?	GI	43	59
10	How do you think being a vocal white nationalist affects your future prospects?	GI	10	15

Figure 33: Top 10 "White Power? Discussion Page" Discussion Starters[465] (Discussion Types-IB = Ideologically-based & GI= Group Identification-based)[466]

---

[465] Aly, A. and Zeiger, S., Op Cit, p.84

[466] Aly, A. and Zeiger, S., 'Countering Violent Extremism Online in Australia: Research and Preliminary Findings', in Aly, A. and Zeiger, S., eds., *Countering Violent Extremism: Developing an Evidence-base for Policy and Practice* (Hedayah and Curtin University, 2015), pp.84–86

In addition to messaging, finally, most participants in the "White Power?" discussion page were at one or other of the phases of engagement with terroristic content known as the captivation (i.e., visiting interactive blogs related to violent extremist material) or persuasion (i.e., participation in communicative exchanges) stages.[467] As a result, users were less susceptible to having their beliefs changed than using exchanges to reaffirm "survivalist" and "victimhood" narratives around white marginalisation and endangerment.[468] According to Zeiger and Aly, the personal identity and social integration functions of social media should be used for future far-right counter narrative campaigns, underscored by trying to not simply meet opinions with factual arguments to be convincing.[469]

Turning back to another insider account of the CAPE "Exit White Power" Project, the 2019 book chapter by All Together Now founder and managing director, Priscilla Brice, shines an interesting light upon what she terms as "the only project of its kind by a civil society organisation in Australia." Brice argues that there was a "counter-narrative shift" early on in the project away from ideology per se and towards an emphasis on lifestyle choices.[470] In terms of rationale, such a shift was instigated through engaging with research—conducted in 2012 by the European Union's Radicalisation Awareness Network (RAN) [471]— which suggested that offering support for entrenched activists to make life decisions was as important as, or was even more

---

[467] For more information, see: Weimann, G & Von Knop, K., 'Applying the Notion of Noise to Countering Online-Terrorism', *Studies in Conflict and Terrorism*. 31(10) (2008), pp. 883-902.

[468] Aly, A. and Zeiger, S., Op Cit, p. 86.

[469] Ibid, pp. 87 & 88.

[470] Ibid., p. 200.

[471] RAN, 'Proposed Policy Recommendations For the High Level Conference', RAN Prison & Probation Working Group, December 2012, online at: https://ec.europa.eu/home-affairs/sites/homeaffairs/files/what-we-do/networks/radicalisation_awareness_network/ran-high-level-conference/docs/proposed_policy_recommendation_ran_p_and_p_en.pdf.

important than, addressing ideology when helping individuals out of far-right movements.[472]

Another key shift, or turning point, in the project's trajectory came at the end of the extension funding awarded to All Together Now. This was a result of heated arguments instigated on the "White Power?" Facebook page by antiracist activists in 2015 in response to some of the discussion topics posed on the forum. Such an unexpected development then "created a challenge for the project's counsellor moderating the posts".[473] It also subsequently resulted in a shift within the CAPE project towards training frontline staff in anti-radicalisation strategies.[474] This episode, in turn, highlights the importance of planning for unintended responses by external groups when it comes to counter narrative initiatives (for example, thinking about who might respond and contingencies that can be put in place to minimise the impact of antagonistic outside groups from hijacking a far-right counter narrative).

Turning further South to New Zealand, one of the best examples of far-right counter narratives, or strategic communications relating to far-right extremism, came in the wake of the Christchurch terror attacks. As a policy advisor from New Zealand's Prime Minister Office expressed at the RRCN project's September 2019 expert workshop, New Zealand is "a diverse and young country, still shaping narratives of who they are as a nation."[475] The same advisor also stated that mass-casualty-style terror attacks are also new in the New Zealand context, with far-right terror attacks tending to be of the solo actor variety more

---

[472] Ibid., p. 203.

[473] Brice, 2019, Op Cit, p. 207.

[474] Ibid., p. 200.

[475] Workshop Participant Presentation, 'Right-wing counter-narratives – York, 24-25 September 2019', RRCN Expert Workshop, 25 September 2019.

recently.[476] Following the mosque shootings in March 2019, priorities in the immediate aftermath explicitly related to nation shaping through narratives and messaging ('what it means to be a New Zealander'), with a strict emphasis on inclusivity and tolerance. Such an emphasis of tolerance was demonstrated through the focus placed on authentically advanced narratives of inclusivity from the Prime Minister, and extended the notion to the local Muslim community that 'you are one of us' in the wake of such far-right attacks and atrocities.[477]

Figure 34: New Zealand Prime Minister, Jacinda Ardern, talking to the families of victims after the Christchurch attack[478]

---

[476] Though some would dispute this: Battersby, J. & Ball, R, 'Christchurch in the context of New Zealand terrorism and right-wing extremism', Journal of Policing, Intelligence and Counter Terrorism, 14:3, 2019, 191-207, DOI: 10.1080/18335330.2019.1662077.

[477] For more on the importance of stories and culture in counter-terrorism, see: Glazzard, A., 'Losing the Plot: Narrative, Counter-Narrative and Violent Extremism,' ICCT Research Paper, May 2017, online at: https://icct.nl/publication/losing-the-plot-narrative-counter-narrative-and-violent-extremism/.

[478] Christchurch City Council, 'NZ Prime Minister Jacinda Ardern visits the Muslim community the day after the Christchurch Mosque shootings', Wikimedia, 16 Match 2019, online at: https://commons.wikimedia.org/wiki/File:NZ_PM_Jacinda_Ardern_-_Kirk_HargreavesCCC.jpg#metadata.

Crucially, another key strand of New Zealand's post-Christchurch response was an emotive element. On the very day of the shooting, New Zealand's Prime Minister and its Police Commissioner directly interacted with the public in order to show "empathy, acceptance and reassurance".[479] This involved talking to the victims and not about the ideology or background of the terrorist perpetrator ("You are *not* one of us"), providing an excellent example of an alternative narrative. As a key strand of this powerful response, New Zealand's Prime Minister, Jacinda Ardern, visibly spent time with the families and victims of the massacre. (Such an act was no mere photo opportunity.) This, again, focussed media attention upon the victims, while assisting with community reassurance ("You are one of us") more broadly in what is an invariably fragile post-attack context.

Finally, a third key narrative in the post-attack response was a push for a "global response". Two months after the attack, for example, Emmanuel Macron and Jacinda Ardern met ministers from all G7 nations and the leaders of key internet platforms (including Google, Facebook, Microsoft and Twitter) in what was dubbed the "Christchurch call for action". This pledge saw New Zealand leading other assembled nations and key World Wide Web stakeholders to adopt a "plan of action" for preventing extremist or terroristic material from going viral online. In conjunction with this, domestically, New Zealand gun laws were tightened, circulation of the shooter's manifesto and attack video were made illegal, and a Royal Commission of Inquiry was set up into the attacks, tasked with learning counter-terrorism lessons from the horrific attack.[480] Such an international agreement and call galvanised a global response around a set of norms which, in turn, have been instrumental in mobilising individual governments and companies to take action on right-wing extremism.

In consequence, the Christchurch attack and New Zealand's impassioned response to it witnessed a proactive shift in seizing the

---

[479] Workshop Participant Presentation (25 September 2019).
[480] This will now report in July 2020 due to an expanded budget and call for evidence. For more details, see: https://christchurchattack.royalcommission.nz/.

initiative against far-right violent extremism. It focused on everyday individuals and victims, thus derailing tabloid-type attempts to place the attacker at the heart of national discussion. Narratives used at the time of the attack by Ardern show a high level of coherence and fidelity,[481] borne out in her interweaving micro-level narratives about individuals affected by the attack, while also operating at the macro level by reaffirming 'inclusive' and 'tolerant' aspects of New Zealand's national identity.[482] Such a weaving of macro and micro ideas of New Zealand national identity demonstrated the power of administering an alternative narrative to foster a new sense of belonging and acceptance, refusing the anti-Muslim, exclusivist ideology of the terrorist perpetrator and instead placing a new onus on including migrant members of New Zealand's national community,[483] and thus using language to demonstrate inclusive notions of New Zealand as a nation ('you are one of us').

Conclusions and Recommendations

This chapter has provided a survey of narratives and potential counter-messaging to far-right extremism in Australasia following the Christchurch terrorist attack. Moving from street-based activism into more direct action and even terroristic forms of political violence, this report has highlighted links with the New Zealand Christchurch attacker and other violent international far-right

---

[481] See Fisher, W. R, *Human communication as narration: Toward a philosophy of reason, value, and action,* Columbia: University of South Carolina Press, 1987.

[482] Ardern, J., 'Ministerial Statements — Mosque Terror Attacks—Christchurch', NZ Parliament, 19 March 2019, online at: https://www.parliament.nz/en/pb/hansard-debates/rhr/combined/HansDeb_20190319_20190319_08.

[483] This was further seen in the media and society through Ardern's wearing a burqa in the week after the attack, as well as the use of Arabic greetings, customs and calls to prayer in public spaces. See: Morrison, S., 'New Zealand women wear headscarves in powerful display of solidarity after mosque attacks', *Evening Standard,* 22 March 2019, online at: https://www.standard.co.uk/news/world/headscarf-for-harmony-new-zealand-women-cover-their-hair-in-solidarity-with-muslim-communi ty-in-a4098196.html.

groups able to be traced back to Australia.[484] It has also highlighted several groups (Antipodean Resistance, Combat 18 & Women for Aryan Unity) whose narratives paint a metastasising threat picture (both in terms of potential and actual radicalisation of Australian and New Zealand's citizens). Furthermore, it is clear that anti-Muslim populist, ethno-nationalist, white supremacist and ultra-nationalist narratives have a broad resonance in the both geographical contexts, suggesting a wider pool of support than Australian far-right extremist groups' collective membership at present, with potentially alarming consequences for mobilisation and radicalisation (especially by white males under 30).

In response to these challenging circumstances, practitioners would be advised to find ways of disrupting permissive environments where, for instance, anti-female and anti-minority viewpoints are left to fester. This is best achieved through tailored and targeted counter narrative projects that help dispel persistent myths and rumours. Here, it is important to note that only one notable programme and strategic communications campaign to date have attempted to distribute far-right counter narratives in the Australasian context; namely, CAPE's "Exit White Power" project and Jacinda Ardern's response to the Christchurch terror attack. Needless to say, there is a great opportunity to both scale up and deepen far-right counter narrative campaigns capable of disrupting and delegitimising far- right populist, ethno-nationalist, white supremacist and ultra-nationalist narratives propagated in both countries.[485]

Going forward, ultimately, such campaigns need to take a targeted approach, especially when dealing with the violent end of far-right subcultures such as neo-Nazism. Accordingly, in order to

---

[484] This is in addition to known links between the attacker and European-based far-right groups. See: Wilson, J., 'Christchurch shooter's links to Austrian far right 'more extensive than thought", *The Guardian*, 16 May 2019, online at: https://www.theguardian.com/world/2019/may/16/christchurch-shooters-links-to-austrian-far-right-more-extensive-than-thought.

[485] This could be done through either tackling the bases of group identification or ideological beliefs inherent to far-right extremism.

counter far-right extremist narratives, this might involve the following:

1. Long-term and sustained work in challenging formulaic or rigid conceptions of Islam, refugees and migrants circulating in far-right extremist milieus (both online and offline);
2. A re-emphasis upon the centrality of domestic institutions and a new vision of democratic participation, in order to counter accusations of so-called 'degeneracy' and 'corruption' among extremist circles as well as the nihilistic tendency among some accelerationist far-right extremists;
3. Counter narrative responses that directly tackle misogynist tropes, especially by placing more of a stress on the positive contribution by feminists and LGBT movement to the life of the Australian and New Zealand nations;
4. Honest dialogue regarding what grievances is is not being listened to, how these might be addressed, and pathways for inclusion in the national conversations of both Australia and New Zealand.

By embarking on far-right extremist counter narrative projects and by including these new and sensitised perspectives into strategic communications work, going forwards Australasia will have a far greater chance in immunising citizens against the perils of far-right extremism and the violent ideology contained therein, as thrown into stark contrast with the May 2019 terror attack.

Chapter 5: Testing the Words vs. Deeds Nexus — A Facebook Pilot Study of UK Far-Right Counter Narratives in the Online Space

Introduction

Over the past decade, counter narratives have often been sourced as an answer to extremist ideologies. Used mainly at the 'upstream' phase of radicalization towards violent extremism, the use of communications campaigns by governments, non-governmental organizations (NGOs), and civil-society actors in order to "[demystify], deconstruct or delegitimise extremist narratives"[486] has come to the fore as a key intervention within the Preventing and Countering Violent Extremism (P/CVE) profession. Such a communications-focused approach has become especially important as extremist organizations and actors have become more adept at using social media in order to radicalize and recruit non-aligned actors to their cause. Moreover, the internet and social media has supplanted traditional forms of media and face-to-face encounters in extremist efforts to spread messages of hatred using sophisticated and targeted propaganda techniques to recruit the right audience.[487] The global far-right is not an exception to this trend. In particular, and as seen through attacks in Poway, Christchurch, El Paso, Halle, and Hanau,[488] the use of manifestos, online

---

[486] Tuck, H. and Silverman, T., 'The Counter-Narrative Handbook', London: ISD, 2016, 65, online at: https://www.isdglobal.org/wp-content/uploads/2016/06/Counter-narrative-Handbook_1.pdf.

[487] Allchorn, W., 'Technology and the Swarm: A Dialogic Turn in Online Far-Right Activism', GNET Insight Blog, 17 January 2020, online at: https://gnet-research.org/2020/01/17/technology-and-the-swarm-a-dialogic-turn-in-online-far-right-activism/.

[488] Helsel, P., 'Suspect in Christchurch mosque shootings charged with terrorism', NBC News, 21 May 2019, online at: https://www.nbcnews.com/news/world/suspect-christchurch-mosque-shootings-charged-terrorism-n1008161; Romo, V. 'El Paso Walmart Shooting Suspect Pleads Not Guilty,' NPR, 10 October 2019, online at: https://www.npr.org/2019/10/10/769013051/el-paso-

meme culture and conspiracy theories can lead to powerful offline effects;[489] the seemingly sporadic and 'solo' actor nature of the attacks masking a more toxic online community of religiously, ethnically and racially-motivated hatred.

Despite this renewed challenge and imperative from far-right right extremist organisations and their concomitant attempts at propagating their viewpoints in the online space, there is a dearth of empirical data on what works and what does not in counter narrative campaigns specific to the far-right. Indeed, the majority of evaluations and report on this topic tend to privilege either an ideologically agnostic approach (i.e., treating specific extremisms as functionally equivalent or co-equal), or one specifically tailored to Islamist extremism.[490] Moreover, approaches tend to privilege individuals who have already moved a fair way down the conveyor belt of extremism, showing either commitment to a specific extremist ideology or group of organized extremist actors.[491] This chapter aims to provide a useful counterfactual to this prevailing tendency. Taking the UK as a case study, it

---

walmart-shooting-suspect-pleads-not-guilty; BBC, 'German Halle gunman admits far-right synagogue attack', 11 October 2019, online at: https://www.bbc.co.uk/news/world-europe-50011898; Hucal, S., 'Racially motivated terror attack in Hanau puts Germany's right wing extremism into focus', ABC News, 27 February 2020, online at: https://abcnews.go.com/US/racially-motivated-terror-attack-hanau-puts-germanys-wing/story?id=69128298.

[489] For a good overview of the 2019 wave of radical right extremist attacks, see: Macklin, G., 'The El Paso Terrorist Attack: The Chain Reaction of Global Right-Wing Terror', CTC Sentinel, December 2019, online at: https://ctc.usma.edu/app/uploads/2019/12/CTC-SENTINEL-112019.pdf.

[490] See: Briggs, R. & Feve, S., 'Review of Programs to Counter Narratives of Violent Extremism', London: ISD, 2013; Tuck, H. & Silverman, H., 'The Counter Narrative Handbook', London: ISD, 2016; Reynolds, L & Tuck H., 'The Counter Narrative Monitoring and Evaluation Handbook', London: ISD, 2016: Silverman, Stewart, Amanullah and Birdwell, 'The Impact of Counter Narratives'. London: ISD, 2016; & Hedayah/ICCT, 'Developing Effective Counter-Narrative Frameworks for Countering Violent Extremism'. Hedayah/ICCT: Abu Dhabi/Hague, September 2014.

[491] See: Briggs, R. & Feve, S., 'Review of Programs to Counter Narratives of Violent Extremism', London: ISD, 2013; Dafnos, A., 'Narratives as a Means of Countering the Radical Right; Looking into the Trojan T-shirt Project.' Journal EXIT Deutschland, 2014; Helmus, T.C. & Klein, K., ,Assessing the Outcomes of Online Campaigns in Counter Violent Extremism: A Case Study of the Redirect

lays out how an iterative, experimental research methodology can be used to test counter narrative content and, most importantly, ensure impactful attitudinal change among far-right sympathetic audiences.[492]

Dialing Back Hatred: Research Context, Objectives, Hypotheses and Methodology for Testing Far-Right Counter Narrative Effectiveness

In July 2020, the Centre for Analysis of the Radical Right (CARR), Academic Consulting Services (ACS) and Hedayah completed research that identified key far-right narratives. The outcome of which was the development of a series of counter narratives that could be used by practitioners in this space. CARR sought to test these counter narratives both online and offline with far-right sympathisers (see Research Objectives below). First, through research with Steven Lacey and The Outsiders, the second using the learnings from these findings to develop content for testing online through Facebook.

Method', RAND Corporation, 2018; & Silverman, Stewart, Amanullah and Birdwell, 'The Impact of Counter Narratives'. London: ISD, 2016.

[492] Here, 'far-right sympathetic audiences' are defined as individuals who have stridently hostile views to immigration, Islam and multiculturalism. They are neither members of a far-right organisation nor heavily ideologised in far-right ideology, but somewhere on the 'tipping point' of becoming more involved (i.e., have expressed support for a far-right influencer or informal followership of such an influence online in the past).

Research Objectives

Goal
To dial down sympathy for FR viewpoints (i.e., moving from scepticism to warm or lukewarm agreeable views towards migrants, diversity/multiculturalism and Islam) and ultimately their engagement with such forms of activism (online and offline).

Theory of Change
By presenting Far-Right (FR) sympathetic audiences in the UK with counter narratives targeted to their attitudinal (i.e., immigration, multiculturalism and Islam sceptic in their outlooks), demographic specificity (male and female white across several age ranges and occupational bands) and interests (e.g., celebrities, pastimes, sports interests (i.e., football, non-Politically Correct or subversive humour), we'll be able to dial down their sympathy for FR viewpoints (i.e., moving from scepticism to warm or lukewarm agreeable views towards migrants, diversity/multiculturalism and Islam) and ultimately their engagement with such forms of activism (online and offline).

Strategic Approach:
Get: Individuals who sympathise with far-right narratives
To: Reflect on and review their sympathies and in doing so reject them
By: Engaging them with counter narrative content which breaks down the basis of beliefs

Social Objectives:
Generate engagement with the campaign content across Facebook.
Test content for effectiveness and resonance in countering far-right narratives.

Research Hypotheses

H1 Greater exposure to counter narrative content will see reduction in sceptical viewpoints towards immigration, multiculturalism and Islam.

H2 Greater engagement with counter narrative content will see a more marked reduction in sceptical viewpoints towards immigration, multiculturalism and Islam.

H3 Counter narrative content that affirms belonging, togetherness and community will see the most positive reaction among the target audience.

> H4 Counter narrative content that challenges views on immigration, Islam and multiculturalism will see the most negative reaction among the target audience.
>
> H5 Counter narrative content where the messengers are from a mixture of backgrounds will see the most positive reaction among the target audience.
>
> H6 Counter narrative content where the messengers are from an ethnic minority background will see the most negative reaction among the target audience.
>
> H7 Video-based counter narrative content will receive the most engagement versus meme-based counter narrative content.

The methodology for this project was therefore informed by an iterative two-step process. The first phase of the project was to conduct ethnographic, focus group testing of far-right counter narrative content with a representative subset of a far-right sympathetic audience to ascertain how they would react to different types of counter narrative content. The second phase of the project was to develop a new, more robust counter-narrative testing methodology that uses a mixture of surveys and social media data in order to track both the attitudinal journeys of users and the performance of counter narrative content in real time and at scale (see Figure 1 below).

> Iterative, Two-Step Methodology: Focus Groups & Experimental Method
> 1. **'Alpha-Testing'** of Far-Right Counter Narratives on RR-Sympathetic Audiences (Offline)
> • 6 focus groups, 5-6 people in each.
> • Mixed and Single Gender groups of people (with highly sceptical views on immigration, Islam and multiculturalism).
> • Locations: North, Midlands and South of England — with scope to expand to other Anglo-phone countries too.
> 2. **'Beta-Testing'** using Survey Experiment methodology on Far-Right Counter Narratives on RR-Sympathetic Audiences (Online)
> • Online Testing various messages and narratives on Facebook by targeting counter narrative adverts at a larger cohort (c. 1000+ individuals) of RR-Sympathetic Audiences
> • Aim is to 'dial down' highly sceptical views on immigration, Islam and multiculturalism of RR-sympathetic audience on mass scale
> • All highly targeted to very specific news feeds and audiences to minimise over-exposure

Phase 1: Focus Group Testing of Far-Right Counter Narrative Content

I. Introduction

As part of the preparation for focus group testing, the project's leads worked in conjunction with global advertising firm M&C Saatchi to source counter narrative memes and videos relevant to the UK-based far-right sympathetic audience in question. Memes and videos were sourced and generated that spoke to each counter narrative theme, and were chosen based on their ability to cut through to audiences in a matter of seconds — captivating the audience as soon as possible. A mixture of messengers was chosen too and an extra set of slides inserted in the deck to see which were trusted the most. A mocked-up counter narrative seed page — used to host the content for the online testing phase — was also inserted in the deck of material tested to gauge initial reactions from the audience about the page.

II. Focus Group-Tested Far-Right Counter Narrative Content

Figure 35: Anti-Muslim Populism Counter Narrative Content[493]

A first set of three memes and four videos were generated and sourced to counter cultural threat narratives that have cropped up in far-right circles — often based on either the Great Replacement or Eurabia conspiracy theory — and to dial down the sense of threat associated with the Muslim community. Topical and historical issues were addressed as part of the content developed — with memes A1 and A2 generated to outline contributions by the Muslim community in the case of the COVID-19 pandemic, but also cast alongside more historical content about the Gurkhas (Figure 34, A4) and Muslim acts of bravery in World War I (Figure 34, A5). Added to this were videos that tried to humanise Muslim shopkeepers (Figure 34, A3) and boxing coaches (Figure 34, A7) as well as how white messengers had been aided in combat by people of other ethnicities (Figure 34, A6).

---

[493] Creative created by M&C Saatchi on behalf of author.

208 MOVING BEYOND ISLAMIST EXTREMISM

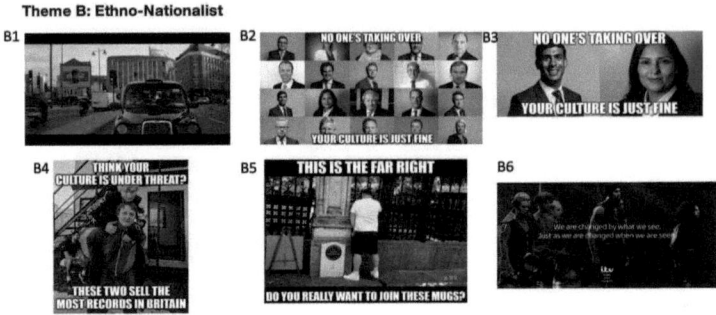

Figure 36: Ethno-Nationalist Counter Narrative Content[494]

A second set of four memes, a video and an ITV advertisement were selected to test in their ability to counter feelings of threat to in-group ethnic identity through immigration and multiculturalism. A video from a recent Coca Cola advertising campaign (Figure 35, B1) was chosen to display racial harmony around football culture as well as memes reassuring members of the audience that their cultural identity was not under threat from minorities or within (Figure 35, B2, B3 & B4). Again, and picking up on more topical issues, creative content was added to the deck that tested the audience's reaction to a picture of a far-right protester in the summer of 2020 urinating on a statue of a police officer killed while trying to stop a terrorist (Figure 2, B5) and an advertisement promoting the Britain's Got Talent Group 'Diversity' (Figure 35, B6) picked up on the reaction to Black Lives Matters (BLM) protests and acts of solidarity with BLM respectively.

---

[494] Creative created by M&C Saatchi on behalf of author.

Theme C: Masculinist

Figure 37: Masculinist Counter Narrative Content[495]

A third set of four memes were selected to test their ability in countering extreme forms of masculinism and anti-LGBT sentiment within far-right circles. The figure of Alan Turing and the Enigma machine was used to elevate how prominent members of the LGBT community had helped fighting patriotic causes (Figure 36, C1) and the role of transgender artists in bolstering regional and national identities (Figure 36, C2, Grayson Perry). Added to this were more feminist leaning memes, outlining how specific instances of how feminine achievement had benefitted the nation (Figure 36, C3) and members of the target audience individually (Figure 36, C4).

---

[495] Creative created by M&C Saatchi on behalf of author.

Figure 38: Populist, Anti-Establishment & Victimhood Counter Narrative Content[496]

A fourth and fifth theme were aimed at dialing down far-right attempts at seizing on populist grievances around anti-elite sentiment, a sense of victimhood and that freedom of speech was being suppressed through an agenda of so-called 'political correctness'. Seizing on crossovers between the cause of leaving the European Union, the populist right and anti-democratic forces within the far-right in the UK, a meme was generated to foster greater faith in democratic process based on the 2016 EU referendum result (Figure 37, D1). Moreover, senses of victimhood were tackled from the elite and popular levels through the use of memes poking fun at prominent far-right leaders who have claimed to be silenced (Figure 37, E3 & E4) through to far-right demonstrators and racist football fans (Figure 37, E1 & E2); the latter picking up on senses of moral duty and conduct when putting across one's viewpoint.

---

[496] Creative created by M&C Saatchi on behalf of author.

Figure 39: Topical Counter Narrative Content[497]

A final set of themes picked up on a set of topical and persistent issues that also came to light later in summer of 2020. Theme F was broached as record numbers of illegal migrants made their way across the channel to see asylum in the UK. This had subsequently led to counter-mobilisations, vigilantism and attacks on hotels and centres housing refugees and asylum seekers in the UK. F1 and F2 tried to humanise such migrants to the audience—suggesting how they had fled to the UK from persecution (Figure 38, F1) and contexts where civil war had endangered their life (Figure 38, F2). A European Youth Campaign against Racism advert (Figure 38, G1) was also added to the deck to capture a shift in the summer of 2020 by UK far-right actors from several decades of focusing on cultural racism back to biological racism.

III. Trusted Organisations & Messengers

A selection of organisations and messengers were collated and put in front of the audience as an additional test to see who would be trusted by the target audience. Brands and charities linked to patriotic and nationalist causes (e.g., Help for the Heroes, The Royal British Legion and the British Red Cross) as well as those either non-aligned (e.g., Coca Cola) or traditionally associated with left-wing causes (e.g., LGBT Foundation) were also selected (see Figure 39 below). Added to this was a list of politicians, journalists and social media influencers again with varied degrees of ideological affiliation (e.g., Keir Starmer vs. Jacob-Rees-Mogg) (see Figure 40 below)

---

[497] Creative created by M&C Saatchi on behalf of author.

212   MOVING BEYOND ISLAMIST EXTREMISM

and extremity (e.g., Gary Lineker vs. Tommy Robinson) (see Figure 41 below).

Figure 40:   Tested UK Brand Messengers[498]

---

[498] Creative created by M&C Saatchi on behalf of author.

TESTING THE WORDS VS. DEEDS NEXUS 213

Figure 41: Tested UK Political Messengers[499]

Figure 42: Tested UK Online Influencer & Media Messengers[500]

---

[499] Creative created by M&C Saatchi on behalf of author.

IV. Mocked-Up Facebook Page

A seed page for counter narrative materials in the second, online phase of the project was also generated on Facebook in order that it might be tested in the focus group 'alpha-testing' (see Figure 42 below). The strapline 'Everybody Makes Britain Great' was used to foster an inclusivity around common themes of nationalism, patriotism and traditionalism. Security and a lack of threat around these key themes were deemed important among the target audience. It was also decided to look beyond a racialised, Anglo-centric focus within the campaign; hence the use of 'Britain' as opposed to 'England' and the Union Jack as part of the branding for the Facebook seed page.

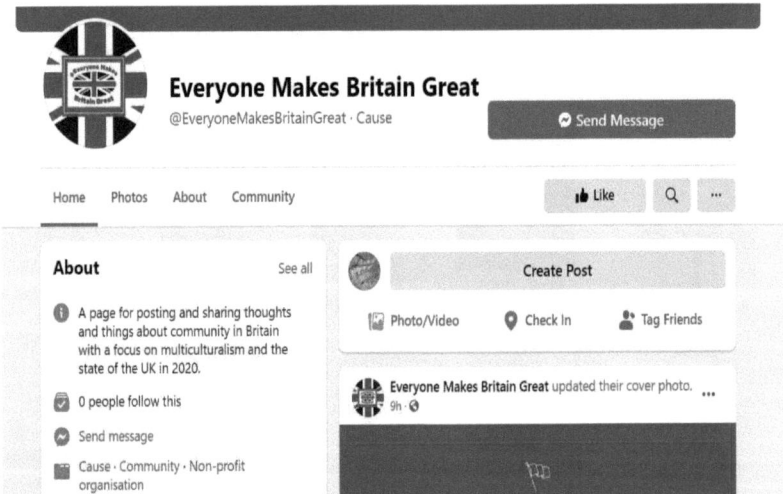

Figure 43: Tested Mock-up of 'Everybody Makes Britain Great' Seed Page[501]

---

[500] Creative created by M&C Saatchi on behalf of author.

[501] *'Everybody Makes Britain Great' Seed Page, Facebook*, online at: https://www.facebook.com/EveryoneMakesBritainGreat.

Findings

I. Issues Important to Target Audience

At the start of each focus group, respondents were asked about issues that concerned or were important to them in 2020. Worryingly (but perhaps not unexpectedly), many of the respondents replied back with social and policy issues that could be exploited by the far-right. They also fit within the authoritarian, nativist and populist tenants that currently animate far-right ideology and included:

- Perceived lack of integration by Ethnic Minorities
- Perceived benefits given by the UK State to asylum seekers
- Immigrants being the cause of crime
- Not being able to celebrate Britishness
- Lack of strict laws on migration
- Anxieties around Crime/knife crime
- Black Lives Matter feeling like a revolution versus an evolution
- Protestors not abiding by COVID-19 Lockdown measures
- Concerns over Attacks on White Policemen

A lack of security and anxieties around crime were therefore key concerns for this audience. As one respondent said: "Here there are gangs, they carry knives. When we were 12/13, we'd go to Birmingham town centre and get the bus, it was no problem, we'd have a Big Mac, cause a bit of trouble, but that was just being like a kid but now they've got knives, it's really scary really." (Mixed sex group, 35–45 years, Midlands). Moreover, the nexus between this crime focus and Black Lives Matter protest in June were still palpable—even several months on: "The gangs, the violence, the whole Black Lives Matter piece; compare that to the police officer that was killed the other day, or the rioting, etc., I just think it's getting out of hand. As a single female I go out walking every day and I'm scared, I look over my shoulder; lads in hoodies." (Mixed sex group, 35–45 years, Midlands)

Below these surface issues were however some deeper and more troubling concerns relevant to this far-right sympathetic audience. The first was the belief that political correctness has gone into overdrive and the belief that their public-facing self has to be censored away from what they really feel. This was especially apparent in how they constructed their relationship with ethnic minorities and race — fearing about being labelled 'racist' and suggesting concerns that they had to assimilate to the culture of migrants and not vice versa. So far had this self-censorship and frustration had gone that some respondents used the language of diversity to describe black privilege and white marginalisation. As one respondent said from the all-female group: "We are now scared to even be white and be proud of being white!" A second response to this concern over stigmatisation and censorship was deep-seated trend of concern for the audience around what they perceived as a 'reverse racism' or a feeling that whites were being singled out for being racist far too easily and the idea of a double-standard when white people express racist ideations. For example, another respondent from the all-female group suggested: "It's not just black people who get racist comments said towards them and it's a completely different scenario when white people get racist comments said to them, so I don't think it's all very fair."

A third deep-seated — but connected and perhaps unsurprising — concern was the belief that British customs and identity were under attack and that the things that made the British exceptional (or a nation to be proud of) were being eroded. Examples of this included a belief in a denial of being able to display vestments of English identity (such as the St. George's flag) or concerns about not being able to celebrate 'English' holidays (such as St. George's day or Christmas) due to a politically incorrect agenda. As one member of the 25–34-year-old group suggested:

> "I'm quite loud and proud, we go to the football, I chav up the house, my teenagers hate me, I don't care. I hate the way that it's sort of shamed on for being proud of being British; Paddy's Day, we put the green flags up and that, St George's Day and that, we're always a bit reserved, we're always a bit too British and it's sad really because we celebrate everyone else's culture but, like you said, we kind of stand back from our own."

Applying these concerns to counter narrative content, it was therefore clear that any content going forward needed to subtly avoid triggering negative psychological reactance through creating content that was non-combative and affirmed in-group identity in a non-racialised form. Added to this was an emphasis demonstrated throughout the initial discussions in the focus groups that lifting up one ethnic group over others would also create counter-arguing and that instead a plurality of racial identities (including white messengers) was needed.

II. Behaviour of Target Audience on Social Media

For the majority of the audience, mainstream, public-facing platforms (such as Facebook, Instagram, Twitter and TikTok) were key platforms that they used on a regular basis. YouTube use was also prolific — with the video-based media platform often seen to report the 'truth' that mainstream media is scared to report. They tended to follow friends and celebrities on mainstream, public social media platforms rather than 'State of the Nation' messengers (e.g., mainstream politicians, journalists etc.) and tended to follow culturally, not politically, charged content online. A small minority used more alternative forms of social media (e.g., Telegram and Gab). For the concern of this project, what was interesting is that they all had followed at least one far-right figure/group on these platforms and trusted these messengers more than the mainstream to tell the truth and to call people out on important topics to themselves. Specifically, the former English Defence League leader, Tommy Robinson (and to a lesser extent Katie Hopkin) was singled out as someone that they have followed — or continue to follow — in the media as a trusted messenger who is able to give voice to viewpoints that the audience felt unable to voice. Interestingly, when meme content was targeted at him in focus discussions, most — or not if all respondents who knew who he was — came to his defence and though factually true questioned the veracity of the statements made within the creative stimulus materials. Attacking the far-right itself therefore proved an unfruitful strategy, triggering excuses in the minds of the target audience.

Added to this there were interesting behaviours reported by the audience in terms of their behaviour on mainstream platforms.

All had a highly critical, reflexive and mediated relationship with social media such that they are highly sceptical of what is presented/don't trust platforms to show pertinent content. As one respondent in the mixed 16-24-year-old group said: "I feel like you have to take every comment with a pinch of salt. I would never read a status on Facebook and then go tell people, 'I've just read this and it's correct.' I'd say, 'I heard it on Facebook but you can't know that it's true'." They were also reluctant to share content on social media over risks of bans or arguments and had started to develop increasingly sanitised habits/profiles as a result of these concerns. As another respondent in the mixed 16–24-year-old group said: "I got a new job recently, and I deleted my old Twitter – not that I'd been ranting and raving about race or explicit things but just in case I'd ever said something that was off-guard, a bit untoward, but the smallest thing, if it's not completely politically correct, then at the minute you can't really say it." Instead, they took their conversations to Instant Messaging-oriented platforms (e.g., Facebook Messenger/WhatsApp/Telegram) and offline to have difficult conversations around ethnicity and race, without the feeling of being stigmatized or self-censored. As one final respondent from the mixed 16-24-year-old group said: "If we're going to talk about it on text, it's a quick text, it's never too much in depth but if we were to meet up in person, that's when we'd speak about it more, so we can spend hours talking about it.". Such a complex relationship was noted as a key challenge for the online 'beta testing' phase– raising concerns about engagement and interaction with counter narrative content on public-facing platforms for an audience that was notably reluctant in doing so.

III. Responses to Focus Group Tested Far-Right Counter Narrative Content: What Worked Well, Not So Well and Fairly Well

As noted above, one of the things that was deemed to work well in the content presented was ideas around unity and the mixing of different ethnicities through commonalities. Not unsurprisingly given the backdrop of a global pandemic, positivity and creating a sense of uplifting emotion worked well with the audience—with emotion itself being the core touch point for how the audience engaged with online content. Moving onto specifics, the focus group research—and analysis by the Outsiders—found that there were pieces and elements of the above content that played well, fairly well and which failed when presented before the target audience. A summary of what was found to work well, fairly well and not so well in this regard is presented in the following section:

1. Far-Right Counter Narrative Content that Worked Well

In terms of the first category of what worked well, the Coca Cola advert (Figure 43), the Open your Eyes to Hate video (Figure 11), Corner shop video (Figure 12), Combination's video (Figure 13) and Gurkha meme (Figure 14) were rated highly among the target audience. More specifically, it was found that the focus on unity, displays of revelry, lack of demonisation of working-class culture and use of sport and community as a source of ethnic commonality worked well with far-right sympathetic audiences across all videos. In particular, the Coca Cola video (see Figure 10 below) received the most positive comments as it was able to execute a feeling of unity in the most successful manner of all the content presented. As one respondent in the all-male group described: "Everyone's coming together despite race, for the love of football really. It was nice, whether you're black, white Muslim, whatever, everyone was just together, happy and it was because of the love of football." There was criticism (for example, for a few non-Londoners it felt too London-centric or didn't appear to be a real reflection of racial relations in the UK) but they were in a minority and of a qualified nature.

Figure 44: Screenshot of Coca-Cola 'Where Everyone Plays' Video[502]

Moving on to the other videos, the above findings held but with some additional insights. For example, the Captain David Wiseman video found that an (admittedly white) messenger was viewed as a good, credible, trustworthy, with the army very well regarded among far-right sympathetic audiences (see Figure 44 below). Showcasing that people from other countries are in the British army, it was particularly well received for creating a feeling that other ethnicities looked after white British soldiers during a time of war and that the ethnic in-group should look after them. Moreover, it even led some respondents (with family in armed forces) to re-evaluate their thoughts and fostered sympathetic feelings towards those of different ethnic backgrounds. As one respondent from the mixed 46+ years group noted: "They were looking after our own, so we've got to look after them ... I think that's a good thing, that's a good thing to show. It changed my outlook!" Again, there were some minor criticisms around an idea of post-racism that 'colour didn't matter' to the identities of the people who helped the soldier in the video but again they were in the minority. These findings suggest a white messenger is crucial in reaching such an audience.

---

[502] *Coca-Cola*, 'Where Everyone Plays' Video, February 2019, *YouTube*, online at: https://www.youtube.com/watch?v=8_XBxcIoZy0.

Figure 45: Screenshot of Open Your Eyes to Hate 'Captain David Wiseman' Video[503]

Other content that landed well with the focus group audience was a film showing the role of corner shops run by ethnic minority owners who helped their communities during the COVID-19 pandemic (see Figure 45 below). While a large number of respondents again negatively evaluated the video because it was too focused on minority groups, individuals based in towns with significant Asian populations saw it as a 'feel good video' that tapped into a kindness and humanity during a difficult time and positively evaluated the corner shop owner spotlighted in the video as a respected messenger doing good amid the circumstances. As one of the respondents in the all-male group alluded to: "I actually thought he was a lovely man with good community spirit, it didn't matter what colour he

---

[503] *Open Your Eyes to Hate*, 'Captain David Wiseman' Video, *Facebook*, 8 March 2018, online at: https://www.facebook.com/watch/?ref=search&v=581451182199701&external_log_id=c055a26b-62da-4ec1-a368-757824995868&q=open%20your%20eyes%20to%20hate.

was, he was just a lovely man, at the end of the day. I liked him as a person."

Figure 46: Screenshot from BBC One 'Cornershop Heroes' Video[504]

Another video to profile a member of the Muslim Community was a short version of Media Cultured's Combinations video that showed the everyday life of a Muslim boxing. This received a positive evaluation because of the kindness of the messenger, the connection with a dearly held sport and its framing of Muslim's being involved in 'something other than terrorism'. Again, criticism centered around Muslims are being elevated above white British members of the UK population. As one respondent from the mixed 16–24-year-old group mentioned: "I've boxed all my life and boxing tends to be people of a lower social class, like a working class all within one environment and it doesn't matter whether you're white, black, what religion you are."

---

[504] *BBC One*, 'Corner Shop Heroes', 12 May 2020, online at: https://www.bbc.co.uk/programmes/p08cxs7p.

Figure 47: Screenshot of Original Content: 'Ghurka' Meme[505]

One final meme-based counter narrative message that received an overall positive response was one depicting the plight of the Gurkhas fighting for their right to stay in the UK during their retirement (see Figure 46 above). Again, this connected with the army which played strongly with the audience but the campaign about the issue was largely only picked up upon and endorsed by older respondents — with younger respondents misidentifying or admitting to a lack of knowledge around the subject. Again, and once explained, patriotic alliances were forged in the minds of the audience as a positive feature of the memes message, with one respondent from the all-female group suggesting definitively that: "I would let them in because they fought for our country, end of."

2. Far-Right Counter Narratives that worked Fairly Well

In terms of the second category of what worked fairly well, these largely gravitated around counter narrative content presented in section B of the deck and tapped into debates around the limitations of free speech. The first of these was a meme depicting racist chanting by white males targeted at a black player during football game, with the tagline "Freedom of Speech is your Right but don't be a

---

[505] Creative created by M&C Saatchi on behalf of author.

racist prick" (see Figure 47 below). For most, older audience members (46 years +), the message appeared too crass but younger audiences found this element amusing. Again, however, the singling out of white people as racists crept in and was deemed a negative aspect of the meme and led to some (rightfully or wrongly) suggesting that the culprits of the racist abuse were never charged. Away from this, most however viewed the 'be kind' nature of the message but some believed that freedom of speech is no longer allowed. As one member of the mixed 46+ year group posited: "'Freedom of speech', they're implying that it's just going to be racist, 'Freedom of speech' means anything but you're reducing it to just racism; it could be about anything."

Figure 48: Screenshot of Original Content: 'Chelsea Football Match' Meme[506]

Another meme tapping into the freedom of speech issue that worked fairly well was a picture depicting a far-right protestor haranguing a group of Muslim ladies' counter-protesting their march, with the words "We are all for Freedom of Speech but don't be a dick" (see Figure 48 below). Again, the be kind sentiment was endorsed as well as the emphasis on the importance of the freedom of speech but the interplay of messengers and the image itself made some people question the veracity of the message. For example,

---

[506] Creative created by M&C Saatchi on behalf of author.

some — who were not perhaps acquainted with the source of the image — felt that it was unfairly demonising the bald white working-class actor in the photo as the racist villain of the piece. As one of the respondents from the 16-24-year group suggested: "He clearly looks like a construction worker, so are they saying that the working class are the ones with an attitude and being dicks?" Moreover, some distrusted the motives of the female messengers within the meme or voiced pessimism around freedom of speech in response to the meme' statement, with one 35-45-year-old group member suggesting that "You're not allowed to speak just yet but here you go, now you can speak but you've got to do it in a way that we'll allow you to do it." It showed that attacking the far-right was largely fruitless.

Figure 49: Screenshot of Original Content: 'EDL March' Meme[507]

3. Far-Right Counter Narratives that Worked Not So Well

A final tranche of results relating to counter narrative content presented to the target audience were those that failed to engage — and at times lead to anger, frustration and active counter-arguing by the target audience — when presented during the focus group phase of testing. These tended to be memes or videos where the messages

---

[507] Creative created by M&C Saatchi on behalf of author.

were too nuanced or clever for the audience to grasp them in an immediate fashion, content that was deemed to attack the far-right, content whose factual veracity was ambiguous or where—as we have seen from the review of the above content—raised one ethnicity above another. Such content often led to fairly extreme levels of psychological reactance and a 'triggering' effect that the project leads were keen to learn from going forward.

TESTING THE WORDS VS. DEEDS NEXUS 227

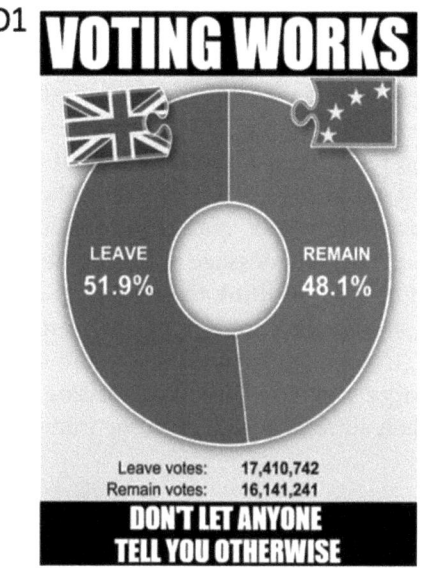

Figure 50: Screenshot of Original Content: Memes on the topics of LGBT equality, Gender equality and the importance of voting in the UK[508]

The first and least problematic section of counter narrative content that failed to resonate were memes in relation to LGBT equality, gender equality and the importance of voting (see Figure 49 above). This was both because audience members found it hard to identify the figures in some of the memes (i.e., the messenger) or simply because they thought that the issues raised by them had been settled in the past and were therefore not relevant for them today. For example, when it came to the memes featuring Alan Turing and Grayson Perry, younger audiences suggested that they had no problem with LGBT rights or equality for women, and believed these are outdated issues for previous generations. Moreover, and for the older group, while there were varying degrees of homophobia on display (for example, being homosexual is "OK" as long as it "isn't

---

[508] Creative created by M&C Saatchi on behalf of author.

in your face"), memes generally created discussion about how it was much worse back then and how far we have come (i.e., this post-feminist and post-racist ideation evident in response to other forms of creative stimulus presented to the target audience). Again, many failed to grasp the relevance of the female equality messages in the two C3 and C4 memes and psychological reactance even extended as far as lambasting the C3 as "xenophobic". Finally, and when it came to voting rights, many respondents claimed that it lacked relevance or that the message of the meme flew straight over their head, causing some to think that it was questioning whether voting mattered at all rather reinforcing the importance of voting in the first place. In such an instance, it was thought that such content should be largely avoided in online testing due to its lack of traction and perceived relevance within the intended audience.

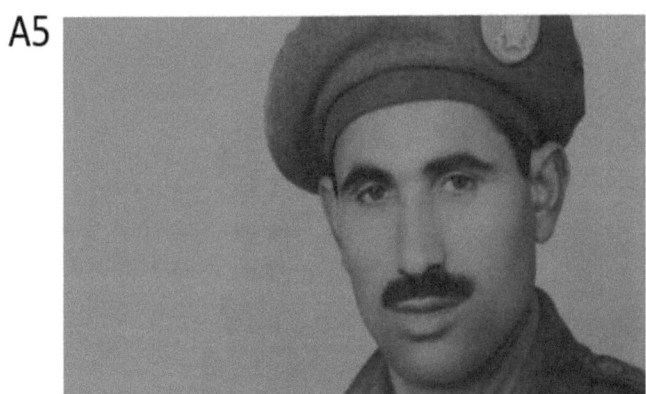

Figure 51: Screenshot of Armed Forces Muslim Association 'Our Heroes: Ali Haidar' Video[509]

The second least problematic section of counter narrative content that failed to resonate were (again) memes and videos that actively raised the status of minorities above the white British in-group in a particularly targeted way. One that received acute attention was the story of a Muslim combatant who had won the Victoria Cross for

---

[509] *Armed Forces Muslim Association*, 'Our Heroes: Ali Haidar' Video, *Facebook*, online at: https://www.facebook.com/1700941716805821/videos/2305489536351033.

bravery in the first World War (see Figure 50 above). Many respondents failed to grasp the peculiarity of the combatant's bravery ("They picked anyone, didn't they ... I can't imagine them saying, 'You're Muslim, you're spared in the war'.") (Mixed sex group, 16-24 years, North) and tied it to themes of white victimhood and marginalisation, saying that: "I think if it was called the 'White British Army' and it showed only white people then everyone would have something to say about that ... if there was a 'Christian Army' and it was just Christians, I think that would be deemed as offensive now." (Mixed sex group, 16-24 years, North)

Moreover, and in another set of pertinent examples whereby ethnic minority health workers and corner shop owners (see Figure 51, A1 and A2 below) were attributed to patriotic acts during the COVID-19 pandemic, most of the audience didn't see the peculiarity of the act or reacted negatively to lifted up one race or religion over the other using reverse forms of racism to counter-argue the point made in the message. For example, in the case of the shop owners (Figure 51, A2), one respondent from the all-male focus group suggested that: "It goes back to the [Coca Cola] football advert, doesn't it? They could do the same here, just put a montage of different shop owners, not just one that's Asian." Moreover, in another response reverse racism was clear — suggesting that the meme "perpetuates stereotypes; this might be saying, 'We do this for you, so don't be racist', or whatever sort of message it's getting across, but I think already it's racist having two Asian people standing outside a corner shop." (Mixed sex group, 16-24 years, North)

Figure 52: Screenshots of Original Content: 'Covid-19 Boris Johnson & Corner shop' Memes[510]

Again, a third problematic section of counter narrative content that failed to resonate were memes and videos that actively targeted the far-right as part of their contents (see Figure 52, B5, E3 and E4 below). Whilst a few thought that the act of a far-right protestor urinating on a memorial to a police officer killed in a terror attack was a disgusting, most people made excuses for the protestor (e.g., too

---

[510] Creative created by M&C Saatchi on behalf of author.

drunk, other races do this too etc.) and disliked the perceived demonisation of the far-right—either identifying with their views or suggesting that it was 'one bad apple' that wasn't representative of the whole movement. As one respondent from the all-male group suggested: "[the meme] suggests that everyone that's in the far-right is a filthy animal like that and in exactly the same way as everyone thinks all blacks that lives in South London are drug dealers, it couldn't be further from the truth." (Male group 16-65 years) On a similar theme, a meme criticising Tommy Robinson also provoked defensive responses, with respondents suggesting that Robinson had been victimised and deserved money for expressing views that others were scared to voice. As one member of the mixed 46+ group stated: "He tells you about things you don't hear about, he talks about all the kids that get trafficked in the north, he does do a little bit of work behind the scenes you know." Added to this there were those whose support moved into disputing the factual veracity of the message of the meme; another problematic area when it came to presenting facts in front of such a distrustful audience. As one of the members of the mixed 16–24-year-old group suggested: "I think they're trying to get something back on him because I wouldn't say he's in the media, he's not on TV, the only way you're going to find him is on You Tube because all the news outlets won't let him onto their channels because they know he's going to say things that people don't like and will disagree with."

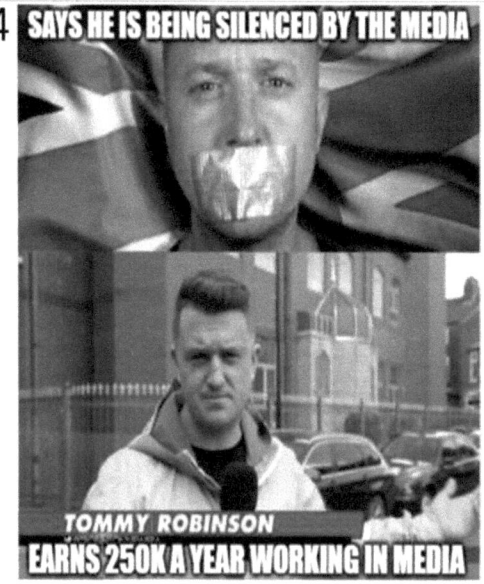

Figure 53: Screenshots of Original Content: 'Far-Right Protestor' & 'Tommy Robinson' Memes[511]

Moving toward the end of content that largely failed to land with the target audience, others that failed to dial down hostility to migrants, Islam and multiculturalism were memes designed to foster empathy for asylum seekers (Figure 53, F1 and F2 below), adverts that highlighted issues of racial inequality raised by Black Lives Matters (Figure 53, B6 below) or other memes that showed the cultural diversity of those who ran the UK (Figure 53, B2, B3 & B4 below). In terms of the first set of memes, there were no counter narratives that changed the mind of the target audience of the issue. All memes presented seemed to dial up their anger towards asylum seekers, questioning why they haven't taken asylum in other countries and actively questioning their motives for coming to the UK. Female respondents (all age groups) were particularly negative regarding refugees and pictures featuring pregnant women/children in the executions worked to exacerbate their 'money grabbing

---

[511] Creative created by M&C Saatchi on behalf of author.

tendencies' beliefs, rather than making them empathize with the plight of the individual in question. In one comment that was particularly representative of views expressed, one female respondent typified the anger felt by other respondents — stating:

> "What really annoys me is the people coming in on the little dinghies from France and the French annoy me for letting them get in the dingy in the first place and then they get to this end, they're half-way through, struggling ... I was watching it on GMTV ... they get half-way and we have to pick them up! We're picking them up, they've not got face masks on! Who's testing them? We don't know! What's happening when they get to the other end? I don't know! What are they bringing into the country? No idea! It's just diabolical, for one, it's unsafe."

F1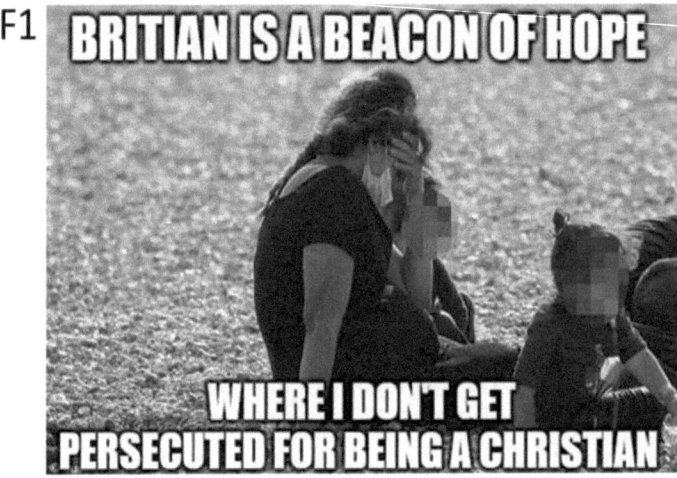

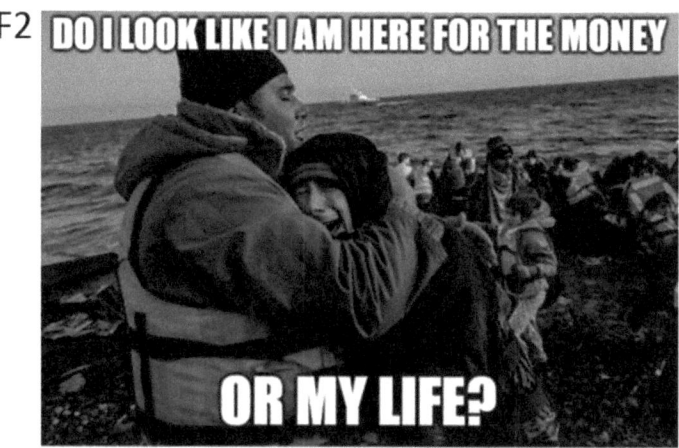

Figure 54: Screenshots of Original Content: 'Channel Migrants' Memes[512]

Turning to a meme showing the cultural diversity of the UK cabinet (Figure 54, B2 & B3 below), again many respondents found that the message was far too coded to grasp and did not trust the messengers that were portraying the message to protect a form of culture that they thought was under threat. As one respondent from the 16-24-year-old mixed group suggested: "I don't really understand it but I think it's sarcastic ... are these people against Islam? ... I don't know ... well, not against it but they're more towards not ... oh, I don't get it" whilst another respondent from the 25-34-year-group suggested: "It makes me feel under threat; why are they telling me it's not? I think it's because it's politicians and politics, they have ulterior motives." A similar meme about two successful white pop artists also drew perplexed comments (and even some ire) from the target audience (B4 below). Many didn't understand the message and thought that it was trying to communicate that you can do anything in Britain today if you 'strive and achieve'. Many from the younger group however took it be poking fun at white British ethnicities, with one of the respondents in the 16-24-year-old group

---

[512] Creative created by M&C Saatchi on behalf of author.

suggesting that: "I think they're taking the mick out of white culture, just looking at them, they're saying, 'These two people are doing really well, you've got nothing to worry about, look at the state of them'! I don't know."

B2

B3

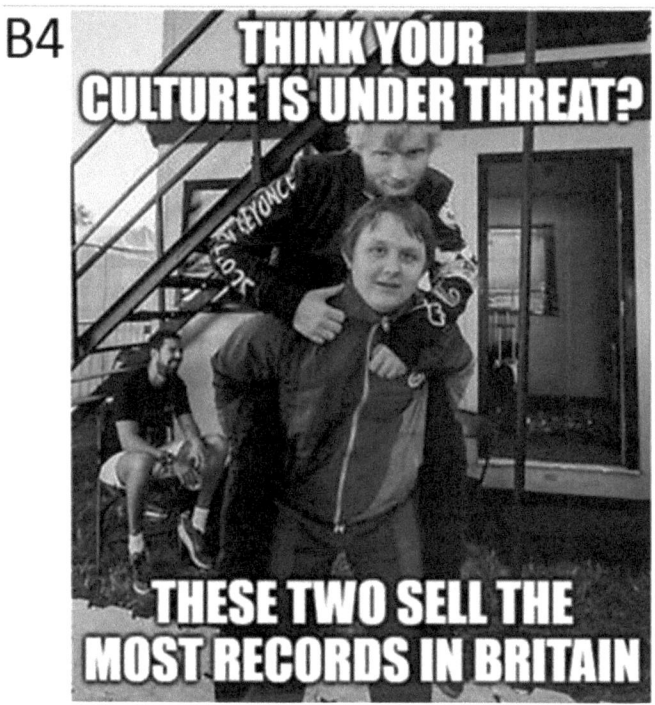

Figure 55: Screenshots of Original Content: 'UK Cabinet' & 'Sheerin-Capaldi' Memes

One final piece of content in this most problematic of content that failed was an advert shown highlighting issues related to the Black Lives Matters movement, showing members of the ITV Britain's Got Talent group taking the knee (Figure 55, B6 below). Again, whilst a significant number had not seen the performance, the majority were hostile to the message that the advert was trying to convey, stating that it was an American issue being featured on British talent show, that it was being political in a cultural space and that it was one agenda too far for the audience. As one of the mixed 46+ group adroitly summarised: "I'd just scroll right past this to be honest, it just winds me up" and another from the all-male group posited: "It wasn't entertainment, it was a political view aired on Britain's got Talent, for a crime that happened in America, that affected nobody here." There was also a sense that they saw the whole BLM actions as a revolution in race relations rather than an evolution –

presenting a threat to British white culture—and therefore it was decided to avoid BLM in beta testing due to the inflammatory nature of the topic for the target audience.

B6

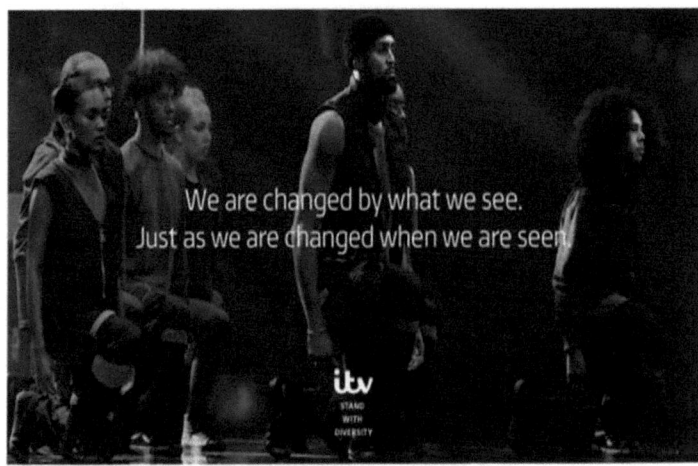

Figure 56: ITV 'We are Changed by What We See' Britain's Got Talent Advert (featuring Diversity)[513]

IV. Focus Group-Tested Responses to 'Everybody Makes Britain Great' Page

Turning to the final set of findings from the focus groups, the last piece of content shown to the target audience outside of the counter narrative content were initial mockups of the 'Everybody Makes Britain Great' seed page (see Figure 56 below). The seed page itself draw a largely positive response from the target audience, due to use of Union Jack (although a few preferred the St George's) and Britain being great. However, they are turned off once they saw the word 'multiculturalism'. This was subsequently changed and it was noted that other 'trigger words' (e.g., BLM, racism and far-right) should be avoided in the online testing of the content.

---

[513] *ITV*, "We are changed by what we see. Just as we are changed when we are seen' Advert, September 2020, online at: h. ttps://twitter.com/itv/status/1307212849643753472

TESTING THE WORDS VS. DEEDS NEXUS 239

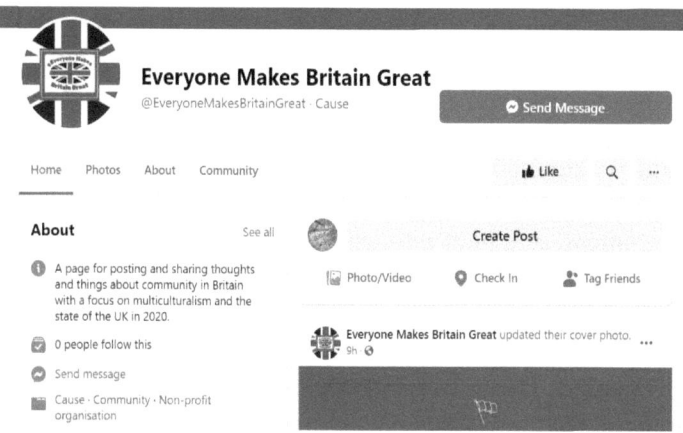

Figure 57: Mockup of 'Everybody Makes Britain Great' Seed Page[514]

Conclusions from Focus Group Testing

To conclude, findings from the initial focus group research were highly useful in the creation of final content for the online section of testing and additionally helped identify the behaviour of the target audience on social media and different segments within the audience (see second methodology section below). Performing such a qualitative deep dive into the thoughts of the target audience had the added benefit of finding what worked and didn't work in a controlled environment and gave the project members a chance to revise content before going online. Most importantly, it was found through the focus groups that messages of unity that foster a sense of common human values, togetherness and kindness worked best with the target audience. In particular, it was learnt that content with a rousing, emotive or 'feel good' factor (such as the Coca Cola advert and Open Your Eyes to Hate video) were preferred over more cerebral content (such as the UK Cabinet or voting memes) that tended to go over the heads of certain sections of the audience. Moreover, if key points of content were introduced, they needed to

---

[514] Extracted from: *'Everybody Makes Britain Great' Seed Page, Facebook,* online at: https://www.facebook.com/EveryoneMakesBritainGreat.

be straightforward and present factual content that were watertight. It was also found that narratives that attacked the far-right, singled out or reified a single ethnicity and were too 'political' failed to engage the audience—and lead to negative reactance. Finally, and to summarise again, some content worked better on some audience members (e.g., females particularly adverse to aggressive content/pregnant refugee, corner shop heroes/Ghurkhas worked better with Northern/older respondents, and historical content didn't run well with younger audience) rather than others but the BLM, refugee, LGBT & voting memes and adverts failed across the board. These lessons were then gathered and incorporated into a revised set of contents presented below.

Phase 2: Online Survey & Facebook Ads Testing of Far-Right Counter Narrative Content

I. Introduction

After the initial focus group stage had concluded, it was apparent what counter narrative messages, messengers and formats worked well with those identified at the tipping point of joining the far-right in the UK. In addition to this, the Outsiders—in conjunction with M&C Saatchi—were able to divide and precisely map the different sections of the larger audience to whom the online beta tested material could be presented (see textbox in section below). New counter narrative material and copy was developed to present to a newly-refined set of target audiences and pre- and post-test surveys were devised in order to measure the extent of attitudinal shift among the online audience. Presented below is the nature of the counter narrative content and online testing methodology used, its success among far-right sympathetic audiences when using Facebook ads tool, and—most importantly—the findings of whether or not the project was successful in dialling down hatred amongst this larger, more representative section of far-right sympathetic individuals.

II. Online-Tested Far-Right Counter Narrative Content

Based on what had performed well in the focus groups, the memes and video used were recast to convey positive aspects (pride, togetherness, kindness) of ethnic and religious diversity related to the themes of kindness, the NHS, the military, football, freedom of speech and other shared passions. These intentionally showed multiple messengers of different religious and racial backgrounds without one particular group being reified above the other and on the most part constituted alternative narrative content — showing how ethnic and religious diversity connected to the campaigns core theme that 'Everybody Makes Britain Great'. Different combinations of in-meme text and advertising copy with different tones developed (short, long, celebratory and commiseratory) in order to see which combinations cut through the most. Below is a copy of each version of content selected for online testing for each theme:

Table 3: Online Tested Far-Right Counter Narrative Content[515]

Advert Name	Creative	Copy
Kindness 1	IT TAKES KINDNESS TO CREATE COMMUNITY	A lot of us have experienced the kindness of strangers the past year, tell us your favourite moment?
Kindness 2	KINDNESS MAKES COMMUNITIES	Kindness makes communities strong. Spread some positivity, share your experiences below 👇👇👇

---

[515] All images created for the author by M&C Saatchi.

Kindness 3	IT'S KINDNESS / THAT CREATES COMMUNITIES	Mother Teresa once said: "I alone cannot change the world, but I can cast a stone across the waters to create many ripples." How can the kindness of people from different backgrounds help build stronger communities? 🖤🤍🖤
NHS 1	NH-YESSS	Diversity makes the NHS what it is, tell us a story about how they helped you 🖤🖤🖤
NHS 2	LADIES AND GENTLEMAN / THE NH-YESS	What makes you proud of the people in our NHS? Share below 📱🎉👤👤👤🎉📱
NHS 3	NH-YESS / EVERYONE MAKES IT THE BEST	Tell us your stories of the diverse staff that have treated you in our fantastic hospitals? 🩺🩺🩺🩺🩺
NHS 4	NHYES / EVERYONE MAKES IT THE BEST	Say it with me NHY-ESS, what do you love about it? 🖤🖤🖤

NHS 5	THE HEROS OF THE / NHYES	Tell us about the best NHS worker you've ever experienced. 👏❤️👏
NHS 6	NHYES	Let's take a moment to celebrate the workers of the NHYESS. 👏👏👏👏
Military 1	FIGHTING FOR QUEEN AND COUNTRY	They put their lives on the line, show them some love 👍❤️👍
Military 2	BRITISH THROUGH AND THROUGH / FIGHTING FOR QUEEN AND COUNTRY	Committed to their core, show these loyal and brave soldiers some love 👊❤️
Military 3	FIGHTING FOR QUEEN AND COUNTRY / WE WILL NEVER SURRENDER	Risking their lives to keep you safe, the army's made up of people from every background, celbrate their commitment below 👊👊👊👊👊

Military 4	FIGHTING FOR QUEEN AND COUNTRY	They put their lives on the line, show them some love 👎❤️👎
Military 5	BRITISH THROUGH AND THROUGH / FIGHTING FOR QUEEN AND COUNTRY	Committed to their core, show these loyal and brave soldiers some love 👊❤️
Military 6	FIGHTING FOR QUEEN AND COUNTRY / WE WILL NEVER SURRENDER	Risking their lives to keep you safe, the army's made up of people from every background, celebrate their commitment below 👊👊👊👊👊
Football 1	WE ALL LOVE IT / INGERLANNND!	When it comes to football it's a passion everyone from every background shares, let us know about your favorite story celebrating England winning 🏆🏆🏆

Football 2	INGERLANNND!	England winning the football unites us like nothing else, bringing people from every background together to celebrate as one, tell us why you think that is 👎👎👎
Football 3	INGERLANNND!	The nervous anticipation waiting for a penalty to be taken, screaming at the top of your lungs, hugging the stranger next to you (pre-covid) and singing three lions at the top of your voice. We all share passions that show us we are actually really similar. Tell us about your stories of unlikely friendships below. 👊👊👊👊👊
Football 4	WE ALL FELT IT	Some footballing moments become etched in our memory. These shared experiences link us together and show our common humanity. Tell about how you've felt whilst

			watching the "beautiful game"? 👇👇👇
Football 5	WE ALL LOVE THE SAME STUFF / WE ALL FELT IT		What experiences have made you change your mind about people of different backgrounds? 👇👇👇
Football 6	WE ALL LOVE IT / INGERLANNND!		When it comes to football it's a passion everyone from every background share, let us know about your favorite story celebrating England winning 🏆🏆🏆
Football 7	INGERLANNND!		England winning the football unites us like nothing else, bringing people from every background together to celebrate as one, tell us why you think that is 👇👇👇
Football 8	WE ALL LOVE IT		The nervous anticipation waiting for a penalty to be taken, screaming at the top of your lungs, hugging the stranger next to you (pre-covid) and

		singing three lions at the top of your voice. We all share passions that show us we are actually really similar. Tell us about when your stories of unlikely friendships below. 🎭🎭🎭🎭🎭
Football 9	WE ALL FELT IT	Some footballing moments become etched in our memory. These shared experiences link us together and show our common humanity. Tell about how you've felt whilst watching the "beautiful game"? 👎👎👎
Football 10	WE ALL LOVE THE SAME STUFF / WE ALL FELT IT	What experiences have made you change your mind about people of different backgrounds? 👎👎👎

Freedom of Speech 1	WE'RE ALL FOR FREEDOM OF SPEECH ... BUT...	Everyone has the right to freedom of speech but it's not an excuse to be unkind, nasty and racist. How do we stop people being racist to the players of what is supposed to be the beautiful game? 😊❓😊
Freedom of Speech 2	WE'RE ALL FOR FREEDOM OF SPEECH ... BUT...	Everyone has the right to freedom of speech but it's not an excuse to be unkind, nasty and racist. How do we stop people being racist to the players of what is supposed to be the beautiful game? 😊❓😊
Shared Passions		Boxing takes discipline and determination, with the skill and dedication of the boxing coach featured in the video being the key to a boxer's success. How boxing coaches like him help bring the community together and make them stronger? 👊❤️🥊

It was also decided that the flow of rollout for the materials would go from 'softer' kindness content that affirmed themes close to the audience's own value system to 'harder' more challenging freedom of speech content that made the audience reflect on ethnic and religious diversity in a way that they might not have encountered before. This again related back to the more iterative nature of the project and provided the hope that this would reduce the 'backfire effect' of later content if it was couched in this way. All audience members also received a chance to respond to the pre-test survey — with the most responsive segments to the Shared Passions video being re-targeted with the post-test survey to save on ad credits and boost responses.

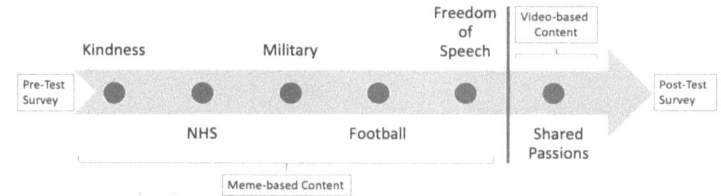

Figure 58: Flow Diagram of Online Far-Right Counter Narrative Rollout

Facebook Ads were used in order to precisely target individuals within each subset of the total audience. Two and four day exposures were first experimented which was then dropped for longer three to six and then five to ten day exposures in order to ensure attitudinal shift and for the platform to learn how to optimise content for the audience in the best way possible.[516] The decision for whether content appeared for a single or double period (i.e., five or ten days) was

---

[516] Such a shift of 5-to-10-day-intervals is also borne out by counter-speech research — with an internal Facebook study on gay marriage attitudinal shift showing that exposures of 2–3 pieces of content per day over a 5–7day period were optimal. See: Erin Saltman, Farshad Kooti & Karly Vockery (2021) New Models for Deploying Counterspeech: Measuring Behavioral Change and Sentiment Analysis, Studies in Conflict & Terrorism, DOI: 10.1080/1057610X.2021.1888404. P.9-10.

weighed against whether the subject was a priority interest for the recipient audience, such that ad credits were used efficiently and that the audience were exposed only to meaningful content tailored to them.[517] Advertising campaigns with an Awareness objective for each theme (e.g., Kindness, NHS, Military, Football, Freedom of Speech and Shared Passions) were run in parallel with a complimentary campaign during the same time period with an Engagement objective, and ad credits were apportioned according to duration and the size of each audience. The reason for running parallel campaigns was to boost attention and engagement scores over the relatively short period content would be served to them, a lesson learnt over three iterations during the six-month period of online testing. Below is a breakdown of the audiences used for the online testing:

> Online Audience Overview
>
> The audiences' profiles listed below were identified from the learnings of the focus groups:
>
> 1. **Working Class Warrior:** Male and female, 18+, North of England and Midlands. Interests match working class, crime prevention, community issues, racial integration, social integration, Sun news, Daily Mail. Key campaign sub-themes identified for the audience included **Kindness** and the **NHS**. (Audience Size: 1,100,000)
> 2. **Youthful Challengers:** Male and female, 16-35, England. Interests match remembrance poppy, British Armed Forces, criminal justice, law enforcement, Remembrance Day, continuing education. Key campaign sub-themes for the audience identified included the **NHS** and **Military**. (Audience Size: 58,000)
> 3. **Embittered Tony:** Male, 35+, North of England and Midlands. Interests match men's humour, social change, political freedom, Piers Morgan. Key campaign sub-themes identified for the audience included **Football** and **Freedom of Speech**. (Audience Size: 51,000)
> 4. **Race Warrior:** Male and female, 35+, England. Interests match Sean Hannity, Bill O'Reilly, Rush Limbaugh. Key campaign sub-

---

[517] An exception was made here for the final post-test survey which went out for ten days and was targeted based on views of the final Shared Passions video.

> themes identified for the audience included: **Kindness** and the **NHS**. (Audience Size: 540,000)
> 5. **Old Timers:** Male, 45+, England. Interests match British royal family, British armed forces, Dad's army. Key campaign sub-themes identified for the audience included: **Kindness** and **Military**. (Audience Size: 180,000)
> 6. **Conspiracy Joe:** Male, 45+, England. Interests match Area 51, freedom of speech. Key campaign sub-themes identified for the audience included: **Military**. (Audience Size: 330,000)
> 7. **Conspiracy Jane:** Female, 16-45, England. Interests match Area 51, child protection, parenting, conspiracy fiction. Key campaign sub-themes identified for the audience included: **Kindness** and the **NHS**. (Audience Size: 130,000)
> 8. **Lefty John:** Male, 16+, England. Interest match University, Master's degree. Key campaign sub-themes identified for the audience included: **Kindness**, the **NHS** & **Freedom of Speech**. (Audience Size: 40,000)
> 9. **Citizen John:** Male, 45+, South of England. Interests match political satire, political movement. Key campaign sub-themes were excluded for this audience as it wasn't considered a priority. (Audience Size: 170,000)
>
> N.B. Working Class Warriors & Race Warriors are the largest (therefore prime) testing audiences. For the purposes of retargeting, Conspiracy Joe/Jane could be combined.

Findings

Facebook Ads Testing: Measuring Levels of Engagement with Far-Right Counter Narrative Content

Main Finding 1: Memes that related to the Military and Kindness received the highest number of engagements, comments, impressions and reactions. Consequently, they also saw the highest spend.

The below table shows the breakdown of reactions to each of the different sub-themes in total across all audiences. As we can glean from below, the Kindness and Military content received the highest number of engagements, comments, impressions and reactions. Consequently, they also saw the highest spend.

Table 4: Summative Cost, Reach and Engagement Metrics from Facebook Ads Testing[518]

ALL AUDIENCES	REACH			ENGAGEMENT						
	Spend	Impressions	Reactions	Comments	Shares	Saves	Engagements	Engagement Rate	Cost per Engagement
Total	US$ 28,513.51	6,277,434	35,473	3,287	2,320	184	41,264	0.66%	US$ 0.69
Pre-test Survey	US$ 746.60	83,401	403	829	82	10	4,166	5.00%	US$ 0.18
Kindness	US$ 5,371.30	1,496,974	7,046	161	433	32	33,071	2.21%	US$ 0.16
NHS	US$ 5,100.01	1,188,638	876	334	69	5	7,453	0.63%	US$ 0.68
Military	US$ 6,483.42	1,417,819	20,924	694	1,452	32	37,407	2.64%	US$ 0.17
Football	US$ 5,300.35	1,220,379	4,172	515	107	76	23,439	1.92%	US$ 0.23
Freedom of Speech	US$ 739.34	231,372	504	467	40	5	17,223	7.44%	US$ 0.04
Shared Passions	US$ 3,426.27	549,156	1,487	140	129	23	265,560	48.36%	US$ 0.01
Post-test Survey	US$ 1,346.22	89,695	61	147	8	1	419	0.47%	US$ 3.21

[518] Data extracted from Facebook Ads manager at time of writing.

Such a result is interesting for several reasons: the first is that—whilst Kindness was weighted double in several of the largest audiences, Military memes were not. In fact, the NHS was the common denominator between all audiences. This might have to do with the larger shares related to this content. In fact, the Military memes were almost three times as likely to be shared when compared to the Kindness material.

Main finding 2: Statistically and anecdotally, it was noted during live testing that the video (Shared Passions) received the most engagements but also unanimously positive and reflective reactions and comments.

Having completed the rollout of memes (that tended to receive a mixed reaction), it was immediately noticeable the size and unanimous positivity associated with the rollout of the Shared Passions video. As you can see from the above summative table and below screenshots, the post was liked in larger volume and received both positive and reflective comments from all audience members. This might be due to the longer form nature of the video—getting individuals to reflect on Britishness and what it means to be Britishness—versus a meme that often evokes a more immediate (and sometimes visceral) reaction. In any case, the overall engagement score for the video speaks for itself (see Table 7 above)—with nearly five times the level of engagement versus static content.

Figure 59: Race Warrior-Shared Passions 1 (Video Optimisation)[519]

---

[519] Post can be viewed here: https://www.facebook.com/111849444007019/posts/345506263974668

Main Finding 3: Majority of viewers (420,346) watched at least 25% of the Shared Passions video before trailing off.

3s views	25% Views	50% Views	75% Views	100% Views
288,043	132,303	21,830	15,783	6,480

Table 5: Views of Shared Passion Videos (Segmented by View Rate)[520]

One of the other encouraging findings was that the majority of viewers watched at least 25% of the Shared Passions video before stopping it completely. This is quite a feat (considering the length of the video (1 minute 9 seconds) versus the recommended industry standard (15 seconds)).[521] It also speaks volumes of the engaging content created by Amjid Khazir at Media Cultured who gets a special mention for allowing us to use an edit of his 'Combinations' video that follows a Muslim boxing coach, Imran Naem, and his love for sport and helping his community.

Main Finding 4: Interestingly, football had the most saves and scored highly in terms of impressions but didn't cut through (i.e., low reactions/engagements). (This could be explained by the sheer quantity of ads.)

---

[520] Data extracted from Facebook Ads Manager at time of writing.
[521] Chen, J. 'Exploring video length best practices for social media', *Sprout Social*, 8 December 2020, online at: https://sproutsocial.com/insights/video-length-best-practices/.

Campaign Name	Spend	Impressions	Reactions	Comments	Shares	Saves	Engagements	Engagement Rate	Cost per Engagement
Football	US$ 5,300.35	1,220,379	4,172	515	107	76	23,439	1.92%	US$ 0.23

Table 6: Summative Table of Cost, Reach and Engagement Metrics for Football Facebook Ads[522]

---

[522] Data extracted from Facebook Ads Manager at time of writing.

Interestingly, the football sub-theme had the most saves and scored highly in terms of impressions but did not cut through when it came to other engagement metrics (e.g., reactions and engagements). This high number of impressions and saves might be accounted for by the sheer quantity of adverts (e.g., ten including all variations) and the timeliness of the material (coming off of a relatively successful European Championship for England's football team). As unpacked in the tables below, only three of the ten adverts (Football 1, 5 & 9) accounted for the lion share of engagement:

258 MOVING BEYOND ISLAMIST EXTREMISM

Football	REACH						ENGAGEMENT			
	Spend	Impressions	Reactions	Comments	Shares	Saves	Engagements	Engagement Rate	Cost per Engagement
Total	US$ 6,453.78	943,828	3,016	420	103	24	20,693	2.19%	US$ 0.31
Football 1	US$ 1,419.82	271,013	879	96	36	9	8,659	3.20%	US$ 0.16
Football 2	US$ 249.21	53,811	427	56	15	2	791	1.47%	US$ 0.32
Football 3	US$ 273.42	70,885	184	6	1	0	686	0.97%	US$ 0.40
Football 4	US$ 506.68	173,013	103	23	2	2	1,369	0.79%	US$ 0.37
Football 5	US$ 1,248.22	207,773	945	157	39	8	7,876	3.79%	US$ 0.16
Football 6	US$ 301.10	84,107	279	38	5	2	741	0.88%	US$ 0.41
Football 7	US$ 2,455.33	83,226	199	44	5	1	571	0.69%	US$ 4.30
Football 8	US$ 3,068.41	49,414	149	6	5	0	462	0.93%	US$ 6.64
Football 9	US$ 444.91	137,661	104	20	2	2	824	0.60%	US$ 0.54
Football 10	US$ 386.51	83,996	903	69	12	8	1,460	1.74%	US$ 0.26

Table 7: Breakdown of Cost, Reach and Engagement Metrics for Football Facebook Ads[523]

523 Data extracted from Facebook Ads Manager at time of writing.

Main Finding 5: High Ranking content that tended to perform better (i.e., scoring an engagement rate of above 2%) had multiple messengers of different ethnicities, had a positive unity message and was presented in a video format.

Of all the content, the most highest-ranking memes and videos—in terms of engagement (i.e., scoring an engagement rate of above 2%)[524]—tended to be ones that had a mixture of messengers of different races and promoted messages of unity and group solidarity. For example, Football 1 and 5 both had multiple messengers and either had entreaties to common shared experiences or value statements in the meme text or copy alongside. Moreover, Military 1 and 2 again had a variety of ethnicities as the messenger and positive text promoting resonant issues with the target audience (i.e., the Royal Family and the Military). This chimed with findings from focus group testing that told us that this audience didn't like content that raised up a particular audience and that needed to include a message of unity in order for it to be impactful. Also, and on the subject of format (as noted above), video content surpassed the engagement rates of all meme-based content (by over twenty times that of static content)—though the shallowness of views as part of that metric does qualify this somewhat (i.e., views are counted for those who have only seen a video for 3 seconds).

---

[524] Even in absolute terms, this is a relatively good threshold in any circumstance for promotional content on Facebook. The all-industry median benchmark for Facebook content is 0.09%. See: Chen, J. (3 February 2021) '36 Essential social media marketing statistics to know for 2021', Sprout Social, online at: https://sproutsocial.com/insights/social-media-statistics/.

260   MOVING BEYOND ISLAMIST EXTREMISM

ALL AUDIENCES	REACH					ENGAGEMENT			
	Spend US$	Impresions	Reactions	Comments	Shares	Saves	Engagements	Engagement Rate	Cost per Engagement
Kindness 1	US$	544,552	2,589	13	75	12	24,469	4.49%	US$ 0.10
Military 1	US$ 1,188.47	223,841	8,014	331	733	6	5,474	2.45 %	US$ 0.22
Military 2	US$ 1,977.82	499,185	4,031	132	258	10	12,499	2.50%	US$ 0.16
Football 1	US$ 1,419.82	271,013	879	96	36	9	8,659	3.20%	US$ 0.16
Football 5	US$ 1,248.22	207,773	945	157	39	8	7,876	3.79%	US$ 0.16
Freedom of Speech 1	US$ 227.14	70,393	133	84	6	1	2,777	3.94%	US$ 0.08
Freedom of Speech 2	US$443.20	160,979	371	382	34	4	14,495	9.00%	US$ 0.03
Shared Passions 1	US$3,616.00	561,386	1,527	103	132	25	289,753	51.61%	US$ 0.01

Table 8:   Highest-Ranking Meme & Video Content Across All Themes[525]

---

[525] Data extracted from Facebook Ads Manager at time of writing.

Main Finding 6: Affirmational content tended to perform better on reach metrics, whereas challenging content tended to perform better on engagement.

Of all the content, affirmational content (i.e., content presented around the themes of Kindness, the NHS, Military, and Football) tended to perform alright in terms of engagement metrics (i.e., some reach over the 2% threshold for what could be considered high-ranking content) but tended to do better when it came to overall reach (out-performing such content by six or seven times when compared with more confrontational content (e.g., Freedom of Speech and Shared Passions content)). This was probably explained by the sheer volume of content (both NHS, Football and Military had several times the number of adverts present in Freedom of Speech and Shared Passions, for example), but also due to its timeline-friendly nature (i.e., evoking positive uniting and non-threatening themes that could then be shared with friends, relatives and colleagues). More challenging content on the other hand tended to see relatively higher levels of engagement — in terms of comments and reactions per advert — than the more affirmational content. This is not surprising given the wedge nature of the issues presented and suggests that such content should be equally balanced with affirmational alternative narratives.

Main Finding 7: Working Class Warrior, Race Warrior and Conspiracist audiences were the largest and most engaged out of all nine audiences. They tended to react, share and comment more than any other audience.

Of all the audiences, when it came to the online testing, Working Class Warrior, Race Warrior and Conspiracist audiences were the largest and most engaged out of all nine audiences. They tended to react, share and comment more than any other audience, and engage in debates in a more sustained and adversarial way. This might be accounted for by their sheer sizes (1.1 million, 540,000, 180,000 and 130,000 respectively) but also their demographics — with a broad base of users, grievances and issue orientations. In particular, the Freedom of Speech adverts seemed to create the highest engagement rates among these audiences—unsurprising given the politicised nature of this topic in the UK at the time of writing.

	REACH						ENGAGEMENT			
Working Class Warriors	Spend	Impressions	Reactions	Comments	Shares	Saves	Engagements	Engagement Rate	Cost per Engagement
Total	US$ 11,559.30	2,852,346	14,662	1,134	938	69	16,803	0.59%	US$ 0.69
Pre-test Survey	US$ 268.78	30965	148	299	31	7	1510	4.88%	US$ 0.18
Kindness	US$ 2,308.00	699,141	2,207	28	99	12	18,164	2.60%	US$ 0.13
NHS	US$ 2,308.00	556,054	312	107	23	2	3,795	0.68%	US$ 0.61
Military	US$ 2,308.00	688,627	9,574	323	703	17	19,895	2.89%	US$ 0.12
Football	US$ 2,308.00	574,665	1,748	108	34	15	11,154	1.94%	US$ 0.21
Freedom of Speech	US$ 226.50	92,445	160	130	4	2	7,800	8.44%	US$ 0.03
Shared Passions	US$ 1,154.00	196,436	462	31	38	13	95,257	48.49%	US$ 0.01
Post-test Survey (3 sec & 50% views)	678.02	14013	51	108	6	1	128	0.91%	US$ 5.30

Table 9: Levels of Reach and Engagement among Working Class Warriors[526]

Race Warriors	REACH						ENGAGEMENT		
	Spend	Impressions	Reactions	Comments	Shares	Saves	Engagements	Engagement Rate	Cost per Engagement
Total	US$ 6,454.02	1,415,549	9,898	1,041	709	68	11,716	0.83%	US$ 0.55
Pre-test Survey	US$ 184.02	20,436	123	245	22	2	1150	5.63%	US$ 0.16
Kindness	US$ 1,311.30	378,747	2,188	59	138	3	6,618	1.75%	US$ 0.20
NHS	US$ 1,274.00	270,240	254	128	21	1	1,711	0.63%	US$ 0.74
Military	US$ 636.00	199,789	5,317	210	439	3	8,344	4.18%	US$ 0.08
Football	US$ 1,638.41	304,643	1,363	239	34	49	7,550	2.48%	US$ 0.22
Freedom of Speech	US$ 106.09	28,041	90	85	6	2	2,359	8.41%	US$0.04
Shared Passions	US$ 636.00	137,971	553	36	47	8	66,462	48.17%	US$ 0.01
Post-test Survey (3 sec & 50% views)	668.2	75682	10	39	2	-	291	0.38%	US$ 2.30

Table 10: Levels of Reach and Engagement among Race Warriors[527]

[527] Data extracted from Facebook Ads Manager at time of writing.

Conspiracy Joe	REACH						ENGAGEMENT			
	Spend	Impressions	Reactions	Comments	Shares	Saves	Engagements	Engagement Rate	Cost per Engagement
Total	US$ 2,937.64	637,204	3,755	528	328	8	4,619	0.72%	US$ 0.64
Pre-test Survey	US$ 111.66	12066	78	157	21	1	715	5.93%	US$ 0.16
Kindness	US$ 444.00	103,585	1,164	39	96	-	1,855	1.79%	US$ 0.24
NHS	US$ 444.00	130,800	107	63	14	-	607	0.46%	US$ 0.73
Military	US$ 974.90	189,708	1,445	81	135	3	2,628	1.39%	US$ 0.37
Football	US$ 444.00	108,765	653	100	32	3	1,914	1.76%	US$ 0.23
Freedom of Speech	US$ 75.08	17,633	72	68	8	-	1,272	7.21%	US$ 0.06
Shared Passions	US$ 444.00	74,647	236	20	22	1	41,022	54.95%	US$ 0.01

Table 11: Levels of Reach and Engagement among Conspiracy Joe[528]

---

[528] Data extracted from Facebook Ads Manager at time of writing.

Table 12: Levels of Reach and Engagement among Conspiracy Jane[529]

Conspiracy Jane	REACH						ENGAGEMENT		
	Spend	Impressions	Reactions	Comments	Shares	Saves	Engagements	Engagement Rate	Cost per Engagement
Total	US$ 1,125.69	266,644	353	31	11	2	14,690	5.51%	US$ 0.08
Pre-test Survey	US$ 27.36	3097	2	6	0	0	67	2.16%	US$ 0.41
Kindness	US$ 306.00	80,616	137	1	2	-	2,061	2.56%	US$ 0.15
NHS	US$ 306.00	62,316	22	3	-	2	452	0.73%	US$ 0.68
Military	US$ 152.00	48,207	131	3	6	-	1,354	2.81%	US$ 0.11
Football	US$ 152.00	47,512	35	-	-	-	914	1.92%	US$ 0.17
Freedom of Speech	US$ 30.33	10,530	17	18	1	-	787	7.47%	US$ 0.04
Shared Passions	US$ 152.00	14,366	9	-	2	-	9,055	63.03%	US$ 0.02

[529] Data extracted from Facebook Ads Manager at time of writing.

Pre- and Post-Test Survey: Measuring the Impact of Far-Right Counter Narratives

I. Survey Design, Rollout & Responses

Pre- and Post-Test surveys—hosted on Survey Monkey—were designed mainly to glean data from the online audiences about their attitudinal profiles but also their engagement with counter narrative material; before and after roll out. For the pre-test survey, each of the nine audiences (listed above) were served the same survey using a Facebook advert with the below image and copy. For the post-test survey, individuals were only served the survey based on their completion rates of the Shared Passion videos (i.e., 3 seconds, 50% and 75% views) and/or whether they sat within the largest and most engaged audiences (i.e., Working Class Warriors, Race Warriors and Conspiracists). In the first instance, all audiences were served the same pre-test survey over 5 days, meanwhile—in the second instance—the post-test survey over 10 days. This was in order to achieve at least 100 responses within priority audiences (i.e., Working Class Warriors, Race Warriors and Conspiracists) (See complete breakdown of survey audience and responses in Table 14 & 15 below).

Table 13: Adverts used to Promote Pre-Test & Post-Test Surveys on Facebook[530]

Advert Name	Creative	Copy
State of the Nation Questionnaire	TELL US WHAT YOU THINK ABOUT COMMUNITY INTEGRATION IN THE UK	It takes less than 60 seconds 👍

---

[530] Creative created by M&C Saatchi for author.

| Everybody Makes Britain Great Questionnaire |  | It takes less than 2 minutes |

Table 14: Pre-Test Survey Questionnaire Name, Audience and Total Responses [531]

Questionnaire Name	Audience	Responses
State of the Nation (2021) Questionnaire 1	Working Class Warrior	353
State of the Nation (2021) Questionnaire 2	Youthful Challengers	4
State of the Nation (2021) Questionnaire 3	Embittered Tony	17
State of the Nation (2021) Questionnaire 4	Race Warrior	271
State of the Nation (2021) Questionnaire 5	Old Timers	66
State of the Nation (2021) Questionnaire 6	Conspiracy Joe	172
State of the Nation (2021) Questionnaire 7	Conspiracy Jane	15
State of the Nation (2021) Questionnaire 8	Lefty John	13
State of the Nation (2021) Questionnaire 9	Citizen John	58
Total Responses		969

---

[531] Data extracted from Survey Monkey at time of writing.

Table 15: Post-Test Survey Questionnaire Name, Audience and Total Responses[532]

Questionnaire Name	Audience	Responses
Everybody Make Britain Great Questionnaire 1	3 Sec Views	876
Everybody Make Britain Great Questionnaire 2	50% Views	100
Everybody Make Britain Great Questionnaire 3	75% Views	81
Everybody Make Britain Great Questionnaire 4	Working Class Warriors – 50% Views	62
Everybody Make Britain Great Questionnaire 5	Race Warriors – 50% Views	82
Everybody Make Britain Great Questionnaire 6	Conspiracists – 50% Views	10
Everybody Make Britain Great Questionnaire 7	Working Class Warriors – 3 Sec Views	15
Everybody Make Britain Great Questionnaire 8	Race Warriors – 3 Sec Views	18
Everybody Make Britain Great Questionnaire 9	Conspiracists – 3 Sec Views	1
Total Responses		1176

The pre-test survey itself was composed of six attitudinal statements to provide an attitudinal 'baseline' for their views on Islam, migrants and multiculturalism in the UK (advertised as a 'State of the Nation 2021' questionnaire) (See Figure 61 below). These were short statements with varying levels of agreement and disagreement based on a five-point Likert scale. The post-

---

[532] Data extracted from Survey Monkey at time of writing.

test survey (advertised as a 'Everybody Makes Britain Great' Questionnaire) was largely the same — with the attitudinal statements served again in order to detect attitudinal shift, but also some summative content evaluation questions to see which counter narrative materials they found most persuasive over the course of the campaign (See Figure 61 below).

Figure 61: **Attitudinal Question Items for Pre-Test and Post-Test Surveys**[533]

*1. The following are some statements that some people believe about cultures, religions and their followers. Can you please tell us how much you agree or disagree with each statement:

	Strongly Agree	Agree	Tend to Disagree	Strongly Disagree	Don't Know
Diversity and multiculturalism are good things for the UK	O	O	O	O	O
I am generally trustful of Muslims	O	O	O	O	O
Islam is a religion of peace	O	O	O	O	O
Your faith, for example whether you're Muslim or not, should not bar you from moving to the UK	O	O	O	O	O
I think immigrants make no impact on levels of crime	O	O	O	O	O
I think immigrants improve British culture by making it more open to new ideas	O	O	O	O	O

---

[533] Screenshots taken from Survey Monkey design portal.

* 2. Which of the following images are your favourite? Please click as many images as you like.

* 3. Which of the following images represent your point of view? Please click as many images as you like.

272 MOVING BEYOND ISLAMIST EXTREMISM

* 4. Which of the following images would you share? Please click as many images as you like.

5. If you have time, please tell us a few reasons behind your choices:

Reason 1:
Reason 2:
Reason 3:

II. Survey Findings

Main finding 1: Whilst those who strongly disagree with positive statements around Islam, migrants and multiculturalism increased slightly, those who disagreed decreased and those who actually agreed or agreed strongly increased.

The main—and most significant—finding from the surveys was a daily significant and detectable attitudinal shift among the audiences relating to their attitudes on Islam, migration and multiculturalism. By combining the number of overall responses to each of the items and converting them into percentages, what we find is that those who agreed or strongly agreed with positive statements to do with Islam, migration and multiculturalism increased. Moreover, and sustaining this positive attitudinal shift, those who disagreed also decreased over the course of the campaign. What was interesting with all surveys was the secular bias among respondents—all choosing to agree that religion either didn't matter or made things worse within society as a whole.[534]

Of course, there are some caveats and negative trends present here also. Not every individual who sat the pre-test survey was exactly the same sample as those who sat the post-test survey but importantly, they were of the same demographic and attitudinal makeup, which makes for a good proxy. Moreover, those who strongly disagreed with the positive statements did creep up slightly and—importantly—remained the modal category of responses. This might be explained by the changing composition of the audience and the further work needed to be done with this audience in order to dial down their hostility further.

Average of ...	Strongly Agree	Agree	Tend to Disagree	Strongly Disagree	Don't Know
Pre-Test Survey	4.26%	14.65%	26.53%	51.39%	3.15%
Post-Test Survey	6.58%	14.83%	23.84%	51.6%	3.12%
% Change	+2.32%	+0.18%	-2.69%	+0.21%	-0.03%

Table 16: Attitudinal Shift Scores (% Change in Average for Each Response Category)[535]

---

[534] This maps onto and coheres broadly with research done on far-right voting in Western Europe. Perhaps counterintuitively, studies show that Christianity actually works as a protective factor against far-right extremism. See: Kai Arzheimer & Elisabeth Carter (2009) Christian Religiosity and Voting for West European Radical Right Parties, West European Politics, 32:5, 985-1011, DOI: 10.1080/01402380903065058.

[535] Calculated by averaging out all responses across all statements, converting them to percentages and seeing the net change in attitudinal scores.

Main finding 2: Memes depicting Kindness and the Military which showed multiple messengers of different ethnicity ranked most highly in the post test survey (with individuals across all sections of the audience selecting these the most when prompted).

Another key result gleaned from the post-test survey was the type of content that the audiences found most persuasive and/or liked. Similar to the online testing, memes depicting Kindness and the Military were key favourites with individuals across all sections of the audience, selecting these the most when prompted. As noted above, this is unsurprising given that unifying themes and multiple messengers of different ethnicity represented performed so well in the focus testing. As part of the post-test survey, open answers were given for respondents to express their rationale for what they liked and didn't like. Some of the answers here were illuminating. For example, one respondent said: "I believe in an inclusive country, but not losing our culture" whilst another "We should be respectful to one another irrespective of differences". Kindness was a key motif in all of the open response answers — with various respondents affirming that "Without kindness there is nothing left".

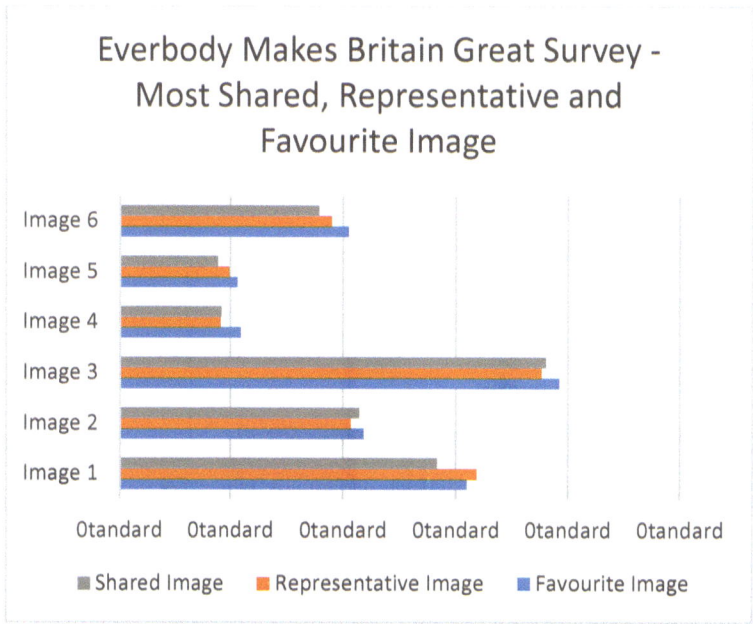

Figure 62: Everybody Makes Britain Great Survey—Most Shared, Representative and Favourite Image

(N.B. Images 1-6 are displayed in Figure 27—going left to right on row 1 and the same for row 2)

Main finding 3: All audiences and levels of video engagement saw consistent attitudinal scores across all pre- and post-test surveys.

As borne out by the percentage changes above, what was evident when comparing all forms of audiences and how they responded overall to the survey were the similarities and consistencies in attitudinal scores across all surveys. As highlighted above, the main trend was to disagree or strongly disagree with the positive statements to do with Islam, migration and multiculturalism—aside from statement four on the irrelevance of religion.

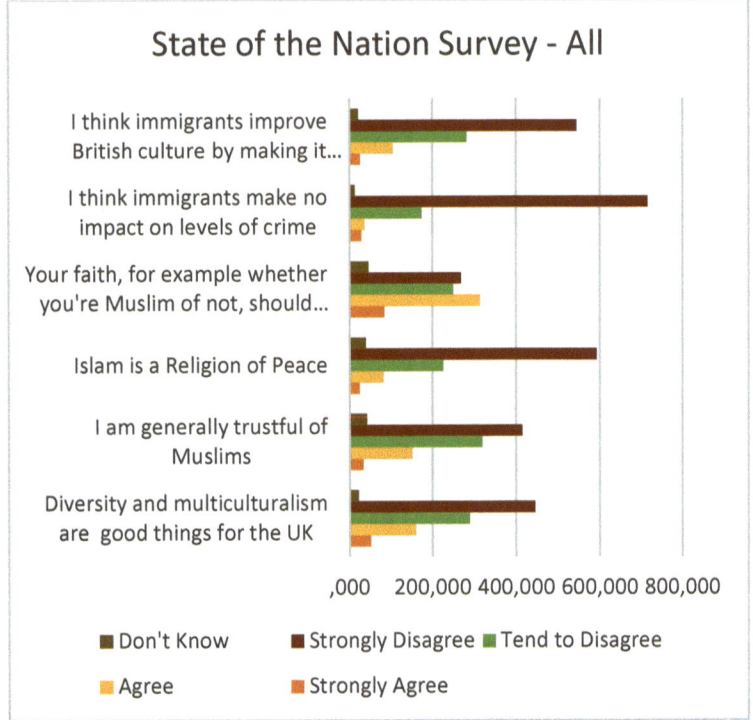

Figure 63: Overall Attitudinal Responses in Pre-Test Survey

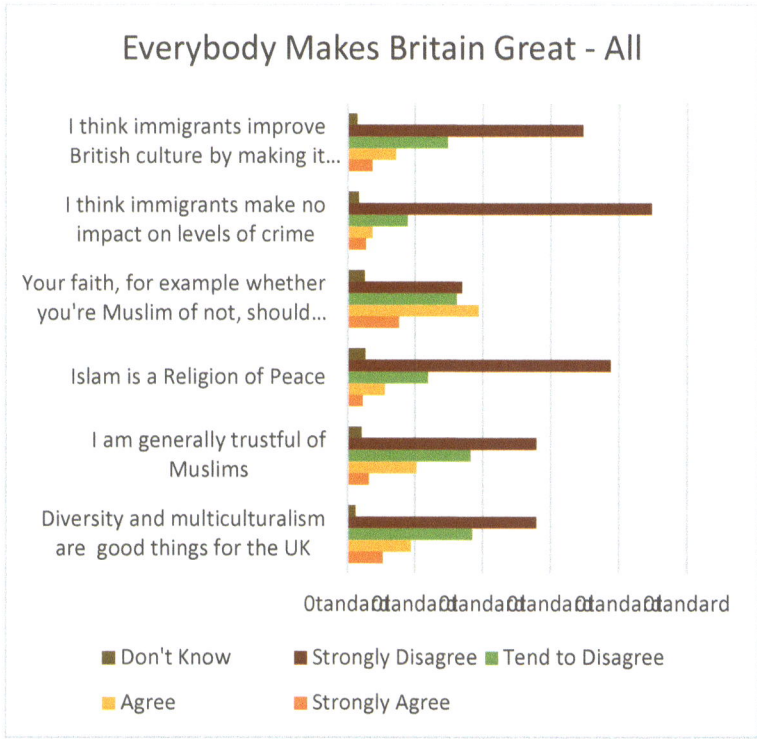

Figure 63: Overall Attitudinal Responses in Post-Test Survey

Looking across all of the surveys, this high level of consistency is born out—with very small variations in responses to each of the attitudinal items on the survey. This is 1) not unexpected but 2) reassuring as this suggests a level of accuracy, reliability and consistency in the demographic and attitudinal makeup in the target audience.

278 MOVING BEYOND ISLAMIST EXTREMISM

Stad. Dev. (%)	Strongly Agree	Agree	Tend to Disagree	Strongly Disagree	Don't Know
Diversity and multiculturalism are good things for the UK	7.30%	6.79%	13.44%	10.16%	2.57%
I am generally trustful of Muslims	5.16%	5.31%	10.98%	7.60%	4.14%
Islam is a Religion of Peace	4.92%	5.31%	17.87%	13.58%	4.19%
Your faith, for example whether you're Muslim of not, should not bar you from moving to the UK	6.79%	7.80%	10.84%	10.94%	2.78%
I think immigrants make no impact on levels of crime	5.075%	7.46%	8.10%	11.48%	1.95%
I think immigrants improve British culture by making it more open to new ideas	5.17%	5.72%	4.36%	5.74%	2.73%

Table 17: **Standard Deviations for Attitudinal Scores (Pre-Test Survey)**[536]

---

[536] Both of the below tables show perhaps a wider variation than expected; this was due to some surveys having very low completion rates (See Table 16 & 17 above).

Stad. Dev. (%)	Strongly Agree	Agree	Tend to Disagree	Strongly Disagree	Don't Know
Diversity and multiculturalism are good things for the UK	3.68%	28.44%	9.94%	17.96%	3.33%
I am generally trustful of Muslims	2.98%	28.67%	12.04%	16.31%	2.56%
Islam is a Religion of Peace	3.67%	4.00%	27.22%	22.036%	4.66%
Your faith, for example whether you're Muslim of not, should not bar you from moving to the UK	5.80%	12.70%	25.57%	12.35%	4.35%
I think immigrants make no impact on levels of crime	3.74%	3.83%	29.37%	24.64%	3.82%
I think immigrants improve British culture by making it more open to new ideas	3.04%	5.37%	26.149%	19.21%	4.12%

Table 18: Standard Deviations for Attitudinal Scores (Post-Test Survey)

Conclusion

As noted in the introduction to this chapter, previous studies on counter narratives have either suffered from a lack of empirical evaluation or lack of ideological specificity. This has raised questions about their effectiveness in achieving attitudinal shifts among extremist sympathetic audiences and — in the cases where such evaluation has taken place — made them so broad as to be virtually useless for researchers and practitioners looking at one form of extremism.

The pilot study reported in this chapter aimed to address that. Using ethnographic focus groups and online mass surveys to develop and test what messages, messengers and mediums work best to dial individuals back from hostile positions on Islam, migration and multiculturalism. Whilst the extent of the attitudinal shift was tentative, it can be noted that the interventions worked and that the tailored nature of the counter narrative content led to very little in the way of 'backfire effects'.

Among far-right sympathetic audiences some key areas and lessons to do with counter narrative content were learnt. Firstly, messages of unity that foster a sense of common human values, togetherness and kindness worked best. In particular, it was learnt that contents with a rousing, emotive or 'feel good' factor were preferred over more cerebral content. Moreover, if key points of content were introduced, they needed to be straightforward and present factual content that were watertight. It was found that narratives that attacked the far-right, singled out or reified a single ethnicity and were too 'political' failed to engage the audience — and lead to negative reactions. Finally, and to summarise again, some content worked better on some audience members rather than others (e.g., females particularly adverse to aggressive content and historical content didn't run well with younger audience). Moreover, videos tended to outperform static meme content, and actually produced more positive and reflective responses from far-right sympathetic audiences.

Moving forward, there is obviously scope to expand on such a methodology to see what works in other geographical contexts and with individuals who are either slightly further up or down the route of radicalisation towards violent extremism. For example, projects with younger far-right users on Instagram or TikTok could use essentially the same method (i.e., focus groups then mass surveys) but would need fine-tuning to their different interests (ie. mixed martial arts or environmental issues) and take into account vulnerabilities that are leading them into more ideological forms of engagement (e.g., mental health, social isolation and self-esteem issues). Additionally, different geographical contexts would also require further fine-tuning for the narratives presented and target groups negotiated. For example, projects with far-right informal or soft supporters in the US and Australasia would need to account for attitudes towards 'first nations' peoples and other immigrant groups that draw the ire of the far-right — being sensitive to the history and perceptions of history therein.

Finally, and going forward, one big question to ask of future testing research is the sustainability of such attitudinal shifts and how counter narratives figure within wider P/CVE approaches. For example, do we need to serve the same audiences a follow-up survey in the month after they've been exposed to counter narrative content to see whether there is sustained attitudinal shift? Can we measure a behavioural shift as a result of counter narrative campaigns? And, crucially, do counter narrative campaigns need deradicalisation professionals on hand to do one-to-one follow-up when an individual shows signs of being at-risk of violent radicalisation? All these innovations could be integrated into counter narrative testing going forward — especially on the far-right.

Conclusion — Revisiting Counter Narratives (Lessons, Recommendations and Ways Forward for Combating Far-Right Extremism)

Over the past ten years, the threat picture around the violent nature of the global far-right has changed drastically. Treating the Oslo massacre as a 'year zero' for the current wave of right-wing terror attacks, the narratives, modus operandi and online cultures of the violent far-right have fused to become more globalised and interconnected than ever before. The first aim of this book was therefore to identify and evaluate the power of far-right narratives (as a phenomenon in themselves) that are echoing around online extremist ecosystems, terror cells and street-based groups at the time of writing. Such developments have obviously raised new policy conundrums and challenges among political elites, law enforcement and civil society compared to the first decade of the twenty-first century. For example, should we pre-emptively ban groups problematic in another geographical context in order to forestall the problem in our own country?[537] How do we detect when online activity will spill into offline attacks? And, are groups and formal organisations meaningful categories for targeting the violent far-right with counter-terror interventions when a lot of so-called 'members' might just be a follower on an encrypted social media channel?[538]

One intervention that has been carried over from previous waves of violent extremism are counter narratives. Defined as "a message that ... [demystify] deconstruct or delegitimise extremist

---

[537] In March 2021, for instance, a UK-based neo-Nazi terror group, Sonnenkrieg Division, was proscribed by the Australian Government based on potential online recruiting. See: Lowrey, T. & Lipson, D.: "Neo-Nazi Sonnenkrieg Division to become first right-wing terrorist organisation listed in Australia", *ABC News*, 2 March 2021, online at: https://www.abc.net.au/news/2021-03-02/sonnenkrieg-division-first-right-wing-terror-group-listed/13206756.

[538] See: Comerford, M. "Confronting the Challenge of 'Post-Organisational' Extremism", *Observer Research Foundation,* 19 August 2020, online at: https://www.orfonline.org/expert-speak/confronting-the-challenge-of-post-organisational-extremism/.

narratives",[539] they have become a key part of western counter terrorism toolkits for tackling Islamist extremism. However, little is known about how we should structure them as a technique for far-right extremism and even less the extent to which they work in stopping individuals from escalating from radicalism to extremist violence.[540] Apart from some notable key exceptions, there are few academic studies aimed at putting counter narratives on a firmer, more empirically rigorous footing.[541] A key aim of this book was therefore to also elucidate better how we might go about leveraging counter-messaging techniques for the new fifth wave epoch and present original data from a UK-based online pilot.

In this concluding chapter, we will summarise the arguments and findings from the preceding chapters and suggest how these could be better incorporated into a more systematic framework when deploying counter narratives against violent far-right extremists globally. Moreover, a commentary on the current state of counter narrative responses will be set out as well as key policy recommendations for practitioners when dealing with the fallout of violent far-right extremist actors. Finally, future avenues of research will be mapped out. In particular, a strong emphasis will be put on a shift away from an obsession in terrorism studies of solely looking at Islamist extremism. Notably, there has been little in the way of empirical studies looking at

---

[539] Tuck, H. & Silverman, H., 'The Counter Narrative Handbook', London: ISD, 2016, p.65.

[540] For an in-depth rehearsal of some of these arguments, see: Ferguson, K., 'Countering violent extremism through media and communication strategies', University of East Anglia: Partnership for Conflict, Crime & Security Research, pp. 10-16.

[541] See the following for cutting edge interventions in this space: Bélanger JJ, Nisa CF, Schumpe BM, Gurmu T, Williams MJ and Putra IE, "Do Counter-Narratives Reduce Support for ISIS? Yes, but Not for Their Target Audience". *Frontiers in Psychology*, 2020, 11:1059. doi: 10.3389/fpsyg.2020.01059; S. L. Carthy & K. M. Sarma "Countering Terrorist Narratives: Assessing the Efficacy and Mechanisms of Change in Counter-narrative Strategies", *Terrorism and Political Violence*, 2021, DOI: 10.1080/09546553.2021.1962308; & Erin Saltman, Farshad Kooti & Karly Vockery, "New Models for Deploying Counterspeech: Measuring Behavioral Change and Sentiment Analysis", *Studies in Conflict & Terrorism*, 2021, DOI: 10.1080/1057610X.2021.1888404;

far-right terrorism and possible responses to it—a problem that this book aims to partially remedy.[542]

Key Findings — Global Far-Right Narratives and Counter Narratives in the Fifth Wave

As noted in the introduction, whilst the academic jury is largely out on whether we are experiencing a fifth wave of far-right terrorism, we can note a significant qualitative and quantitative shift in the nature of far-right terrorism globally over the past ten years. As Augur (2020) argues, the expansion of far-right political violence, the cohesive transnational character of such violence, the similarity of trigger events (e.g., the rising levels of migration and right-wing populist movements), as well as a "common predominant energy" (or cause) around the "awakening the white race to the danger of migration" and changing demographic trends, all provide evidence a step change in global violent far-right extremism.[543]

In chapter one, we therefore zoomed in on narratives—i.e., a story around a set of events that provide the vehicle for ideology—an important form of political persuasion. In this sense, it was noted that far-right terrorist and extremist actors are no different from more mainstream political actors. They use narratives to recruit new members, broadcast their activities and mobilise activists into violent action. In particular, seven threat or crisis narratives were identified as animating the violent global far-right at this moment, including 1) a Cultural Threat Conspiracy Theory Narrative, 2) an Ethnic Threat Conspiracy Theory Narrative, 3) an Accelerationist Narrative, 4) an Anti-Establishment Narrative, 5) a Misogynist Narrative, 6) an Environmental Narratives and 7) a Victimhood narra-

---

[542] Schuurman, B. (2019) 'Topics in terrorism research: reviewing trends and gaps, 2007–2016.' *Critical Studies on Terrorism*. 12(1): 463–480.

[543] Augur, V.A., 'Right-Wing Terror: A Fifth Global Wave?' *Perspectives on Terrorism*, 14(3): 87–97, June 2020, online at: https://www.universiteitleiden.nl/binaries/content/assets/customsites/perspectives-on-terrorism/2020/issue-3/auger.pdf.

tive. Whilst the morphology of the narrative might differ depending on the group and actor (e.g., in particular, the greater and lesser extent of misogyny, accelerationist or environmental motifs), the bracketing of world events culminating in an apocalyptic war or clash of civilizations was noted as common across the board.[544] We then mapped out a seven step process for developing and assessing far-right counter narratives—with a particular emphasis on precision when laying out counter narrative campaigns objectives and the target group that you want to reach.

In chapters two to four, we attempted to put empirical flesh on the analytical and theoretical arguments outlined in the introduction and chapter one by surveying violent far-right narratives and counter narrative campaigns 'in action' in six different geographical contexts. In particular, thirty-two groups and twenty-one counter narrative campaigns were profiled. Overall, what was apparent was the scarcity of counter narrative campaigns when mapped against the abundance of violent far-right groups. Comparing narratives across different contexts, for instance, what was evident from the UK, Germany, and Australasian case studies was the rise in anti-Muslim populist cultural threat narratives that had spurred individuals on to commit violent solo-actor forms of terrorism. Whether that was the Christchurch shooting, the attempted killing of left-wing activists by a Reclaim Australia activist or the Finsbury Park Mosque attack in the UK, all attackers had in their minds broad versions of either the Eurabia or Great Replacement conspiracy theories whereby Muslim invaders were being helped by a corrupted, anti-nationalist elite. Despite this, the Australian and UK contexts had few examples of either NGO or government-sanctioned strategic communications when it came to the violent far-right—with the German case being the exception to this rule.

Turning to the US and Canada, emerging threat narratives of an anti-government nature tended to explain individuals' engagement with far-right violent extremism. The chapter also uncovered concerning overlaps between ideologically distinct groups when it

---

[544] See following for more on crisis narratives: Berger, J.M., *Extremism*, Cambridge, MA: MIT Press, 2018.

comes to narratives of white genocide and demographic replacement in the continent. Despite these differences, one thing that knitted all the case studies together was the presence of online neo-Nazi terror groups and the lack of counter narrative programming going on in this space. Whether that was Atomwaffen in the US, Antipodean Resistance in Australia or National Action in the UK, all so-called post-Iron March groups (for the website from which their ideology and organisations were spawned in 2016)[545] with accelerationist aims to bring down the liberal order were present in almost all the case studies (except New Zealand). Better targeted counter narrative programming to help individuals out from these terror cells and online subcultures was identified as a key practitioner challenge going forward.

In the final chapter, the results from one of the first far-right focused counter narrative testing projects were presented in order to spearhead a broader drive toward a more rigorous and robust methodology in deciding 'what works'. Here a two-step, iterative experimental testing methodology was proposed (separate from the counter narrative development methodology in chapter) to aid practitioners keen on evaluating efforts in this space. This involved more focus group testing of counter narrative content and then using lessons learnt therein to scale up such testing to a much larger online audience. Initial results of the scaled testing — using surveys to track the attitudinal shift of far-right sympathetic individuals in the UK — was promising — with many shifting toward more agreeable positions towards Islam, migrants and multiculturalism as a result of viewing counter narrative memes and videos.

---

545 For more on this see: Counter-Extremism Project, "Violent Right-Wing Extremism and Terrorism – Transnational Connectivity, Definitions, Incidents, Structures and Countermeasures", November 2020, online at: https://www.counterextremism.com/sites/default/files/CEP%20Study_Violent%20Right-Wing%20Extremism%20and%20Terrorism_Nov%202020.pdf.

Lessons and Policy Recommendations — The Current State of Counter Narrative Responses to the Global Far Right

Broadening out, what lessons can be drawn from the above frameworks, case studies and pilot projects? In particular, what we can recommend in terms of counter narrative 'best practice' when dealing with the global far-right? In terms of the counter narratives themselves, they need to be simple, emotive and impactful — with a clear 'call to action' and theory of change for the audience in mind. It is no longer simply possible to put together broad-based counter-messaging campaigns with a loose set of evaluation criteria. Such campaigns will be poorly optimised and might end up exposing the wrong individuals to potentially radicalising content for them. Moreover, messengers of far-right counter narratives need to be 'everyday individuals', i.e., not governments or elites, who have lived experiences to share (i.e., former extremists or victims of extremism) and who can provide an alternative to group narratives themselves. What we're aiming for here therefore is not simply a rejoinder to the right-wing terrorist or extremist narrative but a completely different worldview that doesn't repeat extremist or terrorist tropes. Finally, and when it comes to the medium used, slick, professional and dynamic delivery of counter narrative content is essential. As found in the pilot study above, short-form video content tends to be the most impactful and should be prioritised over static, text-based content. Key innovations here in the future would be using more immersive, story or game-based content that allows the user to either take on the role of a character experiencing extremism or being at risk of extremism and being challenged by its effects.[546]

---

[546] See: Schlegel, L., "Let's Play Prevention: Can P/CVE Turn the Tables on Extremists' Use of Gamification?", GNET Insight, 29th March 2021: https://gnet-research.org/2021/03/29/lets-play-prevention-can-p-cve-turn-the-tables-on-extremists-use-of-gamification/ & Schlegel, L., "Storytelling against extremism: How fiction could increase the persuasive impact of counter- and alternative narratives in P/CVE", *Journal for De-Radicalisation*, No. 27: Summer 2021, online at: https://journals.sfu.ca/jd/index.php/jd/article/view/467.

Moving from the campaign to the policy level, a key policy recommendation based on the findings in previous chapters would be more sustained interest and investment in far-right counter narrative campaigns more generally. Whilst tech companies and NGOs have been leading the way on constructing innovative and ground-breaking programming and campaigns when it comes to combating the violent far-right,[547] little government funding or buy-in has been available in the geographical case studies surveyed above. This can be explained by the new nature of the far-right threat but also painfully embarrassing lessons learnt over government interventions in this space when it came to Islamist extremism.[548]

Another key policy recommendation — that has been highlighted by the findings in this book — is the need for a harder think about how counter narratives might be leveraged for individuals on the far-right who are embedded in online subcultures. A lot of work has been put into redirecting individuals and serving them psycho-social content[549] but further effort and testing needs to be conducted into how counter narratives themselves might lead individuals either away from the ideology itself or into conversations

---

[547] See examples of EXIT Deutschland, Moonshot and Google on these fronts here: EU Home Affairs, "EXIT Deutschland, "Nazis Against Nazis", 2016, online at: https://ec.europa.eu/home-affairs/networks/radicalisation-awareness-network-ran/collection-inspiring-practices/ran-practices/exit-2_en; Moonshot CVE, "Moonshot Redirect Method: How it was Designed", online at: https://moonshotteam.com/redirect-method/; & Jigsaw, "Countermeasures in Practice", 2020, online at: https://jigsaw.google.com/the-current/white-supremacy/countermeasures/.

[548] Cobain, I., Ross, A., Evans, R. and Mahmood, M. "Inside Ricu, the shadowy propaganda unit inspired by the cold war", *The Guardian*, 2 May 2016, https://www.theguardian.com/politics/2016/may/02/inside-ricu-the-shadowy-propaganda-unit-inspired-by-the-cold-war & Katz, R., "The State Department's Twitter War With ISIS Is Embarrassing", *Time Magazine*, 16 September 2014, online at: https://time.com/3387065/isis-twitter-war-state-department/.

[549] MacFarqurhar, N. "White Extremism Faces a Subversive Foe Online: Google Ads", *New York Times*, 30 December 2019, online at: https://www.nytimes.com/2019/12/30/us/white-supremacy-moonshot-google-ads.html.

with trained counsellors who might help to offramp them away from such content.[550]

A final key policy recommendation that needs to be tackled is a serious think about how counter narratives can be used within existing counter-terrorism programming persuade individuals away from joining terror cells and online. Obviously counter narratives and the ideology connected to narratives is only part of the picture but for a term that has been with use for almost a decade and a half there is a woeful lack of thinking about where it sits in existing frameworks — an issue that will be tackled next — and a great deal of hesitancy in the government going anywhere near the method itself.

Concluding Remarks — Immunised Democracy & The Role of Counter Narratives within a Broader Counter-Terrorism Framework

Over the past decade and a half, counter narratives have become a notable part of western efforts to combat terrorism. Placed at the softer end of counter terror (CT) tactics, the use of strategic communications in order to disrupt the ideological grounding of violent extremist causes has come to occupy the 'upstream' space of preventative measures available to governments, NGOs and civil society actors wishing to counter political violence. In preventing violent extremism, or 'PVE', this has become especially important as terrorist organisations have become more adept at using social media in order to radicalise, recruit and disseminate their messages online, thereby circumventing traditional forms of media and face-to-face encounters. In this view, our current moment therefore calls for a 'war of words and ideas'

---

[550] The Institute for Strategic Dialogue has already done a pilot similar to this. See the following for their results: Davey, J., Birdwell, J., and Skellett, R., 'Counter Conversations: A model for direct engagement with individuals showing signs of radicalisation online', (London: ISD, 2018), online at: https://www.isdglobal.org/wp-content/uploads/2018/03/Counter-Conversations_FINAL.pdf.

as much as counter terror actions on the ground in order to combat the threat of globalised, far-right extremist violence (as outlined in the chapters above).[551]

Defined broadly, counter-terrorism relates to the possible policy options that can be used when responding to acts of targeted political violence, and—as alluded to above—takes on both harder and softer hues. As stated below, while the ends of each counter tactic are similar, these two adjectival terms should be kept analytically distinct and separate. The latter refers to legally defined and publicly identifiable foreign and domestic policies seeking to undercut terrorist criminality, lethality, environments and support. The former refers to a suite of more targeted options that take on a military, special operations or (even) extra-judicial set of approaches to dismantle terrorist groups or plots. Common to both approaches, however, is the aim to save lives by disrupting terrorist groups, individuals, activities and milieus acting against the nation state.

---

[551] For more on the importance of building a whole society oppositional culture and ideology to terrorist and extremist propaganda, see: Glazzard, A. 'Losing the Plot: Narrative, Counter-Narrative and Violent Extremism'. ICCT Research Paper, May 2017, online at: https://icct.nl/wp-content/uploads/2017/05/ICCT-Glazzard-Losing-the-Plot-May-2017.pdf & Holbrook, D. & Horgan, J., "Terrorism and Ideology: Cracking the Nut", *Perspectives on Terrorism*, 3:6 (December 2019), online at: https://www.universitcitleiden.nl/binaries/content/assets/customsites/perspectives-on-terrorism/2019/issue-6/01-holbrook-and-horgan.pdf.

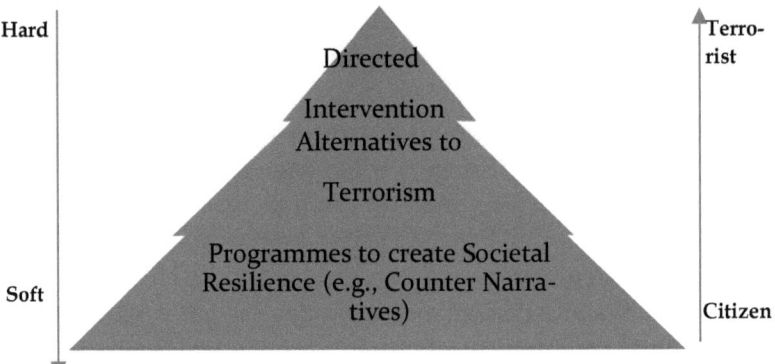

Figure 64: Global Far-Right Counter Narratives within a Broader CT Strategy[552]

As mentioned above (and illustrated in figure 64), counter terrorism does not only operate at the hard edge of institutional responses — direct actions against terrorists and terrorist plotters– but that states might also want to give alternatives to those considering political violence and to act more discursively in teaching key democratic values and the dangers of terroristic violence. This latter approach taps into what terrorism scholar, Ami Pedahzur,[553] calls an 'immunised approach' to democracy and might be instructive in the years ahead tackling the violent global far-right threat. This entails the democratic system addressing violence and extremism through educational initiatives that combat the binary, reactionary and reductive nature of terrorist ideologies. It also includes legal initiatives from above that proscribe, limit and de-legitimise action within extremist organisations. Here, we can see counter narratives playing a key role in countering far-right extremism; both at the hard and soft end of actor profiles — challenging tropes and mes-

---

[552] Adapted from Anne Aly, Anne-Marie Balbi & Carmen Jacques (2015) 'Rethinking countering violent extremism: implementing the role of civil society.' *Journal of Policing, Intelligence and Counter Terrorism*, 10:1, 3–13, DOI: 10.1080/18335330.2015.1028772. P.9.

[553] Pedahzur, A. (2004) 'The Defending Democracy and the Extreme Right: A Comparative Analysis.' In: Eatwell, R., and Mudde, C. (eds.) *Western Democracies and the New Extreme Right Challenge*. London: Routledge. PP. 108–132.

sages that might be disseminated by extremist organisations for upstream actors and providing alternative narratives or possibilities for more downstream actors.

Added to this we can see these approaches being targeted at three different levels. One for those who are already members (top third), those attracted to such groups (middle third) and those who don't have any interest at all (bottom third). This more targeted approach to intervention is key in allocating resources and targeting interventions correctly and successfully — with preventative efforts hitting the lowest common denominator at the bottom third of the pyramid, while more targeted counter measures hit those either sympathetic or active members at the top. Compared to other CT tactics, we can see how counter narratives straddle both preventative and countering violent extremism measures; with tailored and differentiated messages aimed at all manifestations and ideologies of far-right extremism going forwards, the only way to stop the fifth wave of right-wing terror growing apace.

Bibliography

Books and Journal Articles

Allen, C., 'Proscribing National Action: Considering the Impact of Banning the British Far-Right Group', *The Political Quarterly*, 88(4), January 2017, 654, online at: https://onlinelibrary.wiley.com/doi/full/10.1111/1467-923X.12368.

Aly, A., Anne-Marie Balbi & Carmen Jacques, 'Rethinking countering violent extremism: implementing the role of civil society.' *Journal of Policing, Intelligence and Counter Terrorism*, 10:1, 3-13, 2015, DOI: 10.1080/18335330.2015.1028772. P.9.

Arzheimer, K. & Elisabeth Carter (2009) Christian Religiosity and Voting for West European Radical Right Parties, West European Politics, 32:5, 985-1011, DOI: 10.1080/01402380903065058.

Ashour, A., "Online De-Radicalization? Countering Violent Extremist Narratives Message, Messenger and Media Strategy", *Perspectives on Terrorism*, 4(6): 15-19, December 2010.

Augur, V.A., 'Right-Wing Terror: A Fifth Global Wave?' *Perspectives on Terrorism*, 14(3): 87-97, June 2020, online at: https://www.universiteitleiden.nl/binaries/content/assets/customsites/perspectives-on-terrorism/2020/issue-3/auger.pdf & Weinberg, L. & Eubank, W., 'An End to the Fourth Wave of Terrorism?', *Studies in Conflict and Terrorism*, 33(7): 594-602, 2015, DOI: 10.1080/1057610X.2010.483757.

Baele, S., 'Conspiratorial Narratives in Violent Political Actors', Journal of Language and Social Psychology, 38(5-6), 2019, 706–734, 2019.

Battersby, J. & Ball, R., 'Christchurch in the context of New Zealand terrorism and right-wing extremism', *Journal of Policing, Intelligence and Counter Terrorism*, 14:3, 2019, 191-207.

Bélanger JJ, Nisa CF, Schumpe BM, Gurmu T, Williams MJ and Putra IE, "Do Counter-Narratives Reduce Support for ISIS? Yes, but Not for Their Target Audience". *Frontiers in Psychology*, 2020, 11:1059. doi: 10.3389/fpsyg.2020.01059.

Berger, J.M., *Extremism*, Cambridge, MA: MIT Press, 2018.

Bjørgo, T., Grunenberg, S. & Van Donselaar, J., 'Exit from right-wing extremist groups: Lessons from disengagement programmes in Norway, Sweden and Germany', In: Bjørgo, T. & Horgan, J., *Leaving Terrorism Behind: Individual and Collective Disengagement*, London: Routledge, 2009.

Braddock, K., 'Vaccinating Against Hate: Using Attitudinal Inoculation to Confer Resistance to Persuasion by Extremist Propaganda', *Terrorism and Political Violence*, 2019, https://doi.org/10.1080/09546553.2019.1693370.

Braddock, K., *Weaponized Words: The Strategic Role of Persuasion in Violent Radicalization and Counter-Radicalization*, Cambridge: Cambridge University Press, 2020.

Braet, A., "Ethos, Pathos and Logos in Aristotle's Rhetoric: A Re-Examination", *Argumentation*, 6:307-320, 1992.

Carthy, S. L. & K. M. Sarma "Countering Terrorist Narratives: Assessing the Efficacy and Mechanisms of Change in Counter-narrative Strategies", *Terrorism and Political Violence*, 2021, DOI: 10.1080/09546553.2021.1962308

Carter, E., *The Extreme Right in Western Europe: Success or Failure?*, Manchester: Manchester University Press, 2005.

Cobb, S., *Speaking of Violence: The Politics and Poetics of Narrative in Conflict Resolution*. Oxford: Oxford University Press, 2013.

Dafnos, A., 'Narratives as a Means of Countering the Radical Right; Looking into the Trojan T-shirt Project.', *Journal EXIT Deutschland*, 2014, online at: http://journals.sfu.ca/jed/index.php/jex/article/view/98.

Daniels, J., *White Lies: Race, Class, Gender and Sexuality in White Supremacist Discourse*, London: Routledge, 1997.

Dean, G., Bell, P., & Vakhitova, Z., 'The rise of the new radical right', *Journal of Policing, Intelligence and Counter Terrorism*, 11(2), 2016, 121-142.

Dechesne, M., 'Deradicalization: Not Soft but Strategic', *Crime, Law, and Social Change*, 2011, PP. 287–292.

Devine, Daniel, 'The UK Referendum on Membership of the European Union as a Trigger Event for Hate Crimes', 5 February 2018, online at: https://ssrn.com/abstract=3118190 or http://dx.doi.org/10.2139/ssrn.3118190.

Gattinara, P.C., 'The study of the far-right and its three E's: why scholarship must go beyond Eurocentrism, Electoralism and Externalism', *French Politics*, https://doi.org/10.1057/s41253-020-00124-8.

Goodricke-Clarke, N., *Black Sun: Aryan Cults, Esoteric Nazism, and the Politics of Identity*, (New York: NYU Press, 2003).

Fisher, W. R, *Human communication as narration: Toward a philosophy of reason, value, and action*, Columbia: University of South Carolina Press

Gilbert, J., *Patched: The History of Gangs in New Zealand*. Auckland, NZ: Auckland University Press, 2013.

Griffin, R., *The Nature of Fascism*, London: Routledge, 1991.

Groothuis, S., 'Researching race, racialisation, and racism in critical terrorism studies: clarifying conceptual ambiguities', *Critical Studies on Terrorism*, 2020, https://doi.org/10.1080/17539153.2020.1810990.

Gupta, D.K., 'Waves of international terrorism: An explanation of the process by which ideas flood the world,' in Jean E. Rosenfeld, ed. *Terrorism, Identity and Legitimacy: The Four Waves theory and political violence.* (New York: Routledge, 2011), p. 40.

Holmer, G. & Bauman, P., 'Measuring Up: Evaluating the Impact of P/CVE Programmes', Washington, DC: United States Institute of Peace, 2018, online at: https://www.usip.org/sites/default/files/2018-09/preventing-countering-violent-extremism-measuringup.pdf

Holbrook, D & and Horgan, J., 'Terrorism and Ideology: Cracking the Nut', *Perspectives on Terrorism*, 13(6): 2–15, 2019, online at: https://www.universiteitleiden.nl/binaries/content/assets/customsites/perspectives-on-terrorism/2019/issue-6/01-holbrook-and-horgan.pdf.

Jackson, P., '#hitlerwasright: National Action and National Socialism for the 21st Century', *Journal for Deradicalization,* No. 1: Winter 2014/15, https://journals.sfu.ca/jd/index.php/jd/article/view/7.

Kaplan, J., 'Terrorism's Fifth Wave: A Theory, a Conundrum and a Dilemma,' *Perspectives on Terrorism*, 2:2 (January 2008), pp. 12-24.

Kaplin, J., 'Waves of Political Terrorism', In: *Oxford Research Encyclopedia of Politics*, November 2016, DOI: 10.1093/acrefore/9780190228637.013.24.

Labov, W., & Waletzky, J., "Narrative analysis: Oral versions of personal experience", *Journal of Narrative & Life History*, 7(1–4), 1997, 3-38, online at: http://dx.doi.org/10.1075/jnlh.7.02nar.

Lee, B.J., 'Informal Countermessaging: The Potential and Perils of Informal Online Countermessaging', *Studies in Conflict & Terrorism*, 42(1-2), 2019, 161-177, online at: http://10.1080/1057610X.2018.1513697.

Lewandowsky, S., 'Misinformation and Its Correction: Continued Influence and Successful Debiasing.' *Psychological Science in the Public Interest,* 13(3), 106–131, 2012..

Macnair, L. & Frank, R, 'Voices Against Extremism: A case study of a community-based CVE counter-narrative campaign', *Journal for Deradicalization*, (10), 2017, P.155.

McCann, C., *The Prevent Strategy and Right-wing Extremism: A Case Study of the English Defence League*, (London: Routledge, 2019).

Michael, G., 'RAHOWA! A History of the World Church of the Creator', *Terrorism and Political Violence*, 18(4), 2007, 561-583.

Michael, G., 'David Lane and the Fourteen Words', Totalitarian Movements and Political Religions. 10 (1), 2009, 43-61.

Mudde, C., *Populist Far-right in Europe*, Cambridge: Cambridge University Press, 2007.

Mudde, C., 'The Populist Far-right: A Pathological Normalcy', *Western European Politics*, 33(6): 1167-1186, 20210, online at: https://doi.org/10.1080/01402382.2010.508901.

Parker, T. & Sitter, N., 'The Four Horsemen of Terrorism: It's Not Waves, It's Strains, Terrorism and Political Violence', *Terrorism and Political Violence*, 28(2): 197–216, 2016, https://doi.org/10.1080/09546553.2015.1112277.

Pedahzur, A. (2004) 'The Defending Democracy and the Extreme Right: A Comparative Analysis.' In: Eatwell, R., and Mudde, C. (eds.) *Western Democracies and the New Extreme Right Challenge*. London: Routledge. PP. 108-132.

Perry, B. & Scrivens, R, *Right-Wing Extremism in Canada*, London: Palgrave MacMillan, 2019.

Perry, B. & Scrivens, R, 'Uneasy Alliances: A Look at the Right-Wing Extremist Movement in Canada', *Studies in Conflict & Terrorism*, 39:9, 2016, 827, DOI: 10.1080/1057610X.2016.1139375.

Pettigrew, T. F., & Tropp, L. R., ,A meta-analytic test of intergroup contact theory', *Journal of Personality and Social Psychology*, 90(5), 2006, 751–783, online at: https://doi.org/10.1037/0022-3514.90.5.751.

Peucker, M. & Smith, D. (eds.), *The Far-Right in Contemporary Australia* (London, Palgrave Macmillan: 2019).

Piatkowska, S.J., Andreas Hövermann, Tse-Chuan Yang, Immigration 'Influx as a Trigger for Right-Wing Crime: A Temporal Analysis of Hate Crimes in Germany in the Light of the 'Refugee Crisis'', The British Journal of Criminology, Volume 60, Issue 3, May 2020, Pages 620–641, https://doi.org/10.1093/bjc/azz073v

Proshyn, D., 'Breaking the Waves: How the Phenomenon of European Jihadism Militates Against the Wave Theory of Terrorism', *International Studies: Interdisciplinary Political and Cultural Journal*, 17 (1): 91-107, 2015, online at: http://cejsh.icm.edu.pl/cejsh/element/bwmeta1.element.hdl_11089_17468/c/ipcj-2015-0007.pdf. P.105.

Rappoport, D., 'The Fourth Wave: September 11 in the History of Terrorism', *Current History*, December 2001, pp. 419-424.

Rydgren, J., 'Is extreme right-wing populism contagious? Explaining the emergence of a new party family', *European Journal of Political Research*, 44(3): 413-437, 2005, online at: https://doi.org/10.1111/j.1475-6765.2005.00233.x.

Saltman, E., Farshad Kooti & Karly Vockery (2021) 'New Models for Deploying Counterspeech: Measuring Behavioral Change and Sentiment Analysis', *Studies in Conflict & Terrorism*, DOI: 10.1080/1057610X.2021.1888404.

Simon, J.D., 'Technological and lone operator terrorism: Prospects for a Fifth Wave of Global Terrorism,' in Rosenfeld ed., *Terrorism, Identity and Legitimacy: The Four Waves theory and political violence.* (New York: Routledge, 2011), pp. 44-65.

Schlegel, L., "Storytelling against extremism: How fiction could increase the persuasive impact of counter- and alternative narratives in P/CVE", *Journal for De-Radicalisation*, No. 27: Summer 2021, online at: https://journals.sfu.ca/jd/index.php/jd/article/view/467.

Schuurman, B., 'Topics in terrorism research: reviewing trends and gaps, 2007-2016.' *Critical Studies on Terrorism.* 12(1), 2019, pp. 463–480.

Spoonley, P., *The Politics of Nostalgia: Racism and the Extreme Right in New Zealand,* (Palmerston North: Dunmore Press, 1987),

Voogt, S., 'Countering far-right recruitment online: CAPE's practitioner experience', *Journal of Policing, Intelligence and Counter Terrorism*, 12:1 (2017), 34–46.

Zúquete, José Pedro, 'The European Extreme Right and Islam: New Directions?', *Journal of Political Ideologies*, 13 (3), 2008, 321-345.

Weimann, G & Von Knop, K., 'Applying the Notion of Noise to Countering Online-Terrorism', *Studies in Conflict and Terrorism.* 31(10) (2008), pp. 883-902.

Non-Anglophone Books and Articles

Brandstetter, M., 'Parteigründungen als Reaktionen auf staatliche Verbote', *Jahrbuch Extremismus & Demokratie* 28, 2016, 188-206

Exif-Recherche, '«Combat 18» Reunion ', Exif-Recherche, 16 July 2018, online at: https://exif-recherche.org/?p=.

Gräfe, S.,'"Blood & Honour": „Trotz Verbot nicht tot?". Bedeutung in Gegenwart und Vergangenheit' In: Uwe Backes & Steffen Kailitz (eds.), Sachsen – eine Hochburg des Rechtsextremismus? (Göttingen: V&R 2020), 299-314

Gräfe, S., Sven Segelke, 'Rechte Hassgewalt in Sachen, 2011 bis 2016' In: Uwe Backes, Sebastian Gräfe, Anna-Maria Haase, Maximilian Kreter, Michail Logvinov, Sven Segelke (eds.), Rechte Hassgewalt in Sachsen. Entwicklungstrends und Radikalisierung (Göttingen: V&R 2019), 53-136.

Herrmann, U., 'Deutschland, ein Wirtschaftsmärchen. Warum es kein Wunder ist, dass wir reich geworden sind (Frankfurt: Westend Verlag, 2019).

Kocka, J. and Alf Lüdtke. See (f.e.) Jürgen Kocka, 'Ein deutscher Sonderweg: Überlegungen zur Sozialgeschichte der DDR', Aus Politik und Zeitgeschichte 41 (40), 34-45.

Kreter, M., 'Die deutsche Rechtsrockszene. Integraler Bestandteil der rechtsextremen Bewegung oder isolierte, subkulturelle Szene', *Jahrbuch Extremismus & Demokratie* 31, 2019, 159-173.

Wichmann, F., '4 Ways To Turn The Neo-Nazi Agenda On Its Head', *Journal Exit-Deutschland. Zeitschrift für Deradikalisierung und demokratische Kultur* 5, 2017, 93-98.

Wichmann, F., 'Successfully Countering Hate and Far Right Propaganda: The Story of Exit Germany', *Journal Exit-Deutschland. Zeitschrift für Deradikalisierung und demokratische Kultur* 7, 2018, 64-67.

Reports

Allen, C., 'National Action: links between the far-right, extremism and terrorism', Commission for Countering Extremism Research Paper Series, 2019, online at: https://assets.publishing.service.gov.uk/government/uploads/system/uploads/attachment_data/file/8272 32/Chris_Allen_-_National_Action_Post_Publication_Revisions.pdf.

Aly, A. and Zeiger, S., 'Countering Violent Extremism Online in Australia: Research and Preliminary Findings', in Aly, A. and Zeiger, S., eds., *Countering Violent Extremism: Developing an Evidence-base for Policy and Practice* (Hedayah and Curtin University, 2015), pp. 81-89.

Bjørgo, T., & Ravndal, J.A., 'Extreme-Right Violence and Terrorism: Concepts, Patterns, and Responses', ICCT Paper, 23 September 2019, online at: https://icct.nl/publication/extreme-right-violence-and-terrorism-concepts-patterns-and-responses/.

Briggs, R. & Feve, S., 'Review of Programs to Counter Narratives of Violent Extremism', London: ISD, 2013, online at: https://www.dmefor peace.org/peacexchange/wp-content/uploads/2018/10/Review-of-Programs-to-Counter-Narratives-of-Violent-Extremism.pdf.

Cook, J. & Lewandowsky, S., 'The Debunking Handbook' St. Lucia, Australia: University of Queensland, 2011, online at: http://sks.to/debunk.

Counter-Extremism Project, "Violent Right-Wing Extremism and Terrorism—Transnational Connectivity, Definitions, Incidents, Structures and Countermeasures", November 2020, online at: https://www.counterextremism.com/sites/default/files/CEP%20 Study_Violent%20Right-Wing%20Extremism%20and%20Terror ism_Nov%202020.pdf.

Davey, J., Birdwell, J., and Skellett, R., 'Counter Conversations: A model for direct engagement with individuals showing signs of radicalisation online', (London, 2018), online at: https://www.isdglobal.org/wp-content/uploads/2018/03/Counter-Conversations_FINAL.pdf.

Dawson, L., Edwards, C., & Jeffray, C., 'Learning and Adapting: The Use of Monitoring and Evaluation in Countering Violent Extremism', London: RUSI, 2014, online at: https://www.rusi.org/explore-our-research/publications/rusi-books/learning-and-adapting-use-monitoring-and-evaluation-countering-violent-extremism.

Dean, G., Bell, P. & Vakhitova, Z., 'Right-wing extremism in Australia:

Glazzard, A. 'Losing the Plot: Narrative, Counter-Narrative and Violent Extremism'. ICCT Research Paper, May 2017, online at: https://icct.nl/wp-content/uploads/2017/05/ICCT-Glazzard-Losing-the-Plot-May-2017.pdf.

Ferguson, K., 'Countering violent extremism through media and communication strategies', University of East Anglia: Partnership for Conflict, Crime & Security Research, 2016, online at: https:// www.paccsresearch.org.uk/wp-content/uploads/2016/03/Count ering-Violent-Extremism-Through-Media-and-Communication-Strategies-.pdf.

Frenett, R. & Dow, M, 'One to One Online Interventions: A Pilot CVE Methodology', London & Perth: ISD & Curtin University, 2016, p. 14, online at: https://ec.europa.eu/home-affairs/node/7493_en. pdf; and www.isdglobal.org/wp-content/uploads/2016/04/One 2One_Web_v9.

Hedayah/ICCT, 'Developing Effective Counter-Narrative Frameworks for Countering Violent Extremism'. Hedayah/ICCT: Abu Dabi/Hague, September 2014, online at: https://www.hedayahcenter.org/wp-content/uploads/2021/01/2020DEC16_CARR_HowToGuide_FINAL-double-spread.pdf/.

Hedayah Radical Right Counter Narrative Project Germany Country Report, 2021: https://www.hedayahcenter.org/resources/reports_and_publications/germany_radical_right_cve_narratives/.

Helmus, T.C. et al, 'RAND Programme Evaluation Toolkit for Countering Violent Extremism', Santa Monica, Ca: RAND Corporation, online at: https://www.rand.org/content/dam/rand/pubs/tools/TL200/TL243/RAND_TL243.pdf.

Jackson, P.,' Transnational Neo-Nazism in the USA, United Kingdom and Australia', George Washington Programme on Extremism, February 2020, online at: https://extremism.gwu.edu/sites/g/files/zaxdzs2191/f/Jackson%20-%20Transnational%20neo%20Nazism%20in%20the%20USA%2C%20United%20Kingdom%20and%20Australia.pdf

Lewis, J., Knott, K., & Marsden, S., 'Countering Violent Extremism II: A Guide to Good Practice', Lancaster, UK: Centre for Evidence on Security Threats, 24 January 2019, online at: https://crestresearch.ac.uk/resources/countering-violent-extremism-two/.

Macklin, G., 'The Evolution of Extreme-Right Terrorism and Efforts to Counter It in the United Kingdom', *CTC Sentinel* 12(1), January 2019, 17, online at: https://ctc.usma.edu/app/uploads/2019/01/CTC-SENTINEL-012019

Macklin, G., 'The Christchurch Attacks: Livestream Terror in the Viral Video Age', CTC Sentinel, 12 (6), July 2019, online at: https://ctc.usma.edu/christchurch-attacks-livestream-terror-viral-video-age/.

Macklin, G., 'The El Paso Terrorist Attack: The Chain Reaction of Global Right-Wing Terror', CTC Sentinel, 12(11), December 2019, online at: https://ctc.usma.edu/el-paso-terrorist-attack-chain-reaction-global-right-wing-terror/

Mattei, C. & Zeiger, S., 'Evaluate Your CVE: Projecting Your Impact', Hedayah: Abu Dhabi, 2018, online at: https://www.hedayahcenter.org/wp-content/uploads/2019/11/File-16720189339.pdf.

Meleagrou-Hitchens, A. and Standing, E., 'Blood and Honour: Britain's Far-Right Militants', (London: Henry Jackson Society, 2010), online at: http://henryjacksonsociety.org/wp-content/uploads/2013/01/BLOOD-AND-HNOUR.pdf.

RAN, 'Proposed Policy Recommendations For the High Level Conference', RAN Prison & Probation Working Group, December 2012, online at: https://ec.europa.eu/home-affairs/sites/homeaffairs/files/what-we-do/networks/radicalisation_awareness_network/ran-high-level-conference/docs/proposed_policy_recommendation_ran_p_and_p_en.pdf.

RAN, 'Guideline Evaluation of PCVE Programmes and Interventions', Brussels: RAN, July 2018, online at: https://ec.europa.eu/home-affairs/system/files/2020-09/ms_workshops_guidelines_evaluation_of_pcve_programmes_and_interventions_july_2018_en.pdf.

RAN, 'How can online communications drive offline interventions?', *Ex Post Paper*, 22-23 November 2018, online at: https://ec.europa.eu/home-affairs/sites/homeaffairs/files/what-we-do/networks/radicalisation_awareness_network/about-ran/ran-c-and-n/docs/ran_c-n_amsterdam_call_to_action_20181123_22_en.pdf

RAN, 'Ex Post Paper: Current and Future Narratives and Strategies of Far-Right and Islamist Extremism', May 2019, online at: https://ec.europa.eu/home-affairs/sites/homeaffairs/files/what-we-do/networks/radicalisation_awareness_network/ran-papers/docs/ran_pol-cn_most_often_used_narratives_stockholm_05042019_en.pdf.

Reynolds, L & Tuck H., 'The Counter Narrative Monitoring and Evaluation Handbook', London: ISD, 2016, online at: https://www.isdglobal.org/wp-content/uploads/2017/06/CN-Monitoring-and-Evaluation-Handbook.pdf.

SecDev Foundation, 'Extreme Dialogue: Social Media Target Audience Analysis and Impact Assessments in Support of Countering Violent Extremism', March 2016, online at: https://bit.ly/37zacr3.

Silverman, Stewart, Amanullah and Birdwell, 'The Impact of Counter Narratives'. London: ISD, 2016, online at: https://www.isdglobal.org/wp-content/uploads/2016/08/Impact-of-Counter-Narratives_ONLINE_1.pdf.

Tuck, H. & Silverman, H., 'The Counter Narrative Handbook', London: ISD, 2016, p.65, online at: https://www.isdglobal.org/wp-content/uploads/2016/06/Counter-narrative-Handbook_1.pdf.

ibidem.eu